RAZZLE DAZZLE

Other Books by Hank Messick

The Silent Syndicate
Syndicate in the Sun
Syndicate Wife
Syndicate Abroad
Secret File
Lansky
John Edgar Hoover
The Mobs and the Mafia
Private Lives of Public Enemies
Beauties and the Beasts
Gangs and Gangsters
Kidnapping
Barboza
King's Mountain
The Only Game In Town
The Politics of Prosecution
Of Grass and Snow
Desert Sanctuary

RAZZLE DAZZLE

HANK MESSICK

COMMONWEALTH BOOK COMPANY
ST. MARTIN, OHIO
2019

Copyright © 1995 by Hank Messick
Copyright © 2019 by Commonwealth Book Company
All Rights Reserved
Printed in the United States of America

ISBN: 978-1-948986-13-7

For Faye,
    who shared the living
    and the telling.

ABOUT THE AUTHOR

HANK MESSICK (1922-1999) was born in Happy Valley, NC, and educated at the University of North Carolina and the University of Iowa. He began his investigative journalism career in western North Carolina and in 1956 began working at the *Louisville Courier-Journal*, Kentucky's largest newspaper. For the next several years Hank investigated and reported on the Newport, Kentucky, vice industry. He later worked for the *Miami Herald* and the *Boston Traveler*, also investigating organized crime and corruption in those communities. After 1967 he wrote full time, authoring 19 books, mostly about organized crime and its influences in American life.

Hank Messick with wife Faye celebrating their 14th wedding anniversary at the Beverly Hills Country Club (June 9, 1961).

FOREWORD

Hank Messick's *Razzle Dazzle* is an engrossing story. It has all the elements of good fiction, the suspense of a particularly captivating novel of detection. It is filled with fascinating characters, major and minor, who are sometimes magnanimous, sometimes petty, sometimes colorful, sometimes malevolent, all of whom reflect recognizable elements of the human condition.

However, *Razzle Dazzle* is not a work of fiction. The people, places and events are real. It is an account of organized crime in Northern Kentucky; its growth, its power, and, finally, its ouster. Messick traces the many features of the area "across the river from Cincinnati" that led to its derisively affectionate label of "Little Mexico": the religious divisions, the geographic and social alienation from the rest of the Commonwealth of Kentucky, a unique blend of urban realities and rural or small-town values, the shaping force of a dark capitalism that created power blocs and power brokers and a strange morality that separated private and public ethics.

Against this background Messick follows the history and evolution and "organization" of the Northern Kentucky area. In the prohibition era the region played a prominent part in the illegal liquor market, becoming one of the major supply and distribution centers for Cincinnati. The liquor "franchise" was largely that of George Remus, of Price Hill, known as "King of the Bootleggers." Remus raised the practice of bribes and kickbacks to officials to an art form. (Overhead, advertising and public relations cost big money but pay dividends many times over).

Eventually, Remus, his empire and prohibition passed into history.

Sometime near the end of prohibition the national crime syndicate switched to gambling, allotting specific areas to various syndicates. The Cleveland syndicate was given territory that included Northern Kentucky.

In the 1930s Sam Tucker, one of the charter members of the Cleveland syndicate, began to organize and consolidate the region. Local operatives were given the choice of joining forces or leaving the business. Most joined; those who did not were squeezed out. Some of the locals readily moved into new niches. The job of "peacemaker" was given to Red ("The Enforcer") Masterson. The Eastern Syndicate, allowed only a limited interest in the region, was represented by Michael ("Trigger Mike") Coppola, whose interests were in turn represented by another erstwhile independent, Frank ("Screw") Andrews.

By the early 1940s the region was well-organized, and night spots such as the Beverly Hills, the Lookout House and the Latin Quarter provided a plush setting for organized crime. In Newport the less glamorous but more lucrative business of lay-off betting flourished, adding untold amounts of money to the coffers of organized crime and making Newport, KY the national center of lay-off betting.

The evolution of organized crime went smoothly for the most part. Occasionally a candidate for an office, in response to whatever public pressure might be voiced for reform and clean-up of corruption, would run as a "liberal", promising investigations if elected. But such investigations, if conducted, were mere gestures, the political equivalent of wiring antlers on cattle and calling them deer.

There were, however, some groups that were trying hard, if, seemingly, futilely to raise public and political awareness of corruption, notably The Kenton County Protestant Association and the Newport Ministerial Association. When Hank Messick, on assignment for the *Louisville Courier-Journal*, first came into the region, it would be members of the Ministerial Association who would introduce him to the labyrinth and provide starting points for his subsequent investigations and reports.

Razzle Dazzle is not an autobiography, though there are elements of autobiography in the book. Messick does sketch the influences of place and people who shaped his life and career, influences that, in a sense, "prepared" him for what was to prove a special, catalytic role in the reform movement against organized crime.

And his was a special and catalytic part. Messick does not overplay his part, but, wisely, he does not underestimate it either. Messick has covered some of the material of this book in *Syndicate Wife* (perhaps his best-known book, at least in the Northern Kentucky area) and *The Silent Syndicate*. But, I believe, this is the first book in which he draws deeply from his private experiences as both a participant and an observer in the reform movement. And it is the first-person, "insider" account that gives his material a surprising freshness, poignancy and human touch.

Events, when one looks back on them, knowing how they turned out, have a deceptively tidy, monolithic pattern. Hence, it sometimes appears that a great, crusading newspaper, the *Courier-Journal*, standing four-square behind its best investigative reporter, rose in support of outmanned, but unified "reformers," in tandem with state government officials, themselves beyond or indifferent to political influence, to oust evil from an area, good triumphing over evil.

Nothing is ever so tidy.

Messick describes the turf wars within the *Courier-Journal*. He names the editors and staff members who encouraged him, and he names those whose support was at best tepid and half-hearted. His character sketches are masterful, sketches that delineate the integrity of Judge Hill, the hot temper and cold calculation of Charles Lester and the strange, coiled menace of Masterson, hidden behind a quiet, polite manner and expressionless face. Though *Razzle Dazzle* is basically a straight-forward, fast-paced narrative, Messick subtly weaves in the social, political and religious compromises, evasions of responsibility, naivete, witting and unwitting blindness of "good" people that helped foster the conditions that opened the way for organized crime to move in, consolidate and flourish for so many years in the Northern Kentucky area.

As mentioned, Messick's role in the crime and corruption investigation in Northern Kentucky is more clearly drawn than in his other crime books. His feelings and convictions are thus sharper and more focused. One feeling that marked him throughout his investigations was fear. He writes that the hard ball of fear in the pit of his stomach never left him until the night of George Ratterman's election as (reform) Sheriff of Campbell County. That he had the courage to go on in spite of fear (and the courage to admit he was often scared) also testifies to the special role of Messick.

He had good reason to fear. The criminal elements were not stupid. It was not difficult to sense that Messick's stories propped up a slightly sagging, depressed Ministerial Association and that his stories began to link local politicians and officials and police with national organized crime. It was not difficult to assume that if Messick went away, the spotlight would go out. He was offered bribes - fairly substantial ones. When those did not work, he received telephoned threats and other "warnings." Though he learned that top level syndicate leaders thought about but decided against killing him (too much national attention) Messick was always worried that lesser ranked minions, hoping to ingratiate themselves and make a reputation, might not be so inhibited. It seems there was one serious attempt to kill him. Messick tells of a menacing chase along Highway 42, along the Ohio River, where he was boxed in by two cars. The panic he felt and his narrow escape make chilling reading, even today.

Messick is a fine writer. Read a few pages and the title, which at first glance may seem a bit affected, takes on meaning. "Razzle Dazzle" is a dice game, one the bettor is always on the verge of winning - but never does. Razzle-Dazzle could also be a metaphor for the casino, high-stakes, high life style of the area in the gambling era - car-jammed streets, blazing lights, lots of liquor, lots of money and lots of women - but with a Jay Gatsby emptiness under it all.

Messick was (and is) a reformer (not a Puritan; there is a difference). That he thought gambling was, not a sin, but a moral and social blight on any society was one reason for his deep involvement in the reform movement. As he writes in the preface: "This is not to say that widespread gambling is the root of all our problems. Many other factors are involved. Basic, however, is the fact that when people seek to get something for nothing they are playing razzle dazzle with moral standards." A reformer, yes - and a realist. "Victory is never permanent." he writes near the end of the book. He continues: "As this is written, legal gambling is spreading across the United States and voices are urging that gambling boats be legalized along the shores of Kentucky. They have already been authorized on the Indiana side of the Ohio River." Messick the reformer writes: "Gambling, legal or otherwise, has inevitably brought corruption". Messick the realist adds: "History will almost certainly repeat itself as a new generation ignores the past."

Will it? As George Santayana said: "Those who cannot remember the past are condemned to repeat it." He implies that there is some hope in remembering. So here is a chance to remember the past. I hope a lot of people do. The past can be useful as well as fascinating.

        H. Lew Wallace
        Professor of History
        Northern Kentucky University
        September 2, 1995

The mountains tower proudest,
Thunder peals the loudest,
The landscape is the grandest,
And politics the damnedest,
In Kentucky.
- James Mulligan

Those who cannot remember the past
are condemned to repeat it.
- George Santayana

AUTHOR'S NOTE

This is not a work of fiction. Any resemblance to past events and to persons living or dead can be documented.

Several years ago I was stricken with Sjogren's Syndrome, an auto-immune disease for which there is no cure. The moisture producing glands of the body dry up. My eyes were first affected and it became almost impossible to read, to write, to brave sunlight. Confined to a room with a humidifier blowing, I saved my sanity by dictating my autobiography. Over several years it grew to an immense size.

During occasional periods of remission, and with the aid of my wife, I fashioned this history of my experiences in the clean up of Campbell County, Kentucky. I thought it deserved telling.

Hank Messick

PREFACE

About 1 a.m. the wind began to blow. Within seconds, sand from desert dunes turned Las Vegas hellish, blurring the neon and stinging the face.

Down the Strip and along Fremont Street on that night in the early sixties, the sand blew past signs advertising "Liberal Slots" and forty-nine cent breakfasts. It pelted a newspaper rack in front of a pawn shop.

A newspaper came scurrying along the sidewalk where it wrapped itself around my feet. I picked it up. On the front page was a story about school kids carrying knives and guns for self protection (sound familiar?). Inside was an editorial commenting on the story and asking:

"What's wrong with our town?"

The answer seemed obvious to me — gambling and greed, the desire to get something for nothing. I had encountered the same attitudes, the same breakdown of social values and moral authority in Newport, Ky. several years before. Gambling was legal in Newport according to "God's law" which gamblers and politicians said outranked man's laws. The major difference between Las Vegas and Newport was perhaps a degree of sophistication. Both cities were corrupt.

Many things have changed since the sixties when, as John Kennedy put it "a new generation of Americans, born in this century, tempered by war, disciplined by a hard and bitter peace," looked to the stars and believed a better world was possible. Among the changes was an end to the war against organized crime launched by Robert Kennedy which in part was based on the belief that widespread gambling was a threat to society. The moral climate changed as politicians sold the public on the virtues of gambling as a revenue source.

In the nineties gambling, legal and illegal, has become a four hundred billion dollars a year business. Illegal gambling continued unabated while legal gambling emigrated from Las Vegas and the poker parlors of Gardenia to many areas of this country. Off-track betting is no longer confined to bookie joints. The numbers racket blossomed into state lotteries. (In Florida alone, the lottery grosses more than $2,000,000,000 and the "take" is even greater in other states.) Gambling casinos became literally floating crap games as riverboat gambling was legalized in America's heartland.

Greed became fashionable, and with it came fear in equal measure. The streets of America became unsafe. Now citizens worried about crime without a capital "C" forgetting that crime for gain in the last analysis is but an illegal extension of the free enterprise system. It is no accident that when communism crumbled, gambling casinos opened in Moscow.

This is not to say that widespread gambling is the root of all our troubles. Many other factors are involved. Basic, however, is the fact that when people seek to get something for nothing they are playing razzle-dazzle with moral standards.

The book that follows details the author's personal adventures in Newport. A citizen's revolt against crime and corruption in that Ohio River city became my responsibility to report. I learned firsthand of the breakdown of law and order, but I saw how good people can band together to defeat the corruptors. It is a disturbing story, and timely because it may help answer the question people and politicians are asking in the nineties:

"What's wrong with our country?"

HM

RAZZLE DAZZLE

PROLOGUE

14 February '52

It was a bright, beautiful day in the heart of the Great Smokies, but I felt lousy as I pulled into the public parking lot across the street from *The Waynesville Mountaineer*.

And I had reason.

I had worked too long on my book last night, writing until well after midnight. A severe headache had developed costing me sleep and leaving me groggy. Contributing to my mood was the knowledge that I had to find a new job.

A married man with a young daughter should act with more circumspection, I told myself as I parked the Chevy beside a flatbed truck. A prudent guy would've found a job first and then told the editor to go to hell. Well, I had two weeks, and tomorrow, after the paper went to bed, I'd drive down to Chapel Hill and confer with Skipper Coffin. As Dean of the School of Journalism, he'd know who was looking for a reporter.

As I got out of the car I saw a big man approaching. He was a cop. His wife worked in the front office of *The Mountaineer*.

"Hi, Ray," I said.

He blocked my path. His left hand shot out and pulled the glasses from my face while his right fist came around in a powerful swing.

Years had passed since I called myself the heavyweight champion of Happy Valley, but I still had the instincts of a boxer. I ducked. The punch ruffled my crewcut, leaving Ray off balance. I sidestepped quickly around him, getting out of the corridor between truck and car and into open space.

"What the hell is wrong with you?" I asked, although I could smell part of the answer. He was half drunk.

Carefully he placed my glasses on the truck bed, then charged at me with both hands flailing. Dancing away, I resisted the urge to strike back at the easy target. The guy may have weighed 250 pounds, but at least 50 of it was fat. Waynesville's finest didn't get much exercise.

"What's wrong?" I again asked.

"You're a troublemaker," he gasped. "I'm going to teach you not to spread lies about the police department."

Again he charged; again I avoided his punches.

"Didn't your wife hear me give my resignation yesterday? Or wasn't she eavesdropping as usual?"

"You're a liar," he said, but this time he stopped.

"Go ask the great man," I replied. "He'll tell you. He's afraid of cops, you know."

"Damn you." He started forward, then stopped as I moved around him. "All right, I'll ask him, but if you're lying I'll beat your ass off."

I laughed at him, my headache forgotten. "You can try, Ray, but don't bet the farm on it."

He turned toward the street. I picked up my glasses from the truck and followed. I could see female faces watching from the window of the *Mountaineer*. Apparently our little ballet had been observed.

Ray entered, stopping at the counter where citizens bought ads, paid subscriptions, and delivered opinions. I followed, not too closely, and entered the working area. Ray's wife, almost as large as the cop, was crying. The two other women just looked scared.

"Where's Mr. Russ?" I asked.

"He said he was going to the men's room," said Mae Gibson, a tall, attractive woman who kept the paper's books. "I don't think he's coming out soon."

I opened the door to the shop where the toilets and the press were located.

"Mr. Russ," I yelled. "There's someone here to see you."

No reply. I turned back to Ray. "Looks like he's tied up for awhile."

"Damn you," snarled Ray. "I ain't going to wait."

With that he charged into the inner office. His wife screamed, then scurried out of the way. There was plenty of room. I sidestepped. Ray fell across a desk.

"Be careful, Ray," I advised. "You might hurt yourself."

Mae and the other woman began to laugh hysterically. Ray charged again. I got out of the way and shouted:

"Come out, Mr. Russ, wherever you are. You're missing all the fun."

The cop stood in the middle of the floor, looking bewildered. Perhaps he realized how foolish he appeared. In any case, he growled:

"I'll get you later."

And out the door he went.

Calm returned. Everyone resumed his duties. I sat down at my typewriter and began knocking out my weekly sports column. I described how I had won the heavyweight championship of Happy Valley by beating Ab Shuford, an older man even larger than Ray. At the end of the narrative I added this line:

"For some reason that little incident occurred to me today."

Russ never bothered to censor my sports copy so it should get in the paper.

And suddenly he was there, pale of face, red of eye, but stern of voice. A handsome man, Mr. Russ, articulate and intelligent. All he lacked was guts.

"I warned you this would happen," he said. "Your stories make people mad."

He had indeed cautioned me to avoid trouble, to be constructive in my reporting of civic affairs, but he had never suggested that an overweight cop fresh out of prison for moonshining would assault me in broad daylight.

"I didn't do anything. The man was drunk."

My head had begun to ache again. I rubbed it and felt stickiness. Apparently Ray's pinky ring had scratched my scalp when he threw that surprise punch in the parking lot.

"Look," I said. "The damn fool hit me."

Russ touched my head with tentative fingers. "I don't feel anything," he said, and walked away.

I completed what routine work remained, and then went to the courthouse where I swore out an assault and battery warrant before a justice of the peace. The case, I was told, would be heard next day. Then I returned to the office and, with Ray's wife hearing every word, I called Don Shoemaker, editor of *The Asheville Citizen*. When he came on the line, I told him Skipper Coffin had given me his name. Then I briefly sketched what had happened. He promised to get a reporter over for the trial and suggested I drop by some time soon for a chat.

The woman glared at me when I hung up, but I felt better. *The Mountaineer* might not have respect locally, but the *Citizen* was the largest daily in the western part of North Carolina. The cops wouldn't want its reporters snooping around. Of course, I'd have to postpone my visit to Skipper, but hell, maybe when this was over I could get a job with the *Citizen*. They might even assign me to cover Haywood County.

If protection was needed, more showed up just before quitting time. Word had spread about town of Ray's threat to get me later. Eight young men, all veterans of World War II, strolled into the newspaper and announced they would escort me home. Several openly displayed pistols in their belts. Russ had vanished. Both his office and the men's toilet were empty.

Surrounded by guards, I crossed the street to my car. My protectors then returned to their own automobiles and fell in behind me. I felt like I was leading a parade. As we passed the police station they blew their horns derisively.

Halfway to the nearby village of Hazelwood where Faye and I had lived with our fourteen-month-old daughter since leaving Colorado some seven months past, I realized it was St. Valentine's Day. I detoured by a drugstore, my escorts double-parking behind me. They watched as I emerged from the store with the largest heart-shaped box of candy I could find.

I didn't feel silly.

Pulling into the driveway of the rented house, I watched as my friends found spaces for their cars up and down the block. A spokesman advised me to go on in and have supper. No one would bother me.

I kissed my wife and presented the candy. Then I delivered my other gift — the news. Faye took it calmly. We had met at the University of North Carolina where I was studying journalism and she was a graduate student in sociology. She taught at Woman's College of the University just to prove she could be self-sufficient — and, of course, to let me finish my undergraduate degree. A year at the University of Iowa followed our marriage and gave me a master's to match her own. Three happy years at Colorado A&M came next. I taught cowboys how to write and we hunted deer and caught rainbow trout in season. After Marda's birth I decided that if I was to make a living teaching journalism, I needed some actual experience. In those days it wasn't such a radical idea. We returned to my home state where with Skipper's aid I hoped to work on a semi-weekly, a medium sized daily, and finally a metropolitan newspaper. Then I would return to teaching and the writing of great books.

Faye was slender, with auburn hair and blue eyes. She spoke with the soft voice of south Georgia. I loved her very much, although sometimes I felt she deserved better than a hulking hillbilly.

It was a busy evening. The telephone rang constantly. People came and went, all eager to assure us of their support. Some brought their wives. There was a lot of talk, about past conditions, future hopes. The possibility of beginning a second newspaper with me as Publisher and Editor-in-Chief was explored, but no one explained where we would obtain the necessary money. All were eager for change, but their careers — interrupted by war — were, like mine, just getting underway.

My head was aching badly when finally they all left. I went to bed gratefully, and slept without dreams.

*****

The trial was brief. Ray pleaded guilty to simple assault. Mae Gibson confirmed my story, testifying she had seen the cop swing at me in the parking lot and again in the newspaper office. The Justice of Peace fined

Ray $10 and costs. Seven members of the staff attended, but Editor Russ was conspicuous by his absence. He told an Asheville reporter who ran him down, however, that he had not found time to investigate the "incident."

After the trial I drove east along the top of The Great Smoky Mountains. The air was fresh except when passing near Canton where papermills stank up the place, and the rolling hills were peaceful. Spring was in view and the world seemed lovely. It usually does, I reflected, when one gets away from people. I was feeling a bit anti-social that day, I expect.

Don Shoemaker proved to be an amiable man who appeared to eat regularly and well. He listened to my account of events in Haywood County with apparent interest, but when I hinted I'd be happy to carry on the investigation as a *Citizen* reporter, he shook his big head.

"I'm afraid we're not an aggressive newspaper," he said, somewhat defensively. "And after all, why should we be? We have a monopoly situation and that means no competition."

For three years prior to becoming a reporter, I had taught younger minds that the press had a duty to report fully and fairly, to give light so the people could see. Obviously, the publishers of Asheville's morning and afternoon newspapers didn't share that sentiment.

I thanked Shoemaker for his time and wisdom. Neither of us dreamed, I'm sure, that in the years to come I'd be raising hell on *The Miami Herald* while Shoemaker wrote editorials praising my abilities and saying I looked like an "unmade bed."

Leaving the newspaper, I went over to the office of U.S. Attorney T.A. Uzzell. A month earlier he had announced a special federal grand jury investigation of organized crime in western North Carolina. That announcement, perhaps, had made the cops and others in Waynesville somewhat nervous when I began asking about a man called "Dog."

A young assistant was free to talk to me, and provided coffee in a paper cup. He had seen some of my stories, he said, so my good intentions were established. The grand jury probe, he explained, was part of ninety-three ordered by the Attorney General nationwide as a follow-up to the hearings of the Kefauver Committee.

I became interested in Waynesville crime, I explained, when two high school students got drunk on their noon break and cut each other seriously. Little effort was needed to learn that several joints near the school sold moonshine to minors. Some of the veterans to whom I talked volunteered to help and bought seven pints of moonshine at seven different spots within a block of the school. They placed the bottles on display with an appropriate sign in a store window and I managed to get a picture and a story into the paper. My editor blamed me for "engineering the stunt."

After that, more people began to talk to me and I learned the big boss was David "Dog" Underwood. Dog had been a black market operator during the war and served time in federal prison. Upon release, he went to the First Baptist Church and confessed his sins to the congregation which, of course, included Russ. The congregation had been so impressed with his "new born" piety, they made him a deacon. Whereupon, he got busy and organized the moonshine business. There had always been moonshine since the Scotch-Irish who settled the mountains began raising corn, but Dog created an organization.

It was a large enterprise, Ben agreed, but only because Underwood had connections with gangsters in several states. Carolina white lightning was consumed in such cities as Louisville and Atlanta. The boss was believed to operate out of Newport, Kentucky. Some reports named the boss as Frank Andriola, but FBI reports were confused.

It was all very interesting, but there seemed little I could do about it. When I got home, however, I looked up Newport on a map. It was in northern Kentucky, on the Ohio River, across from Cincinnati. Perhaps I'd go there someday, but in the meantime I had to find a job.

The Asheville papers carried a good story about Ray's conviction, and the Associated Press sent it across the state. Russ had no choice come Monday but to print something. I had few illusions about my editor but even I was astonished when below the headline and above the story he placed these lines: Publisher's statement: It is our sincere regret that the incident recorded below took place."

A drunken cop tries to beat up a reporter and the publisher apologizes!

Another week passed before I got free to visit my Alma Mater. It was a long trip in those pre-interstate days and I arrived in the village of Chapel Hill in early afternoon. Parking near the post office, I walked the short distance to Bynum Hall, the domain of the Dean of Journalism.

Visits to UNC were for me a blend of bitter-sweet memories. I had been happy there, made friends among students and faculty, courted my future bride. The wooded campus was lovely, and the ancient buildings solid and enduring. In Kenan Stadium, a natural oval flanked by hills, I had felt as one with the 40,000 spectators who chanted "All the way, Choo choo," as on the field below Charlie Justice ran wild. My desire to write had been encouraged and the very fact of my being on campus seemed to prove that all things were possible. As one of the first veterans at UNC, I found some conflicts with professors accustomed to dealing with beardless boys, but Skipper Coffin had a fondness for hillbillies and protected me.

Short, stout, addicted to chewing tobacco, Dean Oscar Coffin launched a projectile towards a brass spittoon and made me welcome. Joining us were two other members of the Journalism School: Phillips Russell, a courtly slender man who had taught me creative writing; and Walter Spearman, younger and already balding.

They listened as I recounted my adventures in Haywood County. Skipper's wife had been born there so the old man knew the people well. When I finished talking he leaned back with a frown.

"I've known there was dirty work at the crossroads up there for a long time," he said. "Russ is a damn fool."

"Why is he so scared?" I asked.

The Skipper's gaze was suddenly cold.

"You're a young idiot," he said. "When you get your own paper you can make policy. Until then you're supposed to do what you're told to do. You can't clean up a community in a few months. Hell, it took God six days to make the world."

He gave me quite a reaming out, but half through it Spearman winked. I suppressed a smile. When Skipper finished his lecture, he bit off a chew, and relaxed.

"I'll find you another job," he said. "You're ready to move up, I take it."

"I've covered everything from county fairs to high school football games," I told him. "Russ reserved city and county government for himself, but everything else was my responsibility. Yes, I'm ready for a medium daily."

He told me to give Faye his love. Russell followed me out.

"How's your writing coming?" he asked.

The professor had allowed me to take his creative writing course three times for credit, and arranged to have me accepted into the Writer's Workshop at the University of Iowa. More importantly, he had instilled in me the conviction that, with practice, I could become a successful writer.

"I'm still rewriting my master's thesis," I told him. "Since the baby came, there's not been too much time."

Let me have a look at it when you get it in shape," he said.

I cut over to U.S. 70 and followed it back to Greensboro where I departed from my route down to take 421 to North Wilkesboro via Winston-Salem. Reaching the foothills, I scooted up the Yadkin River to Happy Valley and on out Warrior Creek to the old homestead.

The rambling house with its wide porches and high ceilings had been a showplace when my grandfather bought it upon retiring as superintendent of the cotton mill at nearby Patterson, but it had fallen on hard times. When Dad brought rural electrification to a four-county area, he had installed every electrical appliance he could conceive of, and we had joked that only the wiring held the building together.

My parents met me on the porch: mother, tall, thin and worried; father, a pale shadow of his former robust self. He had built the Blue Ridge Electric into one of the largest cooperatives of its kind in the country, but ill health had forced him out after fourteen years and left him shattered. Now his hand was shaking as he grasped mine.

"You mustn't go back," he said. "They'll kill you."

He was crying, I realized in amazement.

Mother explained. "He got a call awhile ago from Waynesville and he went to pieces."

"Who called?"

"He wouldn't say, but they talked for at least ten minutes."

"Not just an anonymous threat then," I commented, "but conversation?"

"It was pretty one-sided. He just kept saying, 'Yes sir.'"

I put my arm around my father's shoulders. "We'll talk about it later," I promised. "Right now, I'm hungry."

We had a dinner of hot biscuits, made only as my mother could, livermush, and mashed potatoes. I'd not eaten since an early breakfast so even the livermush went down quickly. Dad ate very little. I explained I had been to Chapel Hill in search of a new job. Mother told me news of my sister, Mildred, who had won a four-year scholarship to Woman's College of UNC at Greensboro.

After the meal, I helped do the dishes while dad settled down before the old radio to hear the evening news. Television had not yet found its way into the Blue Ridge. He switched it off as I came into the room, and began his plea.

"Call Faye," he suggested, "and tell her to get the baby on the bus and come here. You can go back later for your things. They'll kill you if you go back now. I know those people. Please, listen to me. You can't go back."

I remembered occasions when Dad had accepted my evaluation of critical situations without question and had told Mother:

"Hank can take care of himself."

Now, however, no words of mine could still the fear in his heart. Mother, at last, led him off to bed, giving him something to make him sleep.

Next morning he renewed his efforts, and I was forced to leave my father sobbing as I drove away. To Lenoir I went, thence to Morganton where I picked up U.S. 70 and followed it up past Old Fort and Black Mountain to the top of the Great Smokies. It was a three hour drive, and I carried a heavy heart.

Faye came out to the car as I pulled into the driveway. She clutched my arm as I bent to kiss her.

"Mildred called a few minutes ago," she said. "Your father has had a stroke. They want you to come back."

I took time to shower, shave, and eat a light lunch before returning to Happy Valley. Mildred was home alone. Mother had called my brother in Durham and he had picked up my sister at Greensboro and made record time getting there. Dad was in the hospital at Lenoir and Paul and mother were with him. My sister, eleven years my junior, was morose. Always I had been her hero but now there was accusation in her voice.

"Mother said you were hardly out of sight when he collapsed," she said. "The man who called surely did a good job of scaring Dad."

I knew of only one man in Waynesville who was so full of fear he could so frighten my father, but I would think about that later.

We drove over to the hospital. Dad was under an oxygen tent — a device now as obsolete as the Edsel. Through the clear plastic that covered his head, I could see him breathing regularly. He seemed to be asleep. Mother led me into the hall to embrace me and cry a little.

"He's going to die," she said. "He's going to leave us."

"Was he ever with us?"

"Yes," she said fiercely. "In his own way he loved us. You, especially."

It was no time to argue, and perhaps there were things I didn't know. According to family legend, Dad had been very close to my grandfather and only after his sudden death of a ruptured appendix had he sought consolation with mother who had worked in the cottonmill and sang the "Cottonmill Song."

> Come my love and pay my bill
> Take me out of the cottonmill
> It's hard times in here, my lover
> It's hard times in here.

The doctor came by. He had a black beard and a reputation for profanity. I walked down the hall away from mother and asked the question.

"About the chance of a snowball in hell," he replied. "He may hang on a few days, even a week, but, dammit, there's nothing left inside. He's been dying since he left the co-op. It was his life."

"He's not quite 62," I muttered.

"And you're half that," snapped the doctor. "Don't be a sentimental fool."

Actually, I was not quite 30. If the doctor was right — and why shouldn't he be — there was no question of guilt. There was, however, something else.

My brother, one year my junior, shook my hand. In his muscular body he carried shrapnel collected in France on D-Day Plus-Two, but he was a foreman on a construction crew and husband to a girl he had met in Kentucky. They had two sons with another on the way.

As a boy Paul had declined to compete with me. While we worked together to keep two woodboxes loaded, the cows milked, and the waterbuckets filled, we had never been close. I was surprised to see how bald he had become during my years in Colorado.

Next day Dad was awake. The fear, the excitement was gone. He seemed composed and pleased to see his family. Mother became optimistic. Hitching up the little trailer we had used to move from the west, I ascended the mountains to Waynesville and stopped by the *Mountaineer* to pick up my last paycheck from Mae Gibson.

"I'm sorry you're leaving and sorry about your father." she said.

Ray's wife said nothing. Russ was not in his office. I went to the bank, cashed the check, and drove to the house where my daughter had taken her first step. Faye had been so excited she let supper burn.

We could have left immediately and been down the mountain before dark, but I was determined not to be hurried. I made a few telephone calls to friends and met an ex-Marine under the Cross at Lake Junaluska, center of summer activity of the Methodist church. In prewar days he, by all accounts, had been rather wild and was still on good terms with many of the bootleggers he had known then.

Dog Underwood, he told me, in addition to being a deacon in the church, had recently taken an interest in the pretty young wife of one of his moonshiners. Naturally, in the interest of decorum or something, he visited her only at night when her husband was away at work. No doubt they discussed Scripture.

"It would be interesting if the husband came home unexpectedly," I said.

"It would indeed," said my friend, and we left it at that.

Next day I took my family to Happy Valley. There was plenty of room in the old house, and mother was delighted to have her "one and only" as she called her granddaughter to divert her. Paul went home to his own family, prepared to return on short notice. March winds howled through and around the Messick homestead, and the day inevitably came when the doctor said Dad would not last the night.

Paul and I kept vigil. Dad lay motionless, his shrunken body small on the bed, in a coma. I sipped bitter coffee from a machine and thought bitter thoughts.

I could not hate Russ. The man was a victim as much as Dad. Whether his fear was justified was unimportant; it was real. Objectively, I could not even feel contempt. The editor was more to be pitied than scorned, as the old saying had it. The real bastards were the corrupters, the individuals who had put the press and the police in their pockets. Dog Underwood was on the lower level; the chain led upward to a little town in Kentucky — if the assistant U.S. Attorney knew what he was talking about — and beyond.

The Kefauver Committee had made some startling revelations about the relationship of crime, politics, and business, but in Colorado I heard little about it. The Federal Bureau of Narcotics blamed a shadowy organization called the "Mafia" for most crime. J. Edgar Hoover of the FBI scoffed at the idea. It would be fun to find the truth and thus avenge Dad in a proper manner, but, how could I? My first duty was to my family. It was rather ironic. Dad's casual attitude toward his family had caused me to give mine first priority. And Dad's indifference had been a direct result of his close relationship with his father. Life was sometimes amusing, I reflected, not for the first time.

Slowly the hours passed. I felt a sense of impatience and was immediately ashamed. Paul said little, apparently lost in his own black thoughts.

There was light in the window to the east when our father suddenly stirred, lifting himself. I was on his right, my brother on his left. He turned his head rapidly, looking first at Paul and then at me. Then he fell back and was still.

"He's gone," said Paul, pushing the bell for the nurse.

She came in, a pretty little thing who had attended Happy Valley High several years after me. She shooed us out into the hall. I went to the window and opened it to let cool air wash my flushed face. Paul disappeared in the other direction. In this hour of our mutual loss, we couldn't console each other. Did he blame me for Dad's stroke?

The nurse came out and confirmed the facts. Arrangements were made with the local funeral home. Paul suggested we get home before someone called mother. We drove in separate cars, crossing the familiar road over Warrior Mountain and reached home before the telephone rang. Mother, upon seeing us appear together, collapsed. I looked out the door and saw a neighbor, known familiarly as Aunt Mattie, rounding the curve of the road. She was dressed in black and walked eagerly. Deaths were social events in Happy Valley, I reminded myself.

A front page obit appeared in the local newspaper. It called Dad "the father of rural electrification in North Carolina." The AP picked it up. Russ would read it on the teletype, I assumed. How would he feel? Telegrams and telephone calls poured in. Dad in death had honor but little else, although hundreds of miles of power lines throughout the Blue Ridge stood as a monument to his memory.

Burial was in Harper's Chapel cemetery. While waiting for everyone to assemble, I walked by the open grave to stare at the headstone of my grandmother. The Messicks came to America in 1664 and moved to North Carolina a century later. My great grandfather had been idealistic enough to go north to fight against slavery in the Civil War. After the war, he'd married Mary Hicks and settled in Happy Valley. Two children were born and a third was on the way when Finley Messick decided to move to Texas. Along the way he died of fever. His wife brought her children back to the Blue Ridge where she remarried and lived out her life. Had she gone on to Texas my father and I would have been other than what we became. We might not have been.

It was a sad and hectic time, but eventually it ended and — thanks to Skipper — I found myself working on *The Durham Herald* and living with my family in a rented house on the outskirts of that dirty tobacco town. Not long after moving in, I received a call from Waynesville. The ex-Marine sounded melancholic.

"I'm sorry to report that a certain deacon was visiting a female church member when her husband came home early from work and found them in bed. Being an impetuous fellow, he shot the deacon and being a good shot, he killed him with one bullet."

"When did this tragic event occur?" I asked.

"About thirty minutes ago," said my friend laconically. "You've got a scoop."

"Wish I could write it," I replied, "but thanks anyway."

Several weeks later a follow-up story came in on the *Herald's* wire. A trial jury in Waynesville had acquitted the defendant of killing David "Dog" Underwood, and a large crowd of citizens had loudly applauded the verdict.

Sometimes things work out, I told myself. The next step was to get a newspaper job in Kentucky.

ONE
6 April '57

The small plane banked sharply after taking off, giving me a view of Louisville nestled in a curve of the Ohio River, and then headed east across rolling horse country where allegedly blue grass grew. Our destination was the town of Maysville, also on the Ohio before the river makes its big bend to the northwest by Newport and Cincinnati. In addition to the pilot, a photographer was aboard. Our assignment was to cover a ceremony honoring Stanley Reed, recently retired as an Associate Justice of the U.S. Supreme Court. Reed as a young attorney had practiced law in the river town and folks there wanted the world to know it. The entire court led by Chief Justice Earl Warren was scheduled to attend.

It had taken me five years to get from North Carolina to *The Courier-Journal* and this was my first out-of-town assignment. The fact that I was an overnight celebrity may have been responsible for my selection. Or perhaps no one else was available on a Saturday. On the night before I had appeared on national television when a story I'd written in Raleigh was televised on the "Big Story" series. It had gone pretty well with emphasis properly placed on the young black hero's courage in helping me expose a loan-shark racket preying on city employees. In any case, it had impressed my mother-in-law who had flown up from Atlanta to view it with us. When I casually mentioned I'd be away next day covering the Supreme Court, she had been visibly awed. Her reaction was, of course, very gratifying to a hillbilly from Happy Valley.

RAZZLE DAZZLE

There had been other big stories as I attempted to impress the editors of Kentucky's largest newspaper. Hurricane Hazel had blown into central North Carolina and I'd written the lead story. I had broken a story about Duke University's faculty denying an honorary degree to its law school graduate, Vice President Richard Nixon. There had been stories about school desegregation which were equally unpopular with executive editor Steed Rollins and ultimately I'd been asked to resign. According to Rollins, my stories weren't worth the trouble they caused him. The job loss came as my first son, Hank, was recovering from meningitis and a week before our second son, Jon, was born.

Mark Ethridge, Jr. had welcomed me to *The Raleigh Times*. He had recently been hired by Jonathan Daniels, editor of the morning newspaper, to breathe new life into the *Times*. He wanted aggressive reporting and I gave it to him, the loan-shark story being one of many. Circulation soared, but the happy days lasted only a year before Mark was forced to quit. Almost everyone else quit too. Mark Ethridge, Sr., impressed with his son's recommendation, offered the job I'd long been seeking in Louisville. Upriver, one hundred miles away, was Newport.

We droned along for quite awhile before seeing the blue ribbon of water that was the Ohio again, and we bumped down easily enough on a grassy field which boasted a windsock. A car had been arranged so without delay we headed for downtown Maysville. A biting cold wind blew steadily and the sunlight was pale with little warmth. In the yard beside the courthouse a large platform had been erected and decorated in the national colors. A crowd of several hundred had collected, milling about waiting for the program to begin.

A young man, excitement written large on his face, approached almost respectfully. Upon confirming I represented *The Courier-Journal*, he introduced himself as a reporter for *The Maysville Messenger*.

"This is the second big story we've had in two weeks," he confided.

"Yeah? What was the other one?"

"They're going to build a second story on the Five & Ten," he said seriously.

Well, everything is relative.

There was a stir of excitement and the Supreme Court, each member wearing his robe, appeared and climbed the steps to the seats arranged for them on the platform. Several justices looked very frail; I hoped they had on long johns beneath their regalia. It seemed to be getting colder.

Everyone waited.

"Why the delay?" I asked the reporter.

"We can't start till the Governor gets here."

"Hell," I growled, playing the part of the big-time reporter. "Happy will wait until Warren's balls freeze off. Good politics."

Those were the days when the John Birch Society plastered billboards across the country with the message:

IMPEACH EARL WARREN

The Supreme Court decision on school integration was one reason for the Birchers' dislike, and it was prejudice widely shared by many people. Governor A.B. "Happy" Chandler had always posed as a man of the people. While he stood in no doorways to block blacks, he might have done so if opportunity offered. I had met Chandler several weeks before at a basketball game in Louisville. We discussed the Tarheels' chances of remaining undefeated during the playoffs. The former baseball commissioner professed to be a great sports fan.

The wind blew, the Supreme Court shivered, and forty-four minutes after the designated hour, the Governor rode up in a State Police car. As the crowd thronged around him, he began shaking hands. Smiling, well-fed, and apparently warm enough, Chandler made his way slowly toward the platform. I moved into position near the steps. Happy had a reputation of never forgetting a face or the name that went with it, and I wanted to see if he would remember me.

"How about them Tarheels?" he boomed, and thrust out a hand to pat my shoulder.

North Carolina had remained undefeated, surviving three overtimes in the championship game, to win the national title. The icy wind continued to blow, the Supreme Court continued to shiver, and for five minutes the Governor of Kentucky and I discussed basketball. While proud of my Alma Mater, I really wasn't that interested in the subject, but I was curious as to how much time we could waste.

"Great work," he concluded as if I had some responsibility, and went on up the steps. No one needed to introduce him. A great cheer went up as Chandler stepped to the microphone.

"It's a great honor to introduce Chief Justice Warren," he shouted, and that was that. He shook hands with the man in black, then went back down the steps to his police car, slapping backs all the way.

Meanwhile, the rotund Chief Justice was acting as master of ceremonies, introducing his colleagues who spoke briefly but warmly of their old associate. A bronze plaque bearing Reed's name and likeness was unveiled. It was dated 1956. The reporter explained the program had been originally planned for the year before when Maysville's flood protection walls were dedicated, but Reed had been unable to attend.

Local officials were permitted to speak briefly and then the guest of honor stepped forward. He discarded a prepared speech, a copy of which I had obtained, and spoke of his pride and gratitude. Then turning to a white-haired woman — obviously his wife — he said:

"All the success I have I owe to her."

It was a moving moment despite the cold, and I made notes rapidly. The high school band played "My Old Kentucky Home." All the tears I saw on cheeks weren't caused by the wind.

"Weep no more, my lady..."

Hastily, the ceremony broke up. The distinguished guests, including of course the reporter and photographer from Louisville, were whisked away to a stately mansion where some of the ladies of the town had prepared enough food to feed a plantation. It was served buffet style, and the old men of the law fell upon the table like hungry field hands. Trays on individual folding tables were provided. I found the Chief Justice of the United States huddled in a stairwell, attacking a plate of beaten biscuits topped with ham and washing them down with black coffee.

He didn't want to talk until his plate was empty and then, of course, he refused to comment on current affairs. Somehow, I got on the subject of his days as Attorney General of California, and he told me about his campaign to close down the fleet of gambling ships that once anchored off Los Angeles. The key, he said, had been the syndicate's failure to get licenses for the water taxis that conveyed the suckers out to the ships beyond the three-mile limit.

"Of course our success probably led to the establishment of the Strip outside Las Vegas," he commented, "so what was gained?"

"At least you had fun," I suggested.

His grin made him look twenty years younger.

I let him escape from under the stairs to hunt down some bourbon flavored cake, and went over to Stanley Reed to offer the congratulations of my newspaper.

In answer to a question, he told me: "I'm as healthy as a horse," — and he proved it by living well past one hundred years.

After the photographer and I ate our fill — the biscuits were delicious and the ham sweet — we departed on another chore. Maysville not only had Reed to boast about but it could claim the birthplace of Rosemary Clooney whose song, "This Old House," had made her famous. The Sunday Editor wanted a pix of Rosemary's old home. It proved to be still standing, if just barely, and fitted perfectly the description in the song. Then it was back to our plane. We arrived in Louisville in ample time to meet all deadlines. The editors made one change in my story. I had noted that Happy stopped to talk "to this reporter" while the Supreme Court sat freezing. They changed it to "a reporter." Then I went home to tell Faye's mother about my adventures.

The following week, City Editor John Herchenroeder — big, bald, and bland — gave me a slip of blue paper. Addressed to Executive Editor James Pope, it was signed BB for Barry Bingham, Sr., publisher, and was handwritten:

> I thought Hank Messick did an unusually good job on the Stanley Rèed story. It read as if he had a lifelong background of Kentucky politics and personalities.

Many years later I received another reaction. The young reporter I met in Maysville had moved to a small daily in Ohio and in a review of one of my books he recalled the day the Supreme Court came to town. Messick, he noted, was "the most cynical reporter I ever met."

Well, you can't please everyone.

To be frank, I was rather astonished at the good impression the Reed story created. It had seemed fairly routine, except, of course, for the plane flight. On the other hand, I was constantly being surprised by the "Curious Jumble"—as the *C-J* was affectionately referred to by staffers. The newspaper, which circulated all over the state, sat at Sixth and Broadway, next to the post office. On the fourth floor was the newsroom, divided by a glass partition into two sections, one for the *C-J* and the other for *The Louisville Times*, the afternoon paper. In theory, Pope was executive editor of both sheets, but in practice he left the *Times* to managing editor Norman Isaacs, once known as "the boy wonder." On the floor above was the cafeteria and the studios of WHAS-TV and radio. On the floor below were executive offices and the newspaper morgue — only here it was the library, and, by far, the best I'd ever enjoyed.

Legend dated the newspaper's rise to Henry Watterson who had been editor when it was purchased after World War I by Barry's father, Worth, with money inherited from his second wife. The two men clashed eventually and Watterson was fired. The paper went into a long decline which ended only when Barry took over after his father was appointed ambassador to England. He brought in Mark Ethridge in 1936 who restored its quality.

Many rumors circulated about Judge Worth Bingham, as he was known, and about his rich wife's death. Years later Sally Bingham, Barry's daughter, brought them all out into the open in a rather bitter book. During my years at the *C-J*, however, staff members were content to let the matter alone. Barry was respected. While he left the operation of his papers to Ethridge, he took an active role in the political and cultural life of the city and the state. Newspaper policy was liberal in things national and international and conservative in local matters. The press, in other words, was part of the Establishment.

If Bingham was respected, Ethridge was loved. The word isn't too strong. He was first and foremost a newspaperman. One afternoon he dropped by the City Room and remarked to a group of staffers that he would rather be city editor than anything else — "if Barry would pay me the same." Yet he was always being sent by the President of the United States on special missions to far away corners of the world. His wife, Willie Snow, usually went along and wrote a comic account of their adventures. "It's Greek to Me" was one such book.

My most immediate concern was City Editor Herchenroeder. He looked like the grim, tough editor of legend, but despite his size, Herch had only finished Male High in Louisville. He lived in mortal fear that one of his bright young men would get his job. The staff griped a lot about Herch over coffee, but, in time, I could see the logic of his appointment. He served as an effective brake on the educated reporters, keeping them in touch with journalistic reality.

The real boss after the top brass went home was the man we called "Chief." Slender, elderly, he never wasted words as he tinkered with layout and determined how stories were played. Experience taught him how his bosses wanted things handled and for every situation there was a precedent. If anything, the *C-J* relied too much on precedent, but having achieved its reputation, its editors saw no need to experiment.

It didn't take me long to realize I was a bit superfluous. There wasn't even a desk available. Pope, a soft-spoken Georgian, was perhaps a bit miffed at Ethridge's action in hiring me, but shortly after the Reed story ran he stopped me in the hall to say he was giving me a pay raise.

"You're too far behind the others," he explained.

And shortly after that a veteran reporter died and I claimed his vacant desk. At the desk next to me was Miriam Porter, one of three women on the staff, and another veteran. Ultimately, she would die at her desk.

There were about ten general assignment reporters and another ten who had "beats"— or special fields of expertise such as medicine, religion, or real estate. The newer men and the bachelors were expected to work on weekends, some of them acting as city editor or rewrite editor.

A "university atmosphere" was cultivated by Ethridge and Bingham. Reporters were always winning fellowships or grants to study in Africa or England. That their study proved of little value when they returned to Louisville was considered irrelevant. The newspaper had no foreign correspondents of its own but it subscribed to the news services of *The New York Times* and thus provided its readers with wide coverage of world events. Indeed, the *C-J* modeled itself after the New York newspaper to such an extent that it was usually ranked third or fourth best in the country. Some of my fellow reporters sometimes wondered why more was not demanded of the local staff, but, all in all, they were content with reflected glory.

After my first week on the job I commented to Faye that it was nice to work with people who were your equal and perhaps your superior. That was a hasty judgment, but, on the whole, a sound one. In time I was to recognize that the staff contained its quota of jerks, some of whom had enough sense to recognize their good fortune in being hired and hung on with desperate rancor.

At the first opportunity after arriving, I asked Ora Spaid about Newport. Spaid was the paper's religion writer and he was more cynical than most.

"It's a hell hole," said Spaid, "but we leave it alone. The Cincinnati papers dominate up there in northern Kentucky but they don't do much either. About five years ago they were having a factional struggle in Newport and a cop came down and deputized a busload of private eyes in Louisville for a raid on a joint. We sent along a reporter and a photographer. George Bailey was the photographer. He took a pix of the police chief with his arm around the gambler who was being raided and the cops promptly threw George in jail. He said he thought they were going to throw him into the river. The paper raised hell and the chief was indicted for violating Bailey's civil rights. He was convicted too, and paid a thousand dollar fine and went back to work."

"So?"

"So the *C-J* hasn't sent a reporter or a photographer to Newport since. And it's still considered one of the best papers in the country."

"Did you ever hear of a guy named Frank Andriola up at Newport?"

"No," said Spaid, "but that doesn't mean anything."

I wasn't discouraged by the conversation. Newport could wait. First, I had to get established, prove myself. Others could seek applause by writing thoughtful stories about urban renewal, medical breakthroughs, metropolitan government, but corruption was apparently an open field. Sooner rather than later my opportunity would come.

****

Unable to find a house or apartment to rent in Louisville upon arrival, we settled across the river in Indiana. The small house was located in Jeffersonville, one of three towns on the western bank, and it was actually closer to the newspaper than a home in the suburbs on the Kentucky side. The only obstacle was the traffic on Clark Bridge, but on the 2 to 11 p.m. shift, I missed the rush hour jam. The area needed a new bridge just as it needed new roads and new industry. Economic stagnation existed yet all people wanted to talk about was the upcoming Kentucky Derby — the big event of the year.

Derby Day on the first Saturday in May was always preceded by the annual banquet of the Honorable Order of Kentucky Colonels. A Kentucky Colonel was anyone so commissioned by the Governor of the Commonwealth, and thus included a lot of politicians and campaign contributors. There was a certain romance about it, and I was pleased to be assigned to cover the dinner at a downtown hotel.

Each Colonel had his moment of glory. At the entrance to the big room stood a "herald" with a huge staff. As each individual arrived with his "lady," the herald slammed the staff against the floor and announced in stentorian tones:

"Colonel John Doe and Mrs. Doe."

And with eyes evaluating their looks and evening clothes, in they proudly paraded.

It had become traditional to have as master of ceremony George Jessel, an aging film star who allegedly was both suave and witty. And traditionally he brought along a Hollywood starlet, introducing her solemnly as his "fiance." This entitled her to a seat at the head table but over at the end near the press — which was very nice for the press.

The affair soon seemed silly. Jessel's jokes were inane and the pomp and circumstance forced and artificial. In talking to Karen Hanson, who wore a spectacular low-cut gown of sleek silver, I discovered she didn't even sleep with plump "Georgie."

"He just brought me along for show," she explained. Even more shocking was her refusal to drink a mint julep or anything else with bourbon in it. She gave me a tip on a horse, however. She couldn't remember the name, but it "has something to do with King Arthur."

Neither Bingham nor Ethridge nor any of their friends attended the dinner, but Happy Chandler was there and in good form. It was that kind of gathering.

The race next day was also disappointing. I was given passes that let me roam everywhere from the pressbox to the clubhouse to the paddock, and told to write "My First Derby." In the past, or so I heard, celebrities from movie stars to royalty attended but the event had gradually lost its glamor. The attendance was always given as one hundred thousand, but on this day the infield was largely empty of people. I got into line at a betting window and found upon reaching the window that it was for combination bets. So I put down six bucks on Round Table. He finished in the money and I collected four dollars.

A strange business, I decided, and rode a bus back to the office where I knocked out my story in time to make the first edition. The Chief played it on the front page but, after the main stories were written, it ended back with the want ads. That was all right too. Miss Hanson called to thank me for the nice things I'd written about her in the banquet story, and invited me to come see her in Hollywood. Somehow I never got around to it.

Summer passed and things settled into a routine. Faye and I made a down payment on a house to be built in a new subdivision east of Louisville, but we would have to wait a year or more before it could be ready. The land was covered with huge old oak trees and was close to new schools and shopping. The house would be a tri-level and spacious. We looked forward eagerly to its construction.

One day while covering some sort of public event I thought I had stumbled on a good story. Spotting a white-clad figure, I approached close enough to hear the man boast he would soon be a millionaire. He wore a white goatee to match his Plantation style suit, and he was plump and articulate.

"I just bought this recipe from a black man for only two hundred dollars," he said happily. "It's a combination of herbs and spices he uses to fix the best fried chicken I ever ate. Think I'll franchise it and make millions."

The man he was talking to just nodded, and the two strolled away. Back at the paper I told Herch. He laughed with genuine amusement.

"That's Harlan Sanders," he told me. "Got a restaurant down state and goes around dressed like an original Kentucky Colonel. Always promoting something. Next week it'll be frog legs maybe."

I wasn't convinced. When a man boasts of cheating a black man out of his secret recipe, he must believe it's worth something.

"Got a tip I want you to check out," said my city editor. "Probably doesn't amount to anything either, but maybe we ought to look into it."

It seemed that Logan Shaw, one of our three police reporters and, in my opinion, our only good one, had found an angry sergeant in the Jefferson County Police Department who wanted to talk about cop corruption. Logan, of course, didn't want to get involved since he had to work with the police on a daily basis, but he did tell Herch about it.

When I reached Sgt. Myron Marrs at county police headquarters, we made a date to meet at his home after work. That meant around midnight for he lived east of Shively in one of the vast subdivisions built for veterans after the war. I wasn't too happy about the distance and could only hope I wasn't wasting my time on a nut.

Marrs proved to be a short, heavy man in his thirties, almost defensive in his belligerence. His wife, a pale, thin woman, served coffee and went to bed. Their four children were already asleep.

"So you want the skinny?" said the sergeant. "Well, it's about time somebody did."

"What do you mean by 'skinny'?"

"The naked truth," he replied with a grin. "Let me tell you about it."

The police department was completely corrupt. Traffic ticket fixing was on an organized basis. Robbery had become a science — an alarm at a supermarket set off by cops who then "investigated" and helped themselves. Handbooks accepted bets on horses as openly as pari-mutual wagering at Churchill Downs, and payoffs on pinball machines games were condoned.

Much of his specific information concerned the third district where he had worked until being assigned to headquarters to get him out of the way, but the "skinny" from officers in other districts told the same story. The police chief, Walter Layman, was largely a figurehead, yet even he had intervened to protect his son when the boy was identified in a robbery-by-violence case. The chief had paid off the victim and obtained a receipt. Marrs had taken it from the chief's desk.

"I considered it evidence of a crime," he said unabashedly.

We talked until after two in the morning. He gave me the "skinny" he'd collected: police reports, pictures, and even the chief's receipt. I had enough material for a dozen stories once the data had been checked and confirmed. There was still one question.

"Why are you telling me this?"

He grinned. "Hell, I've been trying to tell somebody this for months. Shaw, at least, listened to me; the others didn't want to hear. As to why, well, I'm a Christian and try to live like one. I moonlight on the side as an electrician so I don't need graft."

I looked up at the large picture of Christ on the wall. The house was neat, clean, and comfortable. It pretended to be no more than it was. Nor did this man.

"Are you alone in this?"

No, I've got about a dozen guys, all veterans, who feel the way I do. They keep their eyes and ears open and pass me the skin. The brass got suspicious, I guess, and tried to put me on ice at headquarters. Some people don't like troublemakers."

"Amen," I said. "Can you set up a meeting so I can talk to your pals?"

"Call me tomorrow." he said.

"Thanks, Sergeant."

"Call me Bub. Everybody else does."

We shook hands. It was a long drive back across Louisville and the Ohio, but I was well content. I didn't dream that in accepting his files I might be committing a felony.

#

10 September '57

Executive Editor James Pope came out of his plain little office and moved to a spot where he could see his reporters at their desks. He caught my eye and gestured with his head. I walked by my colleagues who watched with interest. Pope motioned to the Chief. When I joined them in the hall he handed the copy he was holding to the News Editor.

"We don't want to seem like we're sensationalizing this," he said, "so play it at the bottom of the front page."

The Chief read the lead aloud:

"An 18-month-old story of County police intervention to prevent a criminal charge against the police chief's son has been brought to light."

It was not, perhaps, the most exciting lead the Chief had seen, but it brought a rare reaction from that taciturn man: a low whistle.

"Come in early tomorrow," said Pope. "We may need you." He went back to his office. I went back to my desk.

The decision to go first with the saga of County Police Chief Walter Layman's son had been my own. I told Herch only that Marrs had good information that needed checking out. He told me to go ahead while, of course, not neglecting my new duties as suburban beat reporter.

Jefferson County contained dozens of sixth class cities, one fifth class city, two fourth class cities, and, of course, the only first class city in the state. County police enforced the law in the sixth class cities as well as the unincorporated areas. Attempts to form a metropolitan government such as existed in Dade County, Florida had failed, primarily because the suburbanites distrusted the entrenched political machine that had run Louisville for decades. And, of course, the officials of even sixth class cities didn't want to lose the prestige of office. My attempts to cover this bewildering array of municipalities gave me good contacts throughout the county although it produced few major stories.

The police report given me by Marrs identified Dolph Skaggs, age 20, as the victim of Layman's son. The incident happened on 13 March, 1956. Skaggs had since moved out of the county, and it took some detective work to locate him in the produce department of a supermarket in a town on down the road. He talked willingly enough. Basically he had been followed from work one evening by teenagers in a late model car. They cut him off, pulled him from his car. beat him savagely, and robbed him of his watch and wallet. He called police and gave full information to Detective H.T. Gilmore.

Next day, according to Skaggs, he spotted the car and wrote down the license number which he gave to Gilmore. The car was owned by the police chief's wife. On the following day Gilmore offered a deal: payment in full for his losses in return for signing a release giving the attackers and their families immunity from court action. Skaggs accepted $109.75 but remained angry. When I told him that one of the robbers was the police chief's son, he signed an affidavit.

With the lead story wrapped up, I investigated other allegations. Marrs and his fellow cops gave me the skinny as promised. The last step had been an interview with Chief Layman. He denied nothing, asking me only not to "hurt my boy."

Ed Zingman, a young attorney who worked for the large law firm that represented Bingham's interests, cleared the story for publication albeit a little disdainfully. Either he felt such muckraking was beneath the dignity of the newspaper or was worried about the political consequences of annoying the hitherto all-powerful machine that had selected Layman.

The story ran as Pope had ordered on the bottom of the front page. A copy of the receipt Marrs took from the chief's desk was beside it.

Next morning when I appeared at ten o'clock, Jim Rankin, my old city editor in Raleigh now on *The Times* copy desk, yelled at me:

"Hey, Hank. Layman says he'll resign."

Jim held up the early edition carrying an eight-column banner.

There was considerable excitement on the *C-J*'s side of the building and perhaps some relief at Layman's decision not to make a fight of it. He did resign that afternoon. I let someone else write that while I concentrated on my next story. County Judge Van Arsdale gave me a lead by promising to investigate a traffic ticket racket. With Marrs' help I learned of seventeen persons cited or charged the previous month who had not appeared in court. Some of those cited admitted their tickets had been fixed.

Included in the story was an account of a real estate developer — he had built Valley Village off Dixie Highway — who had been arrested during a "drunknet" operated jointly by county and state troopers. The county cops took the man home instead of to jail, and found another drunk to substitute for him. Captain Carlos Johns was the officer involved. My investigation had disclosed other links between the developer and Johns who commanded the third district. In effect, the cops had acted as the big shot's private army.

That story ran high on the front page next day and the reaction was swift. Commonwealth's Attorney A. Scott Hamilton announced a grand jury probe of all allegations. The county police review board promised an investigation of the cops. Information flowed in from other officers who suddenly found their courage. I was busier than a hound dog with fleas, yet soon I sensed a feeling of unease hanging over the newsroom. Finally, I asked Ora Spaid about it. He laughed rather grimly.

"It's Scott Hamilton," he said. "He's mad at the *C-J* and out to get us any way he can."

I'd heard some scuttlebutt about Hamilton, but no one had seemed interested in giving details. The guy looked like a successful politician should: tall, not fat, with a handsome face and a mane of gray hair.

"It happened before you got here," continued Spaid, who, I had observed, would rather talk than work. "Hamilton tried to be a Kentucky

Joe McCarthy and started looking for Reds. We had a copy editor who was an avowed liberal and had helped a black family move into a white neighborhood. Scott got a search warrant and raided the editor's house. I guess he found a copy of Karl Marx or something, and he claimed the editor was using the newspaper to spread communist propaganda. That scared the top brass even though it was ridiculous on its face. What harm can a copy editor do?"

"Mess up a good story," I commented.

Spaid, who sometimes worked as weekend city editor, grinned and continued: "Hamilton persuaded a grand jury to indict our copy editor on sedition charges. The paper suspended him. All kinds of nuts showed up at the trial — the FBI was cooperating with Hamilton — and our man was convicted."

I recalled a would-be sports writer on *The Durham Herald* who made a career of testifying for the FBI about alleged Reds in North Carolina. Most of what he swore to was fiction.

"Ultimately, the U.S. Supreme Court overturned the guilty verdict on the grounds that sedition was a federal not a state offense. Hamilton was broken-hearted. He had planned to run for governor on an anti-communist platform. So he still hates the *C-J* and so does the FBI."

"What happened to the copy editor?"

"They fired him after his conviction."

"That doesn't seem a very nice thing to do," I remarked.

Ora shrugged. "They didn't want the paper smeared any more than necessary. Right now, I expect everyone is scared Hamilton will try to hurt the paper through your stories."

"How's he going to do that?"

"God knows," said the religion writer. "Scott Hamilton is capable of anything. He's got a big house out in the country with floodlights all around that burn all night. He tells every one the Reds are after him. The man is sick."

The tale made me uncomfortable, but I could see no cause for alarm. I was somewhat surprised, therefore, a few days later upon arriving at work early to have Herch shout: "Where have you been?"

"I got stuck in traffic on Clark Bridge."

"Well, get out of here. Go back to Indiana and stay there. They're hunting you with a subpoena."

"Why?"

"Word is they want to indict you. Scram."

I fled to the safety of another state and told my surprised wife I was a fugitive from justice. A few minutes later the telephone rang. She answered. It was Scott Hamilton demanding to know where I could be found. She told him she didn't know. After all, I was out of sight in the yard. The baby fell down the steps and started screaming. Hamilton got the message.

"I guess you've got your hands full," he said, and hung up.

I sat around wondering and worrying. In late afternoon the phone rang again. Faye handed it to me. It was Herchenroeder and he told me to come to the office.

The place was in a turmoil when I arrived. Word had just come in that the county police chief, his son, and several officers had been indicted on various charges. Even the real estate developer had been hit.

However...

City Editor Herchenroeder and Reporter Hank Messick had also been indicted on charges of knowingly receiving stolen property — the receipt taken from the chief's desk — and Sergeant Marrs had been charged with stealing it.

I'd given the receipt to Herch for use in the paper, and then I'd returned the original to Marrs.

My city editor looked a little pale but he tried to sound confident.

"I don't think we've anything to worry about," he said. "I've already got word the indictment against me will be dismissed tomorrow. Hamilton and I were friends before all the trouble started. Some of the jurors thought that if they were going to indict you they ought to include me, and Hamilton couldn't very well stop them."

"What about me?"

He shrugged. "I guess that'll stand, but don't worry; the paper will back you all the way."

"Like it did that copy editor," I suggested.

He sighed deeply and shook his head.

I was beginning to worry and wonder if I had blundered into another no-win situation when, unexpectedly, Barry Bingham's secretary asked me to come to his office. It proved to be plush indeed, with thick carpets, paneling, and paintings on the wall. There were a lot of books, I noticed, and the secretary was smiling.

Bingham's face was somber but he arose as I entered and stuck out his hand.

"Thanks for coming down," he said, as if I had any choice. "Have a seat, please."

Dressed in English tweeds, he was a slender, sandy-haired man who looked as if a brisk game of tennis would be his cup of tea. His elbows on his desk, he leaned toward me.

"I want to apologize to you," he said, and abruptly I stopped thinking about Steed Rollins. "As you may know, Scotty Hamilton went on an anti-communist crusade awhile back and tried to picture *The Courier-Journal* as a communist propaganda sheet. The Supreme Court slapped him down and he hasn't recovered. To be frank, I think he's a bit demented."

"He surely acts like it," I commented.

Bingham leaned back in his chair. "I know this situation must be a terrible shock. I'm sorry Hamilton struck at the paper through you. It goes without saying that we will back you all the way."

I felt the heaviness in my stomach evaporate.

"In that case," I said, "don't worry about it. I don't mind a fight in a good cause."

Later I was to reflect that it might have been wiser to seem less macho. I should have perhaps expressed shock and dismay. After all, word of my indictment would go out over the wire and people all over the country would hear of it. Getting charged with a felony was a serious business. Bingham, despite his wealth and power, was a sensitive human being and might have felt more responsibility for me had I seemed more upset.

I did take advantage of the opportunity to tell him about Sergeant Marrs. "He's not just a stool pigeon," I said. "He's a good man and he's sincerely concerned about the corruption he's observed. I hope the paper will back him too."

"We will, we will," assured Bingham, but, somehow, the patrician face showed impatience. He stood up.

"Thank you for coming down. If there's anything you need, call me."

As I walked away I noticed that the large office adjoining was dark. Mark Ethridge, Sr., the man who had hired me, was out of town. Well, apparently I did not need him. Attorney Zingman proved his value by taking care of the legal formalities. I was told I didn't have to surrender, be fingerprinted, or enter a plea. All I had to do was wait until the first edition came off the presses, and take a copy home to my wife.

The principal story concerned the police indictments with a sidebar devoted to the good guys: Herchenroeder, Marrs, and Messick. They were well written and factual. A statement from Bingham expressing support for his staffers was included.

Faye concealed her worries and we tried to explain the situation to seven-year-old Marda. Next day some of her second grade classmates tried to tease her and she replied stoutly:

"My daddy didn't do anything wrong."

The only other reaction came from the once-a-week maid who came to work next day and announced she was quitting.

"I have no respect for a thief," she said.

Faye laughed at her. After all, she didn't do windows.

The Courier-Journal immediately launched an editorial campaign for a special prosecutor to handle the Marrs-Messick case. Herch's indictment had been dismissed, as he expected, on Hamilton's motion. This prompted one of the grand jurors to write a letter to the editor which asked:

"Why should an indictment against one newsman be dismissed while the indictment against another is upheld when the evidence against both is exactly the same?"

Herch was a little miffed at that, but, privately, I thought the grand juror had a right to be puzzled. Ultimately, after constant pressure from the media, Hamilton did step aside and allow a special prosecutor to be appointed. His office, however, retained control of the other cases.

The story did get national attention. Even *The New York Times* devoted a full column to it. I began hearing from old friends around the country, including Nick Lindsay, son of the poet, Vachel Lindsay. I had been best man at Nick's wedding back in Chapel Hill and at his urgent request found a minister to replace a justice of peace when the bride's parents arrived unexpectedly. It was sort of reassuring to learn the marriage had survived.

Within a few days the County Police Merit Board began hearings. Our police reporters didn't want to get involved so the reporting was left largely to me. On one occasion Bob Hermann went along. Captain Carlos Johns began giving me hell. Bob took it all down in shorthand so I concentrated on making the cop even angrier, causing him to make even wilder statements. Back at the office, Bob typed up his notes and I incorporated them in my story. A little help from a friend was welcome, but for the most part I worked alone.

One evening after a long hard day, I was relaxing at home when Marrs called. He had been hauled in unexpectedly before the review board and ordered to hand over his badge and gun. Since he was off duty, he did not have them on his person, and had been told to go home and get them immediately.

"Why are they firing you?" I asked.

"Because I told the whole truth. Remember that fake super market robbery? Well, the other bastards were carrying out meat and liquor by the case and I was hungry so I picked up a twenty five cent pack of luncheon meat and ate it. I was hungry."

"And you told the review board?"

"Damned right. I wasn't about to put the finger on the other guys and not tell what I'd done."

Maybe he was a little too honest.

"Take your time going back," I said. "I'll get over there as fast as I can."

I hung up and made a quick call to the paper. Gordon Englehart was working the desk that night and for that I was thankful. A combat veteran of World War II, Gordon was in the running to succeed Pope when that gentleman retired. He was not only a good editor but a good reporter.

"Save some space," I said. "They're about to fire Marrs."

"Okay," he replied.

I drove back over the dark waters of the Ohio to the courthouse which was located a couple of blocks from the river. The review board was meeting in the police chief's conference room. The door was locked.

About four minutes later Bub Marrs came out of the night. He was holding his badge, gun, and handcuffs. Giving me a quick grin, he knocked on the door and was instantly admitted. About ten minutes later he came out empty-handed and looking drained.

"Well," he said, "it's all over."

"Give me a statement."

The stocky man shrugged. "Let it go. I gave it my best shot."

I insisted. He sighed. "Okay, then. Quote me as saying I find it strange the man who tries to clean up the department is the one they fire."

We shook hands. "See you in court," he said, a reference to the fact that his trial was scheduled ahead of mine in about one week.

Ten minutes later the review board filed out. I confronted Chairman John Fulton. He read a prepared statement announcing that Marrs had demonstrated "his unfitness to fulfill a position of public trust" and had been discharged.

"You might try getting rid of some of the real crooks," I suggested.

A power in local politics was Fulton, and he had a proper sense of his importance.

"Don't talk like that," he said, "and be careful what you write."

It was getting late, final deadline was approaching. I drove to the newspaper where I put a new lead on the story I had written earlier and added details. Gordon gave it a good play.

"A helluva thing," he commented. "Go home and get some sleep."

There was reaction the next day. Calls flooded the switchboard and groups of citizens came in person to protest. One such took a large ad which began with a quote from Edmund Burke:

"The only thing necessary for the triumph of evil is for good men to do nothing."

And it proceeded to demand the ouster of review board members.

A legal defense fund was established but proved unnecessary. Frank Haddad, a brilliant attorney of Lebanese descent, took the case for nothing. He explained to me:

"Right after Marrs was indicted he and his wife came to my office with a bag full of silver dollars. They had been saving them for years as a hobby or something. They wanted me to take them as a down payment on my bill, but I wouldn't do it. I'll get the guy off free gratis."

"I hope you do," I replied. "For more than one reason."

The circuit court trial lasted two days. I sat through it under subpoena from the Commonwealth of Kentucky as a possible witness against Marrs. Special Prosecutor Henry Hobson did his utmost to persuade the jurors, even calling Scotty Hamilton as a rebuttal witness, but Marrs could not be shaken. When at last the jury retired to deliberate, Haddad looked at me with a grim smile.

"I think we've got this fucker whipped," he said.

And he was right. The jurors returned in thirty minutes with a not guilty verdict. The crowded courtroom broke into applause. Marrs kissed his wife, shook hands with his lawyer and hugged me.

"God was on our side," he murmured.

Three days later the charges against me were dismissed. The special prosecutor told the judge:

"If the document in question was not stolen, and a trial jury has said it was not, then obviously Mr. Messick isn't guilty of receiving stolen property."

Scott Hamilton issued a statement the following day deploring the dismissal as another example of communist influence at work. The *C-J* printed his remarks and everyone had a good laugh.

When the smoke from the great scandal settled, the final score was: one police chief replaced, a captain, a lieutenant and three sergeants — including Marrs — fired; and another lieutenant demoted to patrolman. A system of numbered traffic tickets was introduced and reform of the police merit system was promised by the political machine. None of the indictments prosecuted by Hamilton resulted in convictions. In fact, the only serious effort to convict anyone was made in the Marrs case.

Still, it was as satisfactory as the political system permitted. Marrs was glad to be out of police work. Many years later I mentioned him in a book and called to tell him. He informed me he had just become a preacher. To me it seemed a helluva waste of a good cop, and I said so. "Praise the Lord," he replied.

In February, 1958, the local chapter of Sigma Delta Chi, the national journalism fraternity, awarded me first prize for the best reporting of 1957 in Kentucky and southern Indiana. I was also nominated by a Columbia University professor for a Pulitzer Prize. I didn't win, but a little later that great communist hunter, A. Scott Hamilton, went home to his floodlighted mansion and blew out his brains.

*****

My adventures as an investigative reporter stirred no competitive instincts in my colleagues. Herchenroeder began assigning all tips about crime and corruption to me, and as more stories appeared, the tips increased in number. After noticing a knowing smile on the faces of some of my colleagues, I asked Ora Spaid what was funny.

"Herch has given you the shit beat," the religion writer said. "He feels obligated to have someone check out these tips but he'd be much happier if you came back without a story."

"What do you mean?" I asked.

"Simple. He just wants to protect himself. If Pope or Ethridge asks, he wants to be able to say he had it checked out and there was nothing to it. Who's going to prove him wrong? Isaacs isn't going to rock the boat. He knows Bingham likes constructive stories."

The conversation didn't bother me. I was learning and I was gaining the confidence of my superiors. The fact that in a "university atmosphere" no one else wanted to do the dirty work simply meant an opportunity for me. All this was but preliminary.

In the months that followed, I combined my routine duties as suburban reporter with various investigations. I discovered a tow-in racket. Democratic headquarters supplied a short list of approved garages, and cops who called one of the garages to tow in a wrecked car received two dollars which was added to the unfortunate motorist's bill. Publicity resulted in County Judge B.C. Van Arsdale — the man who ran the county government — initiating a system of bidding for the right to be called to an accident scene. He did so reluctantly and perhaps only because he was up for reelection. When we received allegations that certain handbook operators were able to use police to eliminate competition, I began visiting bookie joints.

Since the wealthy could go to Churchill Downs at intervals to place bets legally on pari-mutual machines, there was sincere debate within the newsroom as to the propriety of exposing taverns where the working man could lose his cash illegally. As a result, handbooks were tolerated and there were old-timers who boasted they were far less numerous than in the past when one could walk the length of Market Street and never miss the call of a single race. I soon disagreed. Things had indeed changed: the bookies had installed air conditioning and were able to keep doors and windows closed, and there were more books than ever. Obviously, the legal betting stimulated the illegal. After all, the corner handbook was more convenient and some even offered credit.

My forays became routine. I'd go into a joint, buy a beer, talk to someone about sports or politics, and then wander into a back room or up a stairs. The wire service was efficient; the race results were posted within minutes. Several times I actually won, but I soon grew sick of beer and began taking my mug to the toilet and pouring it out. There were just too many bookies. At one intersection on Dixie Highway three of the four corners were occupied by handbooks.

County officials insisted there were only a few bookies operating. I countered by obtaining a list of federal wagering-tax holders of which there were hundreds. Under federal law every bookie was supposed to buy a tax stamp and pay a tax on each bet accepted. The list contained not only names but addresses, and it was public record, open not only to the press but to police. It was difficult to believe people would buy stamps if they didn't intend to accept bets. Purchase of stamps gave them immunity on the federal level and payoffs to police provided protection locally. On several occasions I phoned a tip to police and then returned to the handbook to see the bookie suspend operations before the cops arrived. It was not long before the operators were posting my picture, clipped from the newspaper, by peepholes in the door.

It was embarrassing for the politicians but worse was to come. One day Herch gave me a letter Pope had received. The writer was a Chicago man who said he had recently spent eighteen days in our jail and had been forced to buy food from the jail commissary to avoid hunger. Supper, he explained, was served at 3 p.m. At 8 p.m. a cart loaded with goodies was wheeled around the cell block. His theory:

"Supper is served early so that those inmates with money will be so hungry they'll gorge themselves on commissary delicacies... How about the poor devils with no money? They have to go to sleep on a very empty stomach."

"See what you can find out," said Herch.

My experience with Jefferson County officials had convinced me I wouldn't get an honest answer to an honest question if it concerned corrupt practices, so I decided to try another approach. I asked Carol Sutton to take a letter.

Carol was a very pretty young lady who had begun work in the news department as a secretary and by determination and ability made herself into a good reporter. That some day she would become managing editor, I never for one moment dreamed.

She had some innocent looking blue stationery on which she wrote this letter to the editor:

I want to report on a shocking situation which I hope you will investigate. The prisoners in the jail are being pampered beyond belief. Many of them, I am sure, are getting better food than they are accustomed to. I've heard they even get steaks once a week and ice cream too. Now while I don't believe in being inhumane, I do think these people are common criminals and it is unfair to spend the taxpayer's money to give them things they don't deserve. No wonder many of them like being in jail. They don't want to get out. And when they do get out they come back next week at our expense. Just how much does the average meal at the jail cost the taxpayer?

Do they really get ice cream? I thought people were sent to jail as punishment, not for vacations at our expense.

    A poor taxpayer

When the ink dried, I took myself to the county jail to see the sheriff. In most counties the sheriff was a police official, but Jefferson County, having its own police force, used its sheriff to serve civil papers and operate a jail. Solon Russell, the balding fat man who wore the star, seemed very relieved after reading Carol's letter.

"Pamper them, do we?" he said, "Hardly." He waddled to a file cabinet and returned wlth some papers.

"In June," he began, "the average cost of food per meal per man was 9.46 cents. The cost of preparation, including labor, gas, and steam, brought the total cost to 10.61 cents per prisoner per meal."

The menu for August 9 — the day before — consisted of milk, sugar, sweet rolls and coffee for breakfast; pinto bean soup, onions, bread, and iced tea for lunch; chili, bread, and iced tea for supper. The bread was stale.

I asked a few questions and was given this information:

Supper was served at 3 p.m. "because we have church services and that sort of thing in the evenings sometimes." Prisoners were allowed to keep only two dollars but were allowed to draw upon any other money the jail kept for them as needed to maintain the two dollar level. And a cart containing food and cigarettes was wheeled around the cell blocks in the evenings. No, I couldn't get a picture of it.

It was after three o'clock. Russell permitted me to watch as prisoners went from their dining area to another room. They followed a painted line on the floor and the line carried them in front of the commissary window. Only one man stopped to buy something so soon after supper.

Returning to the *C-J*, I called the State Reformatory at LaGrange. Director Harold Black estimated the state spent twenty cents per meal per prisoner "and we don't overfeed them."

"Could prisoners be fed for ten cents per meal?"

"Well, it would sustain life," said Black.

I wrote my story.

Apparently it struck a nerve on the third floor. The editorial writers followed up with a suggestion the commissary be discontinued or, failing that, profits be used to supplement the regular diet of prisoners. Sheriff Russell stalled for three days before announcing the incorporation of the Jefferson County Jail Commissary and Charitable Fund, Inc. It had several official purposes, none of them to put more food on the table for inmates. It was a hollow victory for, with the heat off, only the prisoners would know if anything had changed for the better. Yet, the following February, the story was awarded the prize for best reporting of 1958. It was the first time any reporter had won in consecutive years.

We moved into our split-level home in Kentucky on Labor Day weekend, leaving Indiana without regrets. The house was in a subdivision called Plantation, and there was a clubhouse with an Olympic swimming pool and other facilities. Nearby was a small shopping center. An elementary school was just down the road and there Marda entered third grade.

Things were looking up.

A few days after our move, Executive Editor Pope called me into his office and asked;

"How would you like to go to Newport?"

"It might be interesting," I replied, and managed not to grin.

THREE
24 September '58

"Why did Pope decide to send you to Newport so suddenly?" asked Faye over dinner that night.

"He's trying to show up Isaacs," I replied.

Norman Isaacs, the managing editor of *The Louisville Times*, had recently imported a flashy young reporter from Las Vegas and sent him upriver to "discover" wide open gambling in Newport. Obviously, he assumed Pulitzer Prize judges would not know gambling in that town had been well documented by the Kefauver committee eight years earlier.

"Pope gave me a little wire story from Newport which said there was an anti-prostitution drive going on up there. 'If they're running the whores out of Newport,' he told me, 'then that's real news.'"

Faye asked, "Isn't Pope executive editor of both papers? Why does he need to show up Isaacs?"

I sipped my coffee. "Apparently Isaacs has a certain autonomy. I don't really understand why, but Pope resents it. Who cares? I've been waiting to go to Newport since Waynesville."

She looked at me with level blue eyes. "Isn't it rather dangerous?"

My shrug was sincere. "Later on, maybe, but not just right now. I'll slip up on them."

"Sometimes I wish you'd stayed a teacher," said Faye, and her sigh was audible.

"Those coeds were nice," I replied, and let it go at that.

Now here I was next day, parked in the driveway of the boarded up Lookout House. The view to the north was of the Ohio River and Cincinnati. It had taken me three hours to drive up Route 42, a two-lane winding road that followed the river. I had parked momentarily to stretch my legs and get my bearings. Until Kefauver, the Lookout House had been a major gambling casino but now it was abandoned. Directly below me was the second class city of Covington with its many church spires. The town was in Kenton County. I let my gaze sweep to the right, to the Licking River which divided Kenton and Campbell counties and Newport from Covington. Daniel Boone found salt licks at the mouth of the river, thus giving it a name.

On the east side of the river Newport stretched across bottom land and up a small hill. The city had less people now than in 1900, about 30,000. In contrast, Covington had grown in the years since Kefauver. Cincinnati, of course, was a metropolis and, relatively, a clean city. Newport was its escape valve. People on both sides of the Ohio called Newport "Little Mexico."

Getting back into the car I drove down the steep hill and followed road signs east. In a few minutes I was on a rusty bridge over the Licking, and then I was driving through "the Bottoms." I moved slowly, looking at the shabby buildings. The street was paved with bricks and a lot of bricks were missing. An air of decay hung over the city.

On the left came a loud knocking. I looked. A woman wearing a red kimono was standing at a window. One hand knocked on the glass, the other supported a large naked breast. When our eyes met, she stopped knocking and waved in a come-hither gesture.

"Welcome to Newport," I told myself, grinned at the woman who was really too large for my taste, and drove on up Fourth Street. By an ancient courthouse, complete with tower and clock, I turned right onto York Street and went by several night clubs. Later I would learn that York was known as "Casino Row." It ran one way south. I followed it to the edge of town, turned left to Monmouth, which was one way north to a bridge over the Ohio. About halfway down Monmouth I spotted a neon sign that said "Glenn Rendezvous." There was a smaller sign that said "Hotel." I parked in front of the building, grabbed my bag and got out. A man stepped from the doorway and put a quarter into the parking meter.

"On the house," he said.

"Thanks."

The man turned away. He was well dressed, well built. I wondered if he had other duties.

There was a desk inside the lobby and behind it the usual pigeon holes for mail and keys. An elderly man looked up at me after I banged on the little bell in front of him. His gaze was wary.

"I'd like a room," I said.

"Don't have no rooms," said the man.

"Any particular reason?"

The old man showed tobacco stained teeth. "The rooms are for customers, not guests," he said.

To my right was the opening to what seemed to be a small restaurant or supper club. It was dark. In front of me was a paneled wall of some light colored material. I could see no opening in it. Nothing moved, the joint seemed deserted. I took my bag back to my car. Cutting down to York again I drove south. The street became a highway. About three miles out I passed a cleared hill crowned by a long low building. Along the driveway leading up to it were block letters spelling: BEVERLY HILLS COUNTRY CLUB. It looked prosperous.

Another two miles and I found a small motel. I parked in front of it, got out, and gazed across the road. Over there was a large brick home and behind it cultivated fields stretched over the rolling hills. Someday Northern Kentucky University would rise out of those corn fields. The brick home would become a hospitality house and I would be honored at a reception there. But of all that, of course, I had no presentiment.

The woman in the motel office seemed glad to see me. After registering, I asked about the country club.

"It's the Las Vegas of the East," she said. "They have a wonderful floor show."

"And gambling?"

"Of course."

"What about the Glenn Rendezvous? I tried to register there, but they said they didn't have any room for guests."

The woman's hair was tied in a bun at the back of her neck, her face was brown. Wrinkles appeared as she frowned.

"That's another story. It's a bustout joint. They've got a little casino and whores. Stay away from there."

I thanked her and went to my room. It was clean and neat. I checked the telephone book for Christian Seifried. He had been mentioned in the wire story Pope had given me and identified as the head of a social action committee hoping to clean up the town. I called the number. His wife answered. In a pleasant voice she told me Chris was still at work. He was a postman and got off at four o'clock.

It was 3:30 p.m. I drove back downtown and located the small post office by the flag flying above it. Somehow the Stars and Stripes seemed out of place. I went inside and asked for Chris. Someone went back and brought him out: a tall handsome man in his forties, with serious brown eyes, dark hair, and very white teeth. I introduced myself.

"Let's go outside," he said.

We went out into the autumn sunlight and stood among the cars. No one was around.

"Do you have any credentials?" he asked.

Digging out my wallet, I extracted my press card. It was the first time in my career as a reporter I'd ever had need to display it. Well, the thing should be good for something.

The postman examined the card carefully, turning it over and reading both sides of it. Seemingly convinced, he returned it.

"So what brings you to Newport?"

"I hear they're running the whores out of town," I said. "My editor thinks that's news."

"It would be if it was happening." He paused. "Let me see your press card again, please."

Once more he looked over my card, and for the first time he smiled.

"Perhaps you're the answer to our prayers."

I almost laughed before I realized he was sincere. "Tell me what's going on," I suggested.

The sun beat down. It was hot and muggy. Seifried told me that more than a year ago an article appeared in Esquire magazine which described Newport as a "Sin City." It gave considerable detail about the attractions offered.

"I've carried the mail for many years in Newport," Seifried began. "I've seen madams fighting with each other over customers. I've seen drunks staggering down alleys, neglected children wandering the streets at night and young girls turned to prostitution. I asked God many times for a chance to do something. When I saw that magazine article I called my pastor."

"Which one?"

"The Reverend Mr. Barkhau."

"And what did he say?"

"He said he'd been here many years and seen reform movements come and go. He wasn't very optimistic but he agreed to talk to the other ministers and see if there was any interest in their congregations."

The problem was apathy, Seifried explained. Newport had no newspapers and most people went to Cincinnati to shop. Nevertheless, a meeting was called and a Social Action Committee was formed.

"That is how it began," Seifried said. "I was elected Chairman. We appealed to City Manager Ralph Mussman. He was a native of Covington and he had twin brothers who were Methodist ministers in Ohio, so we thought he might be receptive. He issued an order to the police to enforce the vice laws or be suspended. The City Council fired him and brought back Oscar Hesch. He refused to do anything and so did everybody else."

"Then what?"

"We've been gathering evidence and we intend to take it to the grand jury. Our greatest need has been some way to inform the people. If they know the truth, they'll get behind us and we'll win. It may take years but we've got the rest of our lives. That's why I said you were the answer to our prayers."

I thought of Norman Isaacs. He'd sent his hot shot reporter to write stories that glamorized casino gambling; advertised it in effect. Not one word about a reform drive. Yet his stories had caused Pope to send me in search of "real news."

We talked for another twenty minutes. He gave me specific information about the Newport Ministerial Association which sponsored the Social Action Committee, and about officials of city and county.

"You'll want to talk to them, I expect, but perhaps you should make your own tour of inspection before you do."

I promised to call him later, and decided I was hungry. Near at hand was the Yorkshire Club so I went there. The place seemed rather elegant. There were white table cloths with napkins to match, and a sprig of flowers on each table. The waitresses were young, mostly pretty, and wore short dresses. The menu was extensive, the prices surprisingly small. I decided my expense money deserved a steak. After all, I'd skipped lunch.

Upon eating I asked the waitress if the casino was open.

"It's always open, sir," and she pointed.

I walked through an open space into a barn-like room about seventy-five feet wide and a hundred feet long. The carpet was thick. Bright lights shone over the tables: dice, roulette, black jack, and several games I couldn't identify. A low hum filled the room. I estimated there were at least one hundred patrons at this early hour.

I was astonished. This was by far the biggest and the most plush gambling scene I had ever observed. It made the handbooks of Louisville look like mountain shanties. There had to be lots of money invested here, and, certainly, complete protection from the law for this entire operation was illegal. Could this be the Cleveland Syndicate the Kefauver Committee had talked about?

Not for the first time since leaving Happy Valley I felt myself to be a country hick, but I quickly rallied. Maybe I was a hick, but I had the state's most powerful newspaper behind me. I walked over to the black jack table.

It did not take long to realize I wasn't going to get rich this night. I moved on to other games. No one took any notice of me. The players were mostly middle class men and women and some of them seemed inexperienced if their conversations and excited faces were an indication.

I broke away after a while, left the building, and crossed York Street to the Flamingo Club, the domain of the legendary character called "Sleepout Louie." There was a dining room and a large bar out front. The bar, I later learned, was unlicensed. The casino was similar to the Yorkshire with one major difference. In back was a handbook with swivel armchairs enabling players to turn from one large blackboard to another as race results were posted. There was even a cashier's window where bets could be made and winnings collected. The book was deserted, but I could guess that in early afternoon the chairs would be full of horse players.

There seemed to be more blue collar types in this crowd than at the Yorkshire, and more laughter. I wandered around, wondering, lost a few dollars at roulette, and went out into the dark. There was one more place downtown I wanted to visit.

Around the block I drove to the Glenn Rendezvous, parking two hundred feet away because both sides of the street were lined with cars. Again someone fed the meter for me. I went into the lobby. The hotel desk was empty. From the supper club on the right came the sound of music. A show was in progress. A man in a tuxedo stood in the center of the lobby. He greeted me with a half bow.

"Good evening, sir. This way, please."

I followed to the expanse of paneled wall. He pressed the wall with one finger. Magically, an elevator opened. I got in. It closed, the elevator moved upward. It carried me slowly. The door opened automatically and I stepped out into a small casino bar. It was not exactly plush, I decided, and there was a grimness about the people I did not understand. A bustout joint, the motel lady had called it. Soon I found out why. One table featured a game called "Razzle-Dazzle." A bar girl with too much makeup explained it to me. Several pairs of dice were used. The player's bet doubled each time with the player promised a payoff of ten times his last bet if he could achieve a certain number of points. He was always on the verge of winning a fortune. I declined to play and also refused an invitation to accompany her to a room where we could "have some fun."

"Jerk," she said loudly as I turned away. A well muscled young man with black hair cut in bangs caught my eye and smiled.

"I'm Tito Carinci," he said. "You're wise not to play that game. Nobody has won it yet."

"Why do you offer it then?"

"Because it makes a pisspot full of money."

"I think I'll go out to the Beverly Hills."

"The odds are better there," said Tito, apparently unworried about losing a prospective sucker. Maybe I didn't look affluent enough.

The elevator door stood open. I walked in and pressed the DOWN button. At the street level I had to plunge through a pack of people who apparently had come out of the supper club and were trying to get on the elevator at the same time.

The night felt cool on my flushed face. To the north the sky was aglow with the lights of Cincinnati. I circled back to York Street and went south, falling in behind a stream of cabs with Ohio license plates. I followed them out to, and up, the long driveway of the Beverly Hills Country Club. The cabs disgorged under a porte cochere, or something, but I drove around them and parked in a huge lighted lot that must have contained two hundred cars. Inside the door I confronted a large circular bar. I went by it, my feet sinking in deep carpet, and looked down into an amphitheater. Guests sat at tables on descending levels. At the bottom was a stage where a line of girls was kicking naked legs. I went back to the uniformed bar man.

"Where's the action?" I asked.

He gestured to a broad corridor on my right. I walked down it and into the largest casino yet.

My mouth fell open. The large room was tastefully decorated in shades of blue. Crystal chandeliers sparkled overhead. Men and women were well dressed, many in evening clothes. A bar man in one corner put drinks on trays which were circulated among the tables by pretty cocktail waitresses. Even the dealers were young and, apparently, selected for their good looks as well as their skills.

This was a class operation, far surpassing the downtown joints in style, in elegance, and in size. This was "The Las Vegas of the East."

I moved around, paid my dues at the blackjack table, and got a free drink. A little overwhelmed by it all, I recovered enough to make conversation with several people. The suckers I discovered came largely from Ohio, but Indiana and New York were represented. It dawned on me that Newport was a regional vice center and the Beverly Hills was its brightest draw. Some of these people had flown here in private planes. Well, it was closer to much of the country than Las Vegas.

The drinks, the excitement, were getting me down. I felt fatigue and decided sleep was in order. I looked at my watch. Hell, it was after midnight.

The bed at my isolated motel was comfortable and I slept like a farm boy after a hard day. Next morning I had difficulty finding breakfast — all the gambling joints were still closed so I ate at a pancake house near the bridge in Covington — and then headed for City Hall. It was housed in the same rococo style structure that contained the circuit court. City Manager Oscar Hesch was an unpleasant little man with a bowtie. In answer to my questions he stated:

"We're conducting a drive to rid the city of undesirables. We're taking first things first and are working on the most undesirable features. We will continue until conditions are satisfactory.

"What kind of conditions?"

"Vice conditions," he snapped.

"Does that include gambling?"

"You define it."

"Are you going to close places like the Yorkshire Club?"

"If we find sufficient evidence."

"All you have to do is walk into the back room."

"I don't know; I've never been in there."

I tried a few more questions but the city manager remained evasive. After thanking him, I went in search of Police Chief George Gugel. His office, I discovered, was in a second building behind the courthouse which contained police headquarters and the jail. Entrance was from Columbia Street and up a flight of stone stairs.

A white haired man in an expensive, pin-striped suit, Gugel had a fleshy face and unrevealing eyes. This was the man who several years earlier had thrown a *Courier-Journal* photographer in jail for daring to take his picture. After introducing myself, I said:

"I understand you have a vice drive underway. Can you give me details?"

"No," said Gugel. "You'll have to see Leroy Fredericks. He's Chief of Detectives."

"Are you going to crack down on gambling joints?"

He stared at me for a full ten seconds. Then, without a word, he got up and left the room. I waited for several minutes but he did not return to the little office so I began searching for Fredericks. A sergeant at the booking desk said Fredericks was "unavailable." I asked for the names of all persons arrested so far in the vice drive and was told they were also "unavailable."

Feeling somewhat frustrated, I returned to the courthouse in search of someone willing and able to talk. I found such a person who asked only that I swear on the grave of my mother I would not reveal his name as a source. My mother wasn't dead, but I agreed anyway.

The individual, who had been an official for some years, said there were three factions in Newport. One was the Cleveland Syndicate which operated the Beverly Hills and the Yorkshire among other things. Albert "Red" Masterson was their enforcer. He hung out at the Merchant's Club across the street. The second faction was the "Independents" which included "Sleepout Louie" Levinson at the Flamingo, and the heirs of the late Peter Schmidt who ran the Playtorium and the Snax Bar. Attorney Charles Lester was the mastermind of this group and he was constantly intriguing to gain total power. The third group included the prostitution racket and numbers. The latter was dominated by "Screw" Andrews, a known killer.

Persons favoring vice were known as "liberals" even though politically they tended to be right-wing. Those opposing vice were called "do-gooders" or hypocrites.

The vice drive had been inspired by the Syndicate which feared that unrestrained bustout gambling and prostitution would bring heat and cause the do-gooders to rebel. The drive would gradually fizzle out, he predicted.

"Is there anyone in town known as Frank Andriola?"

The official frowned. "The name sounds familiar, but I can't place it."

Footsteps sounded in the hall. My source froze. "You'd better leave now. Someone might see us. Remember what you promised."

"Thanks," I said.

I left the building and drove to the First Baptist Church where I had an appointment with the Reverend Dudley Pomeroy, pastor and secretary of the Newport Ministerial Association. The minister was a far cry from the hell-fire-and-damnation Baptist preachers I'd known in Happy Valley. He looked like a college professor, sharp of eye and soft spoken. Seifried had prepared the way so we wasted no time.

"The so-called vice drive is eyewash," said Pomeroy. "It's meant to divert us from the gambling joints where the real money is made."

"Sorta like Razzle-Dazzle."

"Correct. Apparently they learned of our social action committee and decided to beat us to the punch. We aren't fooled however. Our churches represent more than eight thousand voters and we intend to continue our efforts until even the gambling syndicate leaves town."

"What's your next step?"

"Can we talk off the record?"

When I agreed, he told me the Campbell County Grand Jury would be meeting early next month. His group planned to make a pro forma appearance before key city and county officials and then go to the grand jury to ask that those officials be required to enforce the law.

"We don't want out plans known in advance," said Pomeroy, "but you're forewarned."

I asked why he expected the citizens to back reform when they apparently had known no other way of life.

"The problem," he replied, "is that the area is about equally divided between Catholic and Protestant. There is a certain bitterness that goes back to Know-Nothing days when Catholic churches were burned up and down the Ohio. The Catholics tend to be more tolerant of gambling. We need their help but we're not going to wait for it."

At Pomeroy's suggestion I ate lunch in the Glenn Schmidt

Playtorium, a combination bowling alley and restaurant. In the past, there had been a casino in the basement but when the legitimate attractions began to make money, it had been moved next door to the Belmont Snax Bar. No point in putting all the golden eggs in one basket, had been the advice of attorney Lester.

After eating, I went next door and entered a small lobby. A lunch counter was on the left. There were no tables. A door slid open in front of me. I walked through and into another huge casino-handbook. Not more than a dozen men were in the room and they paid no attention. I walked around, counted four dice tables, five blackjack tables, and two roulette wheels. Then I went back to my car. It was Friday afternoon, time to travel.

Three hours later I was at the *C-J*. No one commented on my absence. I wrote my story, leading with Pomeroy's "eyewash" quote, and took it directly to Pope. The executive editor read it, editing instinctively as he went along but cutting nothing. He looked up with a satisfied smile.

"This is about what I expected. We'll run it Sunday."

"This is going to be a continuing story," I said. "The good guys up there need all the help we can give."

"It's your baby," said Pope. "I'm making you responsible. Keep an eye on things and go back whenever there's hard news."

I called Faye to tell her I'd be home for dinner. Then I called Chris Seifried and told him to read the *Courier-Journal* on Sunday. I had noticed racks containing the *C-J* in front of City Hall and most of the gambling joints. After all, the newspaper served the entire state.

My story ran under a six column headline at the bottom of the front page. The trip to Newport had indeed been interesting. I was just a little unhappy about my failure to find the trail of Frank Andriola, but I would keep looking.

FOUR
13 October '58

The house was dark except for a tiny red eye burning on what appeared to be a side porch. There was no sound yet the Reverend Donald Baker assured me that this was the most notorious house of ill repute in Newport. Baker was a young man, small in size, and fresh out of the seminary, but he was president of the Newport Ministerial Association. A bachelor, he had elected to accompany me on a tour of Newport vice spots. Tomorrow the grand jury would meet and Chris Seifried would ask for indictments.

We walked up a sidewalk to the little red eye. It proved to be a lighted bell button. I pressed the button and a door opened. A large heavy featured woman stood outlined against the light. This had to be Vivian.

"Come in, come in," she said and we obeyed.

The entrance was to a dining room. The woman led us through it and into a much larger room lined with couches, soft chairs, and bright with light. The windows, I noted, were completely covered by black curtains. Sitting in a semi-circle at the end of the room were twenty-one — yes, I counted them — women. They wore low cut dresses and showed plenty of leg yet there was nothing vulgar about them. In fact, they might have been girls dressed up for a date with a bank teller.

"Go back and talk to them," suggested Vivian. "See which one you like best."

The girls were smiling encouragingly. I started forward, heard a muffled sound behind me, and looked back. The Reverend Mr. Baker had not moved; he seemed to be choking. His face was as red as the lipstick on the girls.

"What's the matter with your friend?" asked the madam.

"It's his first time," I explained hurriedly.

The girls began to titter and then to laugh openly. Apparently they enjoyed seeing an embarrassed young man. Perhaps it was a novelty. Their laughter increased as, without a word, Baker bolted from the room. Even Vivian chortled.

"Hell," I said, "I'll have to go out and calm him down."

"Why bother?" asked Vivian. "You've got your pick of the stable."

I hesitated. One girl in a blue dress caught my eye. She had dark hair and a small if well formed figure. There was a glow about her, a freshness, and I remembered the girls of the Blue Ridge. They bloomed early and faded fast. This girl might have come straight from the hills.

Vivian confirmed my theory. "That's Lela," she said, noting the direction of my gaze. "She's new."

Duty before pleasure, I decided. I did want to talk to some of the women about prices, but I was concerned about my companion.

"I'll be back," I told Vivian, and retraced my steps.

Baker was waiting in the car. He looked at me without embarrassment.

"I just couldn't stay in that place. It was a sin just being there."

"We weren't going to do anything but talk," I pointed out.

He shook his head. "I just can't do it."

Preachers, I decided, were no doubt safe companions, but perhaps on my next tour I'd better ask for a church layman to accompany me. This minister said he would show me some other places and let me do the investigating. Down the block we went on foot. The night was very dark and the town had few street lights. At a bar on the corner where Baker said laymen had found prostitutes, a fat man greeted us with outflung hand.

"A *Courier-Journal* reporter came to town and all the girls left," he said.

It hadn't taken Vivian long to figure out who we were and spread the word.

Baker and I headed along a side street towards another joint.

"We've got company," said the young minister.

I looked back. A huge man wearing overalls was behind us. He stopped when we stopped.

"One of the Bridewells, I think," said Baker. "There's a large family of them. They operate bustout joints."

"Just what is a bustout joint?" I asked.

"It's a joint you don't get out of until you're busted financially. If they can't cheat you, they'll put knockout drops in your drinks and rob you. Either way you go out busted."

We walked on, the hulking figure still close behind. As we approached a corner, I muttered to Baker, "Run."

We dashed around the corner past a door and ducked into an alley where we hid behind a clump of garbage cans. Bridewell, if that's who it was, charged after us, lumbering past the alley. We waited. A few moments later he returned. We could hear the door to the bar open and close.

"Guess there's no use going in there," said Baker.

I agreed. We wandered on. Up ahead we spotted a group of boys. They appeared to range in age from eight to fourteen, or thereabouts. The smallest kid of all rushed ahead of his fellows and came up to me.

"Hey, mister," he said, "I'll show you a cat house for a dime."

I didn't want to encourage delinquency but I was curious to see if he could deliver. I fished out a quarter and handed it to him. A larger boy came up and tried to take it away from him but the kid squirmed away and pointed at a little red eye in the darkness. It was Vivian's. Inadvertently we'd circled around to our point of beginning. Well, the child was honest, that I could confirm.

A police car slid up to the curb and a man in plain clothes stuck his head through the window and shouted:

"Gino, you son of a bitch, come over here."

The taller boy, apparently the leader of the gang, ran toward the car. The cop dressed him down.

"Damn it, Gino. I told you to stay off the streets while the grand jury is meeting. Who the hell do you think you are? All the casinos closed. If you ever want to amount to anything, you've got to learn to obey orders. Understand?"

The boy mumbled something.

"That's Pat Ciafardini, a big shot detective," said Baker.

In the glow of a distant street light the detective's face was sharply handsome. He had white teeth and a lot of black hair. Now he spoke to the kid again.

"Get off of the streets, you little fucker," he said.

The boy trotted back to his companions. He was grinning. I realized the kid was proud of being singled out. He waved his arm and everyone disappeared across a vacant lot. The cop car pulled away into the night. I pulled out my notebook and recorded the conversation.

"Good stuff," I commented, "that 'whorehouse for a dime' may go down in history."

Baker's face was white. "It was depraved," he whispered.

We checked out several additional taverns only to be told that there would be no action while the grand jury was in session. About eleven p.m. I took Baker to the Evangelical United Brethren Church, of which he was pastor. He explained he had been made head of the ministerial association because his church membership was small and he had no family. We said good night and I drove north across the Ohio to the Netherland Plaza Hotel. It was more expensive than the motel I'd used before, but I felt safer in another state. Moreover, I had quoted the motel operator in my previous story and that place might have been checked out. From my room the lights of Newport seemed in another world. A barge moved on the river. I took a shower and went to bed.

*****

The day dawned bright. I ate breakfast in the coffee shop, paid my bill, and drove back to Newport. Entering on York Street I passed the courthouse *et al.*, and put my car in the huge parking lot across a side street from the Playtorium. It was a short walk to the scene of action. I climbed the stairs to the second floor, passing a huge painting depicting civic virtue. In a small courtroom Chris Seifried towered above his allies. The Reverend Dudley Pomeroy and Baker I already knew, and I was introduced to the Reverend George Bennett, minister of the First Presbyterian Church. George was a medium sized man with brown hair worn in a crew cut. He wore glasses with heavy plastic frames. Like the others, his expression was serious.

The grand jurors, an undistinguished group in dress and appearance, assembled in what was ordinarily the petit jury box. A fat bailiff in a police uniform with sergeant's stripes ordered everyone to stand up. Circuit Judge Ray Murphy came through a door behind the bench. I was surprised to notice the absence of a robe; the Judge wore a dark business suit. He was a tall, lanky man nearing fifty with a florid Irish face. Seating himself, he rapped for order. From the back of the courtroom came Commonwealth's Attorney William Wise, a heavy man and handsome despite oily black hair and a fleshy face. He and Murphy, I later discovered, had taken office in 1940, shortly after the Cleveland Syndicate took control of the Beverly Hills Country Club from Peter Schmidt.

Judge Murphy asked the grand jurors to stand. He administered an oath, then introduced Wise who he said would advise them on points of law and present witnesses. There was, the judge added, no outstanding matter to come before the jurors but a representative of the ministerial association had asked to talk to them. He had that right, added the judge, and he was sure the jury would listen carefully.

At a signal from the bailiff, the jurors stood up and followed the uniformed man to a side room. The judge rapped his gavel, looked down at the ministers with open curiosity, and vanished into his chambers. Wise spoke briefly to Chris and then headed for the grand jury room.

"He wants to brief the jurors for a few minutes," said Chris. "Then he'll call me."

George Bennett laughed. "Wants to get them properly cynical, I expect," he said.

I walked over to Chris "What do you hope to achieve?" I asked.

"I'm going to ask for indictments. Realistically we will settle for the jurors to put officials on notice to enforce the law."

Twenty minutes later Wise opened the door of the grand jury room and beckoned to Seifried. Several ministers patted the back of the tall figure as he walked across the room holding a brief case containing, so I had been told, reports of investigations made by members of the Social Action Committee.

After he moved inside, I checked out two strangers who'd been standing by silently. They proved to be reporters from the Cincinnati papers, and they thought the whole affair was a great joke.

"Nobody's going to change this town," said the *Post*.

"Without gambling, Newport would be a ghost town," said *The Enquirer*.

These guys might just as well be working for Norman Isaacs, I mused.

We waited. I used the time to find out more about the individual ministers and about the town's history. The preachers weren't much help. All were relative newcomers. The only veteran was Dr. Harold Barkhau, pastor of St. John's United Church of Christ. Much older than his peers, he seemed restless and after an hour, broke away. I followed him out the door and when we were alone, I asked him what he really thought about it. The old man shook his head.

"Right now my congregation is planning to send me to visit the Holy Land. I think that trip will be more productive than this exercise in futility."

I watched him descend the staircase by the mural of civic virtue and I thought of the Reverend Don Baker. He had been almost physically ill upon finding himself in a whore house while this old man had learned to live with organized vice and could still look forward to a visit to Jerusalem. There was surely some sort of lesson for me there, I decided, but instead of thinking about it, I went back into the courtroom where Bennett introduced me to three church laymen: Jack Cook, Jack Steinman, and Cesare Bernardini. They had come in case Chris needed their backup testimony. Cook was a heavy set young man who worked as a roving foreman for the telephone company and could usually be reached quickly. His brother, Henry, had briefly been U.S. Attorney for the Eastern District of Kentucky. Steinman belonged to a wealthy family which owned a large business in Cincinnati. He was tall and somewhat reserved. Bernardini's demeanor spoke of his Italian ancestry, as did his swarthy skin and unruly black hair. These men had been active in mapping out the mean streets of Newport, locating each brothel, bustout joint, and handbook.

Chris emerged promptly at noon to say that he had not finished and would return when the jury reconvened at 2 p.m. The jurors, he said, had listened politely but seemed hostile. We walked in a group to the Playtorium for lunch. Even though there was a casino next door, the Playtorium was considered respectable. It had been built, Cook told me, after the Cleveland Syndicate took the Beverly Hills Country Club away from Peter Schmidt.

The conversation was generally optimistic. No one expected results from this grand jury but all felt a foundation was being laid. I ate a bowl of green pea soup which was delicious. The waiter apparently knew who I was for when he served my soup he said, "Enjoy, Mr. Messick."

After the luncheon we shook hands all around and I crossed the street to the parking lot. My car was the Chevrolet we bought in Durham. On the way out of town I drove up Central Avenue past the Sportsman's Club, an old but large barn around which there was no sign of activity. The area around it had been cleared for an urban renewal project and the building itself was rented from the city. Screw Andrews bossed the numbers racket in Cincinnati from this building, but I would need to wear black face to get in. Well, I was in no hurry.

The trip went smoothly for the first sixty miles and I was telling myself I would arrive in plenty of time to meet the first edition deadline, when abruptly the motor began to cough and the car to slow. The motor stopped. I looked at my gas gauge. It was half full. I pressed the starter and got the motor running again, but after a hundred yards, it once more sputtered to a stop. This time I couldn't get it going. I looked under the hood but could see nothing amiss. I wasn't much of a mechanic anyway. There were no houses in sight but after ten minutes a man in a pickup truck came along and stopped when I waved at him. He told me the nearest service station was in Carrollton and offered to take me.

Carrollton was a county seat and boasted a couple of street lights and a courthouse. The service station operator had a tow truck and suggested we'd better take it out to the car. Sure enough, it was necessary to tow the Chevrolet back to town. I was beginning to feel a little sick, so I managed to get a 7-Up out of the machine nearby. While I drank it, the mechanic began examining my car. Another mechanic was busy running wires to temporary lights at the back of a boat trailer. The owner, a short man with a cigar, was attending to every detail.

"He's the editor of the local paper," said my mechanic. "Always goes fishing after he puts the paper to bed."

Some ten minutes passed before my mechanic, a red haired middle aged man in greasy coveralls, let out a shout of triumph. He waved to me.

"They've sweetened you, my friend," he said. "Put sugar in your gas tank. Look."

He held the cap to my gas tank. Sugar was plainly visible on the inside of the cap and on the lip of the tank.

"It's an old trick," the mechanic said. "Stops up the fuel line so the gas can't flow. This car won't be going anywhere today."

I used the station's phone to make a collect call to the *C-J*. Pope didn't seem surprised, and promised to send the company plane to get me. The pilot, he said, just happened to be at the airport, so it wouldn't take long.

When I came out of the station, the local editor had walked over and was looking at my car. He turned to face me with a smile of pure pleasure.

"Serves you right for getting out of your territory," he pronounced.

"The *C-J* covers the whole state," I replied. "Anyway, you've got yourself a scoop."

"I've got better things to do," said the editor. He walked over to his car and drove away pulling his fishing boat behind him.

Someone volunteered to drive me to the airport which proved to be a grassy field with a wind sock hanging from a pole. I sat down on a rock and waited. The queasy feeling had intensified and I ached all over. The plane arrived quickly. I climbed beside the pilot. We were barely above tree level when I began to vomit. It made quite a mess. I'd never been air sick before but this was much worse than an upset stomach. I was barely conscious when we touched down at Standiford Field.

"Take me home," I muttered.

The pilot complied. Faye helped me into the shower and then into pajamas. I lay down on the bed and went to sleep. I awoke somewhat better, but weak. I called Pope who had already heard from the pilot. I could write the story if he would send someone to pick it up. He promised to do so. By the time John Meehan arrived I was feeling better. John brought some wire copy which quoted Commonwealth's Attorney William Wise as saying Hank Messick would not be called to testify. "The jurors," said Wise, "thought that *The Courier-Journal* is trying to promote itself in northern Kentucky in circulation and Messick is a reporter trying to make a name for himself as a feature writer."

Obviously, Wise didn't know the difference between a feature story and a news story. Nevertheless I revised my copy to include his comments and Meehan, who seemingly enjoyed playing copy boy, took the story back to the paper.

It was too late for the street edition but the story would make the state edition which went to Newport, and that was what mattered most.

I went back to bed.

*****

My telephone rang shortly after I reached the city room next morning. Wise was calling. In polite, formal tones he advised me the grand jury had reconsidered and now wanted me to testify. Would I agree to appear the following day?

Abruptly everything seemed to make sense. My car had been "sweetened" and my body poisoned. Now I was being, in effect, dared to come back to Newport. The unspoken threat was obvious: if I did come back, something worse might happen to me. On the other hand, if I didn't return, I would be discredited and the drive on vice would be handicapped.

"I'll be there tomorrow afternoon," I said.

On the following morning Faye drove me up to the highway and I flagged down the northbound bus. Getting off in Carrollton, I found my car ready to roll.

"You should'a seen this place yesterday," said the service station man. There was sugar all over."

He handed me a strange looking contraption which had a clear plastic container caked with sugar.

"Your fuel pump," he said. "If they hadn't put in so much, it wouldn't have choked up like this and more sugar would've gotten into the engine. They must have poured in five pounds at least."

Pope had agreed to pay the cost of repairs so I gave the mechanic a check, put the fuel pump in beside me, and proceeded up the lonely road.

My nausea and weakness had gone away, but now in my stomach fear was growing. This time they knew I was coming. That fear, that dread, would increase on subsequent trips and become a cancer. Yet something within me was stronger — perhaps an instinctive revolt against anything that threatened my independence of action.

I arrived in the grimy little town about 1 p.m. and parked boldly in front of the courthouse. The car had seemed a little reluctant to make the trip. Perhaps some remaining sugar was gnawing at its vitals. By parking out in the open, the car and I were making a combined statement.

I climbed the stairs to Wise's office. His secretary was out to lunch and the inner room was unguarded. Wise was having lunch at his desk, I thought, as I saw him pour bourbon into a cup of black coffee. He sipped the coffee and put the bottle away without asking me to drink. Just as well; I intended to be more careful with whom I ate or drank in Newport. The grand jury would be back shortly, he informed me. I could wait in the courtroom.

Feeling somewhat lonely, I called the Reverend Mr. Bennett and asked for company. Within minutes, Jack Cook appeared. He told me that several ministers had testified the day before, including Don Baker who had told the grand jury about our tour of Newport night life. Officials had also testified.

At 1:35 p.m. Wise invited me into the grand jury room. A dozen individuals, men and women, sat around a long table. None of the men wore neckties. The women were middle aged and dowdy. I entered carrying a large paper bag and after I'd sworn to tell the truth, I opened the bag, and placed my fuel pump on the table.

"This," I said, "is what happens to innocent people who come to your town to do a responsible job of reporting."

I had not mentioned the sugar episode in my story nor had I told Wise about it.

The man nearest me picked up the fuel pump and looked at the sugar inside the plastic gizmo. He grinned widely. The device went down the table. Several people actually frowned. Wise looked at the pump with impassive face.

"I first came to your city late last month," I began, "and acquainted myself with its night life..."

I talked for at least an hour. No one interrupted. No one had questions. When I finished, no one thanked me. One woman smiled. I picked up my fuel pump and left the room. The car was still sitting in front of the courthouse. Cook made a production of looking under the hood and said he could see no evidence of a bomb. I shook hands with him, got back in the car, and drove home.

On October 21 the grand jury made its final report. By Newport standards it was a shocker. The jurors stated:

"We found a laxity in law enforcement with regards to the operation of taverns, prostitution, and gaming."

The jurors also said that several members voted to indict officials, but the majority opposed.

"Because of this divergence of opinion," the jurors wrote, "the conclusion is that although there was evidence of law violation, the evidence falls short of sufficiency to return such indictments at this time; however, city officials charged with enforcing the law should take heed, and forthwith inaugurate a stringent program of law enforcement."

Even more amazing was a final recommendation that if the city should be unable to cope with the problem, state police "should be granted the privilege of coming into Newport and lending their assistance in the correction of these conditions."

State law prohibited state police from entering incorporated areas other than sixth class cities, but tradition had long made all of Campbell County off limits. No politician of either party wanted to annoy voters by violating that tradition. Yet an official request would undoubtedly be honored.

I contacted Newport Mayor Mayberry in San Francisco where he was attending a convention. When asked about the grand jury's recommendations, he replied:

"We don't need the state police and we don't want them. I won't call them in unless the higher ups tell me to."

"Who are the higher ups?"

"That's for you to find out," said the Mayor. "You're a reporter, aren't you?"

"Could the higher ups be the syndicate gamblers?" I asked.

"You're not a reporter, you're a smart aleck," snapped Mayberry, and that pretty well terminated the interview. It made a good little sidebar to the main story, however. Meanwhile, the *C-J* bought itself a new plane. The old one still stank.

*****

On a dark night in early December I returned again to Newport. At Pope's suggestion, I left my car behind and flew up, landing at the Greater Cincinnati Airport on the Kentucky side of the Ohio. George Bennett met me and we went to a church where others were waiting. They filled me in on recent developments.

The Social Action Committee, I was told, had planned to follow up the grand jury's recommendations with a request to Governor Chandler that state police be sent to Newport. However, the move had been postponed when Reverend Barkhau received an invitation to lunch across the river with City Manager Hesch. At that meeting, Hesch told Barkhau:

"I asked you to meet with me because you have been here longer, you are older, and I think you know the situation better. Would you ask your group to withhold going to a higher authority for a couple of months. Mr. Wise and I have had a conversation and we're determined to wipe out prostitution."

Barkhau had taken the offer to the ministers and after heated debate the group agreed to compromise. Instead of asking for state police action, they had gone instead to Alfred Portwood, Chandler's Commssioner of Alcoholic Beverage Control. Portwood told them that seventeen special investigations had found no violations of the liquor laws in Newport, but he agreed to send in an agent to make the rounds with the Social Action Committee acting as tour guide. The tour was to take place later this night. Chris, George, and I made a preliminary inspection. All joints were operating as usual.

At 11:30 p.m. we met Tom Powell, an ABC agent from neighboring Kenton County. A short stocky man in a trench coat, Powell had a red face and a harassed manner. We began our tour. At the Stardust Club we found the gambling tables covered with sheets. Powell, his coat pushed open to expose the gun on his belt, greeted the manager, James Harris, an old friend. George grinned at me. We had expected a farce and were getting one. "Nothing here," said Powell.

Back on the street we headed for the Glenn Rendezvous, the nightclub in the Glenn Hotel. I suggested Powell ignore the supper club on the first floor and head for the elevator. He agreed, but on arriving, he stopped in the lobby to check his coat. The gun, of course, was plainly visible. When, after chatting with the hatcheck girl for a few minutes, he at last walked toward the concealed elevator, a man with white hair and a pallid face blocked our way. He was Charles Lester, the attorney who represented many of the independent operators.

"You can't go up without a warrant," said Lester.

"You're right," said Powell.

We visited several other joints without results. The word was out. Growing tired of the charade, Powell suggested we call it quits for the night. I insisted that he visit the Flamingo Club on York Street.

"There's no use to go there," said the ABC agent. "It doesn't have a liquor license."

"Well, it sure as hell has a bar," I said, "and it was running earlier tonight.

"Okay," he said, "we'll take a look."

The neon was glowing brightly above the entrance to the joint, and the front room contained a half a dozen well dressed men and four overdressed women, but the long bar at the back of the room was empty of bottles. A vase of flowers sat on the bar in lonely splendor.

A fat man with diamond rings on both pinkies and a ruffled shirt beneath a sky blue sport jacket walked forward as if to greet us. This was the famous "Sleep out Louie" Levinson, operator of the joint. He'd won the nickname, according to one story, by engaging in marathon poker games and occasionally "sleeping out" a hand to conserve his strength. A brother, Ed, formerly his partner, had moved on to the Fremont in Las Vegas.

"The back room is closed, gentlemen, but would you like a glass of milk?" he inquired graciously.

As if on cue, the hardbitten men and women at the tables raised their glasses in salute. The glasses contained milk. Bennett and I began laughing. Chris was expressionless, and Powell looked self-righteous.

We declined the milk and started for the door. Behind us someone said loudly:

"Sneaking preachers!"

Powell wanted to go home, but I was determined that Chandler's man wouldn't leave town without finding gambling. We walked to the Dream Bar. It was a narrow building with a back room where a nonstop poker game had been in progress since my first visit to Newport. The door to the back room had always been open with the action visible from the street. It had been open earlier tonight but now it was closed.

"Let's go in and have a drink," I suggested.

Powell's beefy face lighted up. "Why not?"

We went into the bar. Powell ordered a beer, and began to discuss the recent World Series with the bartender. I walked to the closed door; the sounds of a game within were audible. Bennett walked over, grinned at me, and apparently stumbled against the door. It flew open. Six men sat at a round table, cards in their hands, and money in front of them.

"Look," I said, "gambling!"

Powell turned, hesitated, and then strode into the room. He threw his wallet on the table, the badge it contained exposed.

"This place will be cited," he said, "for allowing gambling on liquor license premises."

George and I shook hands. Even Chris was smiling. Powell made some notes, picked up his wallet, went back to the bar, and finished his beer.

"Good night," he said, and went out the front door.

George drove me across the river to the Netherland Plaza where earlier I'd made a reservation. En route, he confided that someone had been making threatening calls to Mary Jane, his pregnant wife. Other individuals whose names had been publicized were being harassed.

Next day I returned to Louisville by American Airlines. The flight required about thirty minutes, less time than needed to reach the airport My story about Powell's law enforcement efforts made Portwood and Chandler look a bit ridiculous, all of which suited the *C-J* brass very much — they were supporting Wilson W. Wyatt, a former mayor and counsel to the newspapers. It also produced from Happy Chandler a quotation that was to become famous:

"The people of Newport have a right to have it dirty."

23 February '59

The Reverend George Bennett noted in his diary:
"It was a fit day for the grand jury hearings, very dark and rainy. Gray. Everything was gray. Hank Messick was there and the grand jury regulars. Chris wasn't called until about eleven. Came out at 12:45. Then Hank, I, and Don Baker testified. I dropped the evidence all over the floor and fumbled around a bit. The jury seemed not just tired and bored but definitely hostile. Mary Jane and I talked later. I feel uneasy. People are trying to scare Mary Jane. It would have been nice if someone had offered to visit with her while I testified."

Four days later, I stood in the courtroom while the foreman of the grand jury made its report to Judge Murphy.

"Regarding the request of the Social Action Committee to indict certain officials, there was sufficient disagreement as to render indictments impossible... The residents of a given community are entitled to have the service of the men they elect to office..."

"We note with some approval the statements attributed to Alfred Portwood, chairman of the Alcoholic Control Board, that much of the publicity concerning this county is exaggerated; that 'downriver' news writers sensationalize facts with the possible motive of selling their papers in the northern Kentucky market..."

"Our experiences, reason, and personal evaluation of human failings, incline us to the off-repeated belief that man's frailties and weaknesses cannot be completely legislated away. Mankind, having been born in sin will ever be a prey to the temptations of sin."

"The devil can quote scripture for his purposes," I remarked to Seifried. The tall man nodded, concealing his disappointment.

"You mean the Commonwealth's Attorney, don't you?"

Some ten minutes later I intercepted three women jurors on the way to their cars. They recognized me and stopped to talk. One of the women pointed to the parking lot in front of the Playtorium and Snax Bar casino.

"Look," she said, "they're starting up already."

Somewhat startled, I observed that the women must believe the ministers were right about gambling.

"What would Newport be if gambling were gone?" a juror questioned.

"A ghost town," replied a second woman.

"How about Sunday drinking?" I asked.

"Mr. Wise says the people in Cincinnati need a place to come to for cocktails," said the first juror.

"How about prostitution?"

The smiles vanished. "Mr. Wise and the other officials assured us they have cleaned up prostitution in Newport. It doesn't exist anymore."

I met Bennett as planned and told him of the conversation. He laughed.

"Not only is there prostitution, but it is well organized into night and day operations. C'mon, I'll take you to a day place within a block of the police station."

That night, Bennett wrote in his diary:

"Messick fast-talked me and Chris out of some advance information on our next steps. Then I drove him to the prostitute place at 212 Columbia. He went in, sailed out the back door in a few minutes, bug-eyed and sweating. 'Goodness, that's the most aggressive woman I ever saw,' he said. He left for Louisville."

A few days after I encountered the "aggressive woman," I was sitting in the city room enjoying the peace and quiet. Unexpectedly, the three main members of the Capital Bureau stalked in and headed for Pope's office. They did not condescend to banter a few words with us underlings. Obviously their mission was serious. After about thirty minutes they came out accompanied by Executive Editor Pope and took the elevator down to the top management level. Bingham and Ethridge were being consulted which meant it was a serious matter indeed.

An hour later Pope returned alone to his office, and, after about ten minutes, came to the front of the newsroom and motioned to me. Startled, I obeyed. Seated in front of Pope's desk I heard a strange story.

The Capital Bureau had received unimpeachable information, albeit secret, that Governor Chandler was planning a trip to Cuba to recover campaign funds held there by Fidel Castro who had taken over the country January 1. Several hundred thousand dollars were involved. The money may have come from Newport gamblers and been taken to Havana in 1958 for safe keeping.

Politics in Kentucky had not been so dramatic as in Cuba, but the *C-J's* man, Wilson Wyatt, had been forced to take second place to Bert Combs in the campaign to oust Happy Chandler's nominee. Kentucky governors could not succeed themselves so Chandler was backing Harry Lee Waterfield. The newspaper was a deadly enemy of Chandler-Waterfield and welcomed any dirt that might discredit them.

Rumors had reached me during my forays around Little Mexico that a squad of state police detectives visited Newport in the summer of 1958. Allegedly they went to every brothel, handbook, bustout joint, and casino. The detectives had been under the impression they were working undercover in preparation for a giant raid. No raid occurred. A man named Frenchie, armed with all the data collected by the detectives, followed on their heels. According to the rumor, Frenchie shook down the operators on behalf of the Chandler campaign. In return for the "contribution", he promised the policy of no interference in local affairs would continue. Perhaps that was the money now said to be in Cuba, but why had it been necessary to take it so far away?

Pope was not concerned with where the money came from or how it got to Cuba. He was interested in covering Chandler's efforts to recapture it.

"Does Chandler know you by sight?" he asked.

My impulse was to take a chance and say "no." If the governor was going to meet with Castro, it would be a wonderful story. It might even win a Pulitzer Prize. But I recalled that cold day in Maysville. Chandler had recognized me there.

"I'm afraid he does," I said with regret.

"Too bad," said Pope. "I'll have to make other arrangements. Keep this under your hat."

I promised.

Chandler did go to Miami Beach but apparently a meeting with Castro did not take place. The tale soon spread, however, and a lot of people found it funny. On May 23 the final rally of the Combs-Wyatt campaign was held in the Flag Room of the Kentucky Hotel in Louisville. More than a thousand people were there. Burt Combs got the faithful laughing as he described a story he said was "going around the state." Supposedly, Chandler went to Miami Beach, waded out into the Atlantic and with hands outstretched, shouted:

"Castro, oh Castro, give me back my money."

It was, I thought, an episode typical of Kentucky politics. The alleged shakedown of Newport vice lords was considered routine. Presumably, the gamblers had also given money to Chandler's opposition so that point could not be the issue. No one knew enough about organized crime to realize the Cleveland Syndicate had operated in Havana as well as Newport, so that angle remained unexplored. In the end, it all amounted to a joke on a par with Chandler's use of the expression "ankle blankets" to describe the spats city boy Wilson Wyatt allegedly wore.

Came the primary election and the Combs-Wyatt team won easily. John D. Breckinridge, scion of a famous Kentucky family, running as an independent Democrat, got the nomination as Attorney General. In Kentucky, the Democratic nomination had been tantamount to election since Reconstruction.

Election year frenzy and the long months of lame duck rule by

Chandler effectively stymied the reform drive in Newport. I kept my investigative talents alert by probing the Louisville Police Department. Two brothers, a captain and a lieutenant, named McDonald, owned a horse farm, I discovered, and had stocked it with race horses bought from Andrew Ormes, a notorious gambler with Newport connections and a long record. After I had exposed the relationship, the *C-J* called him "the equivalent of Chicago's Tony Accardo," and suggested it was improper for police officers to be associated with him.

I also learned that while slot machines had been driven out of Louisville years before, pin ball machines were being operated as gambling devices. Federal wagering tax stamps were often posted on the wall besides the machines, an obvious statement of intent. Operators won local immunity by giving free food to cops.

Again there were investigations, grand jury reports, and a minor shake-up of the police force. I gave an affidavit about handbook gambling to the city's public safety director and he bypassed the Chief and busted up three joints. Chief Carl Heustis decided he needed a leave of absence for health reasons. He never returned and was replaced by a man who reorganized the department.

It was progress of a sort but, by now, I realized the management at the paper really didn't care about gambling per se. The lesson was reinforced one day when I was sent to cover the annual Steeplechase held by and for the bluebloods of the city on a farm nearby. Grandstands had been erected and fenced off to give horse owners and their friends a degree of privacy while they watched their daughters guide horses over various obstacles. And inside that fenced area, a portly man was making book openly. My press pass got me inside. I asked the bookie how he happened to be there.

He was, he said, imported each year for the occasion. Proud poppas wanted to bet on their children, after all, and the bets were quite substantial. The county cops, in whose domain the event occurred, never bothered him.

I hesitated but then became angry at myself. If I could write about working men betting in handbooks, I should be free to report on the landed gentry. If I was to be believed in Newport, I had to pull no punches in Louisville. I told the photographer assigned to me to shoot the bookie in action. The man was agreeable, supremely confident his sponsors would protect him.

The news editor wasn't happy with my story. He growled to himself as he read the copy and then picked up the telephone. Nevertheless, he ran the story complete with pix. It was the last time we covered the Steeplechase. If any gambling went on, the newspaper didn't know it.

I had learned at *The Durham Herald* that ignorance is sometimes bliss insofar as editors are concerned, and I had noticed the smiles on the faces of my fellows when I came in with an exposé, so I sometimes wondered why Pope allowed me to return again and again to Newport. Perhaps he retained a strain of Puritan ethics. Gambling bothered him only when he was given proof of accompanying corruption. He couldn't launch a crusade, however, and each visit to the city upriver had to be in pursuit of a specific news angle. I understood that if in carrying out my assignment I gave aid to the reform drive, well, that was all to the good. Yet it was apparent that Pope was largely reacting to the superficiality of Isaacs. The men had different philosophies and perhaps Pope worried about the future of the *C-J*. Unless something dramatic happened, Isaacs would succeed Pope as executive editor of both newspapers. Obviously someone was grooming him for the job. I couldn't believe it was Mark Ethridge — he was too good a newspaperman — so it had to be the big boss, Barry Bingham.

Jim Rankin, my former city editor in Raleigh, provided ample proof of Isaacs' incapacity. Stuck for months on the copy desk while he "learned the town," Jim finally wangled a reporting job. Within days, he developed a good source who put him on the trail of a hot story involving a rather prominent citizen. Not only did he confirm the wrong-doings but he obtained pictures. Isaacs refused to run the story and began cursing Jim for embarrassing the citizen. Rankin, a much bigger man, looked down at the editor and growled:

"Don't talk to me like that."

Isaacs shut up, but the best reporter *The Louisville Times* had known in years walked out. Pat Kelly, our former managing editor in Raleigh and now a big wheel in Atlanta journalism, found room for Jim. Soon he was a city editor and Louisville a bad memory.

Occasionally I wondered if I would follow Rankin when Pope retired, but, meantime I used the operational freedom he granted. In July, photographer George Bailey and I drove to Newport, arriving after dark. Bailey was the man who had been jailed several years earlier while taking pictures of Police Chief Gugel, so he was understandably nervous. We parked some distance from the courthouse behind a church and well out of sight of the street. The occasion was a City Commission meeting at which Chris Seifried appeared with a group of high school students. Chris presented a list of 140 wagering-tax-stamp holders which he had matched with a list of persons holding liquor licenses.

The students asked embarrassing questions of officials and Mayor Mayberry promised to investigate the new allegations. Someone asked me where we had parked. In keeping with the farcical nature of the proceedings, I replied:

"We figured none of the bad guys would go near a church."

Bailey, meanwhile, fell into a conversation with City Manager Oscar Hesch, and mentioned his short sojourn in Newport's jail.

"So you came back?" said Hesch in a wondering tone.

After the meeting, George and I walked back to his car.

"You shouldn't have told that guy we parked at a church," said Bailey.

"You shouldn't have told Hesch you were the guy Gugel jailed," I replied.

We found the car where we had left it. Bailey detoured up the Licking River to an even more ancient bridge to prevent anyone downtown from seeing us. I thought he was being overly cautious but it was his car and he was driving. We said little during the long ride home.

Next afternoon in the City Room I was handed a bit of wire copy that had just come in from Cincinnati. A car had been torched the previous night behind a Newport church.

The vehicle, according to AP, belonged to a new minister who had arrived in town only the day before. According to Newport police, it was just an accident. A sneak thief, obviously, had dropped a lighted cigarette while ransacking the car.

Having been told about the vice drive, the new minister disagreed. It was arson he said, and he was getting his wife and children away as quickly as possible.

Bailey sauntered over and read the wire copy.

"I told you so," he hissed. "They thought that was our car."

My stomach turned over. He was probably right, but, dammit, nothing would have happened if he hadn't told Hesch he was the photographer Gugel once jailed.

In a strange way, I became more stubborn as I became more scared.

****

On September 13, a "United Effort Day" was held in Newport churches. All pastors preached on the evils of vice and the police corruption that permitted it. They also distributed pledge cards to their congregations, binding all who signed them to support only political candidates who promised to enforce all laws.

I arranged in advance for Bennett to collect suitable quotes from his fellow ministers, and with another photographer — Bailey was unavailable — drove again up along the Ohio. Dr. Barkhau, just back from the Holy Land and resplendent in his academic robes, provided the best picture although we visited several churches to confirm a united effort.

"Our society is contaminated from top to bottom," said Pomeroy at the First Baptist Church. "Because we have been careless, corruption is too much in evidence. It's time to stand up and be counted. If you sign these cards, we'll know whether or not we'll have good government."

Two blocks away, the Flamingo Club was operating. Even at that morning hour, dozens of people were in the handbook betting on baseball games. One dice table was running and money was stacked on a card table. I got brandy in my coffee in the front room from the unlicensed bar where, on my last visit with Tom Powell, I had been offered milk.

"The point of this sermon," proclaimed Bennett at the First Presbyterian Church, "is that we must recognize our town as His house and realize it is a den of thieves and not a house of prayer. And then let our conscience guide us."

Liquor stores near the bridges to Cincinnati were doing a rousing business. Their front doors were locked but side doors were open. In the story I wrote later that day, I noted the only question asked was: "What'll it be?"

"That question," I concluded, "in a broader sense, was what Newport citizens were trying to answer Sunday."

More than 700 cards were signed that day and thousands more in the weeks that followed. Ministers in neighboring counties and in Cincinnati joined in the chorus and I was reminded of revival time in Happy Valley. Only the Catholics stood apart — and, as a result, a lot of people kept insisting that "God's law" did not prohibit gambling. Back in Louisville, Religion Writer Ora Spaid congratulated me on attending so many sermons and happily rewrote my story for the Religious News Service for which he was a stringer. He, at least among my colleagues, hoped the Newport battle would continue for it meant extra money in his pocket.

In addition to asking citizens to support law-abiding candidates, the ministers sent questionnaires to twenty-two candidates for the Newport City Commission and three candidates for Mayor asking if they favored enforcement of laws against prostitution, Sunday liquor sales, and gambling. Only one candidate for City Commission bothered to reply, and he was considered unelectable. The ministers were disappointed in the lack of response from the mayoralty candidates for among them was former City Manager Ralph Mussman.

Immediately upon being fired as city manager in 1958, Mussman had been appointed County Juvenile Officer by County Judge A.J. Jolly. He'd served in that post until September 1959 when he resigned to run for mayor. A graduate of Newport High School, Mussman had a master's degree from Morehead State College and had done graduate work at the University of Maine. Sports had provided him with an avenue into politics: he had coached football and basketball teams before becoming Newport Recreation Director and then City Manager.

Because of this background, the reformers hoped that if elected, Mussman would again become their ally. He was elected in November but had apparently learned a lesson: one sound apple in a barrel of rotten ones will also rot. Much later Mussman told me:

"If you run for office and you think you know what the people want, you go along with the will of the people if elected. I ran as a 'liberal' not as a reformer."

Even before taking office, Mussman formed a real estate and insurance company and started making deals with Screw Andrews, but all that did not become public immediately. A new decade was about to begin and with new state leadership in Frankfort and renewed unity of purpose in Newport, the reformers looked ahead with fearful anticipation.

On New Year's Eve, Faye and I prepared to celebrate in our traditional fashion — by making love — but after the children were in bed, we talked about the decade just ending. It had begun in Colorado with Marda's birth and it had taken us back to North Carolina and finally to Louisville. I had ceased to be a teacher and become an investigative reporter on a great newspaper that, unfortunately, didn't consider investigative reporting fashionable. What lay ahead?

"Newport is becoming dangerous, isn't it?" asked my wife.

I shrugged and made the best of it. "Not really. The bribe and the frame replaced the bullet up there a long time ago. Sometimes the Chief grumbles because the boys aren't shooting each other like they used to do in Chicago. It would make better copy."

Faye smiled. She looked unusually lovely in the blue wrapper that matched her eyes. It had been a Christmas present.

"Why do you want to keep going back to Newport?" she asked. "Is it because of your father?"

"Not entirely in the way you think. I keep remembering when Dad was trying to start the REA co-op. He was almost alone and up against a powerful enemy. Chris Seifried and his friends are almost alone too. No one believes they can win but they intend to keep trying. They need my help.

"Will the paper back you?"

"As long as Pope and Ethridge are there," I said with more confidence than I felt.

"Just don't forget you have a family," she said softly.

"I'm not likely to do that."

I took her hand and we went to bed.

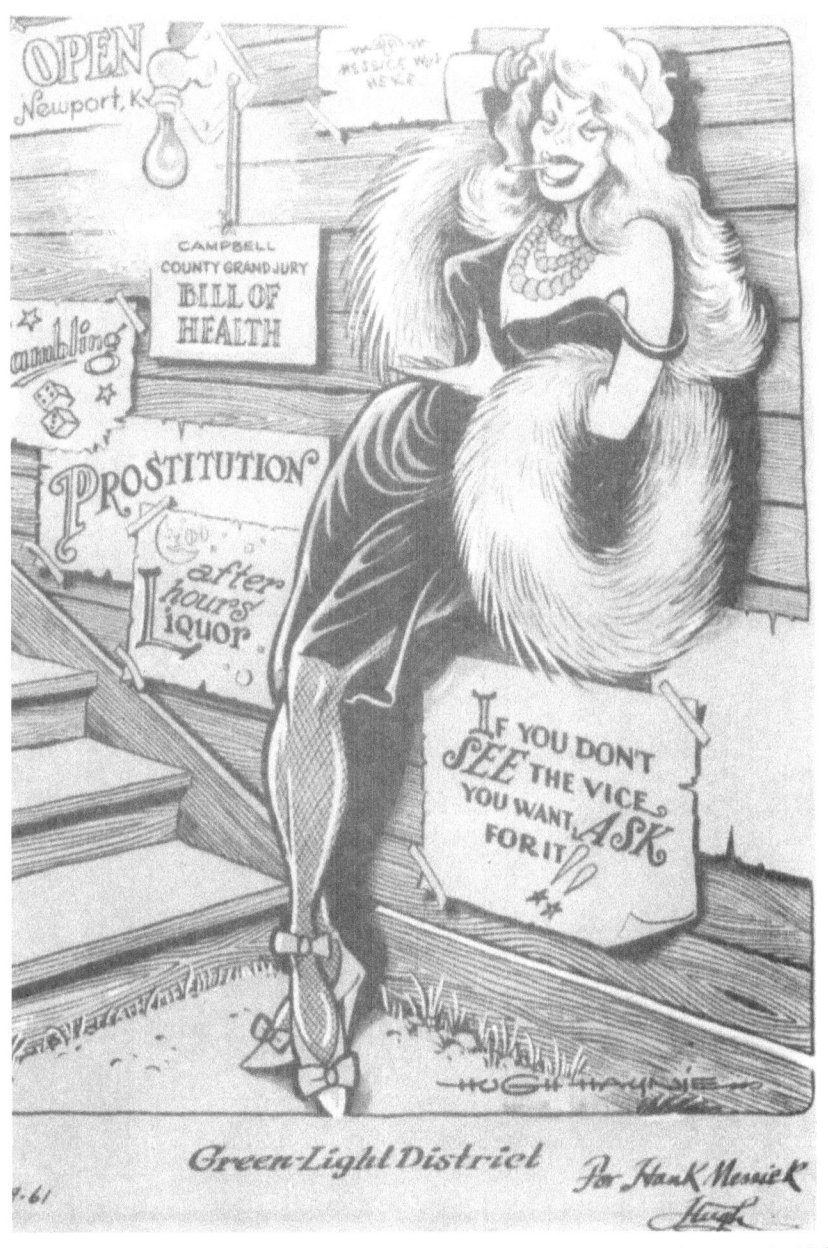

Louisville Courier-Journal editorial cartoon by Hugh Hayne on February 19, 1961

Hank Messick, 1961

George Ratterman, 1961

(Top) From left: Special Commissioner John L. Davis listens as Chris Seifried, Chairman of the Social Action Committee, testifies

(Left) Rev. George Bennett, First Presbyterian Church, an early leader of the Social Action Committee.

Downtown Newport Clubs in relationship to the Police Station and City Hall. See next page for corresponding list.

Downtown Newport in Relationship to the Police Station and to City Hall*

A   Police station and Jail
B   City Hall and Courthouse

1   Vivian's - 21 West Third - Night house of prostitution
2   Mabel's - 26 West Second - Day house of prostitution
3   Goldy's - 28 West Second - Day house of prostitution
4   Kitty's - 30 West Second - Day house of prostitution
5   Harbor Bar - 201 Columbia - Night house of prostitution and bust-out joint
6   Florence's - 212 Columbia - Day house of prostitution
7   Columbia Cafe - 101 West Fourth - Night house of prostitution and bust-out joint
8   Fourth Street Grill - Corner of Fourth and Columbia - Night house of prostitution
9   345 Club - 345 Central Avenue - Night house of prostitution and bust-out joint
10 Wanda's - 213 York - Day house of prostitution
11 Florence's #2 - 208 Central - Day house of prostitution
12 Old Alibi Club - 310 Central - Negro nightclub and gambling
13 Original Sportsman Club - 202 West Southgate Alley - Numbers and casino
14 Old Copa and temporary Sportsman Club (raided in 1961) - 339 Central Avenue - Numbers and casino
15 Old Dogpatch and New Sportsman Club - Second and York - Bust-out joint as Dogpatch, "bust" as Sportsman
16 Bobben Realty Company - Finance Builidng, Fourth and York - Lassoff's "layout betting" clearinghouse
17 Merchants Club - 15 East Fourth - handbook and casino
18 Schmidt's Playtorium - East Fifth - handbook and casino
19 Belmont Snax Bar - 12 East Fifth - handbook and casino
20 Office of Charles E. Lester - Fifth and York
21 Spotted Calf Cafe - West Fifth - handbook and bust-out joint
22 Yorkshire Club - 522 York Street - Handbook, casino,, layoff betting
23 Flamingo Club - 633 York Street - Handbook, casino, layoff betting
24 Tropicana, Glenn Hotel, Glenn Rendezvous - Monmouth Street - Gil Beckley's "layoff" headquarters, bust-out joint
25 Galaxie, Frolics, Stardust, Silver Slipper, Stark Club, etc. - Monmuoth Street, "bust-out joint", B-girls
26 Newport Library - Fourth and Monmouth - books
27 Wiegend's Bar - 313 Monmouth Street - Handbook and bust-out jont
28 Esselman's Cafe - 904 York - Handbook and bust-out joint
29 Stables Cafe - Monmouth Street - Second home of Lassoff brothers, "lay-off betting", handbook
30 Embassy Bar - 606 York Street - Handbook and bust-out joint
31 Ray's Cafe - 116 West Fourth - Second home of Hattie Johnson, prostitution

*These represent the major places in downtown Newport mentioned in the text,, but they are by no means inclusive of all illegal operations in the area shown in the picture. The Bawdy Houses mentioned except for Number 11, were operating in 1959-60. The much mentioned Beverly Hills and Lookout House were outside the city proper.

Frank "Screw" Andrews, head of numbers empire in the 1950s and owner of the Flamingo Club in Newport, KY

Winding Up . . . Frank "Screw" Andrews, ex-numbers king of Newport swings at *Cincinnati Post & Times-Star* photographer Bryon Schumaker. The incident happened during a 1962 visit by Sheriff George Ratterman at the then closed Flamingo Club on York Street.

(Top) Artist Kristina Bach's rendering of Tito Carinci

(Bottom) At George Ratterman's Police Court trial, from left: April Flowers, Tito Carinci and Rita Desmond

(Top) Police raid of the Hi-D-Ho Club in 1952 discover a secret room and occupants in the ceiling of the Club

(Bottom) April Flowers' promotional photo, circa 1960

Aerial view of Old Lookout House in 1952.

(Top) Raiders led by Sgt. Jack Thiem examine the take at a blackjack table during a raid on the Merchants Club in 1951. From left: Edward Gugal, "Dovey" Polinsky, Thiem, and veteran patrolman Jack Schnelle.

(Bottom) Heave-Ho at the Hi-D-Ho, 1951.

(Top) Hattie Jackson testifies at Ouster Hearings. From left: Newport Police Chief George Gugal,, Attorney Jiggs Buckman, and Newport Detective Chief Leroy Fredericks. Questioning Hattie with back to camera is Kentucky Attorney General John B. Breckinridge.

(Bottom) Ex-Madam returns . . . Hattie Jackson, flanked by John Breckinridge, left, and State Police Sergeant B. L. Sherrard, returns to the Campbell County Circuit Courtroom in Newport to testify before the 1961 special grand jury.

(Top) Attorney General Robert F. Kennedy waging a war against organized crime and racketeering in the 1960s.

(Bottom) Gilbert Lee Beckley, Newport lay-off bettor, 1959.

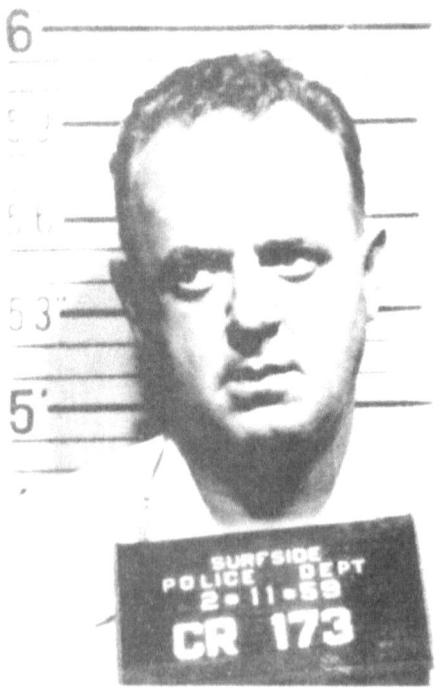

Jack Thiem testifies at 1961 Ouster Hearings in Frankfort.

Charles E. Lester, left, with his former rival, Daniel Davies, during a recess in the 1963 federal court trial of Lester and five others charged with framing George Ratterman.

(Top) Faye and Hank Messick, 14th wedding anniversary at Beverly Hills Country Club.

(Bottom) More Indictments . . . Special Judge Edward G. Hill hands over a new batch of indictments returned by a special Campbell County Grand Jury to Mrs. Virginia Drahmann Hesch, court clerk. Her husband, City Manager Oscar Hesch was indicted later.

York Street, Newport, KY looking North, Flamingo Club (633) on right, Yorkshire Club on left.

(Top) Kentucky Commonwealth Attorney William J Wise before Kefauver Committee, 1951.

(Bottom) Cleanup Begins . . . Home of Newport's most famous madam, Vivian Schultz. Moving Day November 8, 1961.

SIX
4 May '60

The Reverend George Bennett wrote in his diary:
"Hank Messick came about 2:30 p.m. We went to the Terrace Hilton in Cincinnati and checked him in. It seemed strange, another world, to be suddenly in one of those push-button, modernistic rooms on the 17th floor with Kentucky in the distance looking like the suburbs of a city that were of no interest to me. I got Bernardini to agree to go with Hank tonight..."

My boss had found another "news angle" as an excuse to send me back to northern Kentucky. Grand juries had been impaneled in both Kenton and Campbell Counties. In Kenton the presiding judge had told the jurors:

"All of us have witnessed in Kenton County a frightful era when gambling was at an all time high and law enforcement at an all time low. We will not return to that era. If the gambling interests are given the proverbial inch, they will soon want, and take, the well known mile. The solution is apparent--they must not be given that first inch."

Less than a mile away, Judge Murphy noted only that nineteen criminal cases confronted the Campbell County Grand Jury. The Judge made no mention of a recent *Saturday Evening Post* article that described Newport as "Kentucky's Open City".

In Louisville Pope read the sketchy wire and called me to his office. The assignment: compare conditions in Newport and Covington. So I got on a plane.

Cesare Bernardini was a drug company representative who had grown up in Cincinnati and who credited his escape from poverty to a mission church, a Presbyterian group set up in the middle of an Italian colony. After tonight the gamblers would call him "Little Caesar" and Attorney Danny Davies would tell all who would listen:

"There are two people you can't trust — a married whore and an Italian Presbyterian."

The short, swarthy Bernardini made a good companion. We started at the Snax Bar and found the door to the gambling room closed. The grand jury was in session. Someone told us we could find women at the Harbor Bar on Columbia Street. The bartender there didn't look up from his *True Detective* magazine but mumbled:

"The girls and slots are upstairs."

We found the stairway, climbed it, entered a hall that opened to a "sitting room." Eight girls greeted us with enthusiasm. They wore a strip of fishnet around their breasts and another around their hips. From a bedroom we heard a woman trying to calm an irate customer who was protesting he had been robbed. The girls swarmed around us, reaching, rubbing, pleading.

Apparently business was bad. What with the grand jury in session and the madam out of the room, competition ran riot. In self-defense, I turned to three slot machines standing against a wall, and dropped in a nickel. The ancient machine clacked loudly as I pulled the handle. A handful of coins gushed out and spilled on the floor. Immediately the girls scrambled for them. I glimpsed Bernardini — his face was flushed and he was sweating.

"Damn it, Hank, you can see their hair!"

He meant pubic hair and he was right.

Abruptly the girls ceased to chatter as an elderly woman emerged from the rear with an angry young man still demanding his money back. He left without it and the madam turned to us with an apology. We followed the unhappy customer down the stairs.

"There are nine brothels within two blocks of the police station," said Bernardini, "but some of them are day houses. Where do you want to go next?"

Day houses catered to the luncheon trade from Cincinnati and men needing a "quickie." They were open from ten in the morning until five in the afternoon.

We tried the Fourth Street Grill, just across the street from the police station. A lone waitress sat at the counter playing solitaire. I thought I recognized her from Vivian Schultz's place Don Baker and I had visited in 1958. She looked young then, fresh from the mountains, and her name was "Lela." We asked for coffee. Reluctantly she took a pot from a hot plate — the only cooking facility visible — and told us to put a quarter in the jukebox. When I obeyed, she pointed to a rear door and announced:

"The girls are in back."

"How about you?" asked Bernardini.

"I got the rag on," snapped the girl from the hills. "Why do you think I'm out here?"

In back we found a blonde, brunette, and redhead, a big cake bearing the words "Happy Birthday, Alice," and a fat woman with purple hair whom I recognized as Vivian. She sat apart from the girls and smiled benignly.

"Which one is Alice?" asked Bernardini.

"She hasn't got here yet," said the redhead.

"She's too old anyway," said the blonde.

"Alice is retired," said the brunette. "Let's get sexy."

Two of the girls wore slips, the other white shorts. They told us the price was ten dollars. We told them we'd think about it and come back later. No one seemed to mind.

"I guess we're not their types," said the brunette as we walked out.

Down Fourth Street one block from the police station was the 345 Club. Two groups of men moved ahead of us into the building. Five were in the first group, all wearing business suits. Six kids of high school age followed them. A bartender directed traffic up some stairs. I was prompted to ask how many girls were available.

"Enough," said the bartender.

As we climbed the stairs, the color of the walls changed from green to pink to a blushing red. A large room was full of people. The business types stopped to talk to girls wearing shorty nightgowns while the teenagers, laughing shrilly, clustered around a row of slot machines. About the only vacant place was a blackjack table. A large, heavily rouged woman sat behind it, and she had nimble fingers. The chips I bought vanished so quickly I scarcely had time to palm one for evidence.

We went from the 345 Club to the Glenn Rendezvous where a tuxedoed goon said the floor show was in progress despite the grand jury so we should wait in the casino upstairs. The concealed elevator carried us up and I wasted some more of the *C-J's* money at blackjack. We watched an obviously drunk patron playing Razzle-Dazzle. He was up to ten thousand and trying to double his money. He didn't, and with a shaking hand, wrote a check to cover his losses. He seemed to think it was funny. I wondered how he would feel next day.

I spent the next day checking Covington, finding only a couple of handbooks. All the cab drivers in that city and in Cincinnati that I talked to assured me "the action" was in Newport. I did find some oldtimers who discussed "the good ole days" when the Lookout House was open and Covington had more class than its sister city.

The following day I flew back to Louisville. Pope gave my story good play and, on the day after it ran, I received a call from a man who said he was foreman of the Campbell County Grand Jury. Would I come back and testify? There were enough votes to indict this time.

I drove up on the day designated in the new Nova station wagon which had replaced our sweetened Chevrolet. Intending to say my piece and get out of town quickly, I was forced to wait until late in the afternoon. Commonwealth's Attorney Wise, so I learned later, tried to persuade the jurors I was a troublemaker and unworthy of their attention. He failed and when I entered the Grand Jury room I was greeted with broad smiles. Almost, I felt welcome and I talked for almost two hours.

When they finished with me, Bernardini was called. In a mood of optimism I waited until "Little Caesar" completed his testimony. He talked me into attending a general strategy session with Chris and some of the ministers. It was almost midnight before I got away. I got in the new car, enjoyed the healthy sound of the motor's roar, and headed home.

The night was very dark. I drove as fast as the curves would permit. The good feelings of early evening had faded into fatigue. Upon leaving the urban area I entered blackness broken only by an occasional house light far off the road. There was almost no traffic and I felt alone on the planet as the miles went by. After an hour I noticed headlights in my rear view mirror far behind me. When I looked again, the lights were closer and now there was a second pair. Probably high rollers on their way home from the Beverly Hills Club, I decided, but then I realized even that rug joint had closed in honor of the Grand Jury.

Curious now, I watched my mirror. The cars were closing in. Where were they going in such a hurry?

Now the cars were behind me, bathing me with light. One car swept around and dropped in front of me. I assumed the other would follow, but it did not. Nor did the car ahead pull away. I realized I was boxed, in the middle. Two men were in each car and the cars were large, powerful looking. The hoods of Newport drove only the best.

Pressing the accelerator, I tried to pass. The driver moved to the middle of the road and stayed there. I slowed. He slowed. Now there could be no doubt that I was the target, but what was their purpose?

I was sweating. Fear gathered in my stomach. Aware of it, I laughed. Back in Happy Valley I had dreamed of high adventure, of narrow escapes, and desperate deeds. Now I had my chance. I should be enjoying this.

We passed a road marker and I realized my location. Abruptly an answer came to me. Up ahead the road ran close by and parallel to the Ohio River. There was no guard fence and in the past cars had occasionally gone off the bank and into the water. I could remember writing such a story while working the graveyard shift. These bastards were going to shove me into the river and call it an accident.

What to do? I couldn't think of anything. Then, as if the gods of adventure had intervened, I saw a car approaching from the south. The car in front moved over to the right at the sight of the oncoming lights. I waited, gauging our speed and the speed of the northbound car, and then I stepped on the throttle. My new car surged forward. I slipped left and went around the car ahead. Light blinded me, then was gone. Now everyone was behind me and darkness was ahead.

My maneuver had been unexpected, apparently, for I gained a hundred yards before the two cars seemed to recover. Just beyond was a curve and a side road to the left. Maybe, just maybe, I could get into it without being seen. As I turned into the curve, I flipped off my lights. There was enough starlight to see the gravel of the road on the left. Braking heavily, I turned into it, drove a hundred feet or so and stopped.

Behind me the Newport cars roared by. I held my breath. Would they give up upon not finding me on the road ahead or would they make a search? I drove without lights down the gravel road, found a wide spot and turned around to face the highway. Ten minutes passed; I saw lights from the south. Two cars thundered by. I waited fifteen minutes before driving slowly onto the paved road. It was only after passing through sleeping Carrollton that I began to relax.

Nothing happened to impede my progress. Exhausted physically and mentally, I reached home and climbed into bed. Faye did not awaken. I lay there trying to summon sleep while my mind insisted upon reliving the ride down the river. I realized I could not tell Faye about the episode. To do so would cause future worry. It then dawned upon me that I couldn't write the story either. Pope, to say nothing of Bingham and Ethridge, would not permit me to return to Newport if they knew about the chase. The damned town had been a hell hole for a hundred years; it wasn't worth a reporter's life.

Two days later the grand jury reported to Judge Murphy:

"We were impressed with the evidence relating to prostitution, and two instances of slot machines. On the basis of this latter testimony, we have returned indictments."

*****

About a month later, Commonwealth's Attorney William Wise called me at the *C-J* to ask in formal tones if I would return to Newport voluntarily to testify against the defendants or would it be necessary to go to the trouble and expense of subpoenaing me? I promised to call him back after consulting with Pope. My executive editor looked solemn. It was one thing, he noted, to sneak into town, get a story and beat it back to Louisville. It was quite another matter to be there in public view for several days.

I thought about my wild ride home on my last trip, but I didn't say anything. Pope told me to demand a police guard while in Newport. Moreover, he would send Kyle Vance from the Frankfort Bureau to watch my guards. We might get a good story, he observed. When I called Wise back, he agreed and wanted to know what name to register me under at a Cincinnati hotel. Currently popular on TV was a private eye show featuring a character called Peter Gunn. One of my favorite fictional characters was Dashiell Hammett's Sam Spade. Combined, they made an interesting name: Peter Spade.

Wise didn't even chuckle. He was playing it very straight.

Arriving by plane in Cincinnati on Sunday afternoon, I took a cab to the Sheraton-Gibson. Awaiting me were Newport Chief of Detectives Leroy Fredericks and Detective Grover Johnson. We checked into a double room on the eighteenth floor. Wise's assistant, Gardner Reed, a slender young man, arrived with an unopened bottle of bourbon. Fredericks said he wouldn't spend the night but would stay until we were settled in.

Dinner in the hotel dining room was a strained affair. Johnson, who looked like a country boy in his first city suit, was plainly uncomfortable. Halfway through the meal he threw down his napkin and said:

"I hate this place. It puts on airs."

We retired to our rooms and sat around looking rather blankly at each other. The phone rang. Fredericks picked up the receiver and seemed startled.

"It's for you, Pete," he said.

No one in Newport was supposed to know my *nom de guerre*. The caller was Vance. He wanted the expense money Pope had entrusted to me. I had planned to slip it to him next day in the court room, but now, with Fredericks watching, I could only tell him to come on up. Two minutes later Vance, considered an expert on Kentucky politics, was in the room. I introduced my companions and Fredericks poured the newcomer a drink. I took Vance into the next room, gave him his money, and told him:

"You've blown your cover. You'll be a marked man in Newport."

Vance laughed. He didn't believe me. The harsh realities of the police beat were too far behind him.

Shortly after Vance departed, Wise arrived. He explained he only wanted to make sure I was safe. Fredericks soon got him into the other room and talked long and low. Vance was mentioned several times. The Commonwealth's Attorney downed his drink and left.

Again we sat looking at each other. I got up and wandered to the window. Far below I could see the lights of moving cars. It was a long way down. I remembered a New York hood named Kid Twist who became known as "the canary who couldn't fly." He'd gone out of a hotel window while under police guard. Something of the terror I had experienced on the long ride home now returned. I'd put myself in the hands of men I distrusted. Suddenly I was glad that Vance had blundered into the scene. At least they knew they were being watched. I took a deep breath and began to relax.

In the course of the evening Fredericks received several calls. I could guess from the conversation that he was talking to Wise. Finally, he turned to me and asked:

"You don't know what your friend's plans for the evening were, do you?"

The truth began to penetrate. These guys thought Vance was up to something. My suspicions were confirmed an hour later when Vance called me. He'd gone to Newport and dropped in at the Glenn Rendezvous. He was having a drink and the bartender was telling him about "the room upstairs" when a "big bouncer" came in and ordered him to leave.

"We know who you are," the bouncer told him.

Realizing my warning had been valid, Vance had returned to his car and driven over to Covington as if leaving the area. When he was sure no one was following, he had returned to Cincinnati and was in the same hotel. Was he safe there?

Now I knew why Wise had been calling. Vance's disappearance had puzzled them. They hadn't counted on scaring him so easily and when he didn't visit another joint they became worried. I advised Vance he could sleep soundly, hung up the phone, and told Fredericks:

"You can tell Mr. Wise to relax. My friend is in his room. He said he had an interesting evening."

Fredericks stared as if waiting for more, then shuffled into the other room and dialed the phone. I announced I was going to bed. Fredericks finished his call and departed.

Next morning we breakfasted in the hotel and drove over the muddy Ohio. The courthouse was crowded. Sylvester Highchew, allegedly the new owner of the Harbor Bar, although there was nothing on record to prove he'd bought the place, was to be tried first.

"He's fronting for Ralph Bridewell," Bernardini told me.

Vance was in the crowd, I noticed, but he didn't come near me. After an hour or two of confusion, Wise advised the selection of a jury would take the balance of the day. I need not hang around. The problem was what to do with me. Since almost every bar had a handbook there was no innocent place to take a do-gooder. Reed and Johnson conferred and decided to go out to the Newport Gun Club. Its members were largely cops and wouldn't be around. We'd get lunch from vending machines.

The club proved to be nice enough and I stuffed my white briar and asked Johnson for a match. He plucked a coffee can full of matchbooks from the bar and handed it to me. The match books advertised The Spotted Calf Cafe at Fifth and York. On the back of the matchbook were hearts, spades, diamonds, and clubs. On the front was a horse's head. On the break were a pair of dice.

"You suppose they might have gambling there?" I asked.

"Nah," said Johnson. "Not a chance."

Nevertheless, when they weren't looking, I put a handful of matchbooks in my pocket. Later, after visiting the joint, I showed them to three grand juries and told of the large handbook and small casino at The Spotted Calf.

Dinner was even more of a problem, but, after much debate, we drove up the Licking River to a fish camp that boasted a bowling machine inside and a stinking privy out front. Johnson felt right at home. I met some interesting fishermen wearing hip-high waders, and was given a shot of good bourbon from the owner's private stock.

Next day I was called to testify. Wise asked about my visit to the Harbor Bar. My recital took about ten minutes after which I was cross examined for more than an hour by Attorney Davies. Apparently assuming I had to be a puritan — after all, I was a do-gooder — the lawyer tried to embarrass me by demanding I describe in exquisite detail the bodies of the girls I had seen. When I realized what he was attempting, I became amused. Nevertheless, he tried the same tactic on the "Italian Presbyterian" — who followed me on the stand. Bernardini got red in the face, but he answered the questions until Judge Murphy ordered Davies to move on.

We were followed by a string of Social Action Committee members who had visited the Harbor Bar several times in the course of their investigations. The trial spilled over until the next day. It was obvious the evidence was overwhelming, but the spectacle of citizens coming forth to testify was more important than the ultimate guilty verdict. The jurors, however, after less than an hour, did provide a surprise. They found Highchew guilty of maintaining a house of prostitution, a verdict which carried a minimum sentence of one year in jail. This was unprecedented and caused the crowded courtroom to buzz. A lesser charge of disorderly conduct had been routine in the past. Plainly shocked, Wise conferred at the bench with Murphy and Davies and then asked all witnesses in the pending trials to step into his office. We crowded in and were told that when the case of Highchew was separated from the others, Davies had agreed there would be no delay. The attorney had now requested the other trials be postponed.

"In view of the supercharged atmosphere," said Wise, "I've agreed to a delay."

"Why?" asked Bernardini. "As prosecutor you ought to like the atmosphere."

"It isn't fair to the defendants," said Wise. "A new jury panel will be able to consider the cases more calmly."

In a normal world his reasoning would make sense — in the world of Newport it also made sense but of another kind.

Highchew, as a stand-in for Ralph Bridewell, had tested the quality of the jury panel and of the prosecution witnesses. The verdict proved they had scored high. Since the remaining defendants had no stand-ins, Davies wanted to change the lineup. The witnesses couldn't be reached but new jurors could be obtained.

There was nothing we could do about it. I wandered out into the courtroom. Wise's assistant walked in with a new glass of coke for his boss. He sat it on the table. No one was looking so I tasted it. Good bourbon.

Someone touched my arm. I turned to look at a tall, lanky man with greying black hair. He wore a blue shirt and khaki trousers.

"Can I talk to you a minute?" he asked.

"Why not?" I replied.

He took me over to an empty corner of the courtroom and introduced himself. His first name was Howard, the last name doesn't matter.

"I thought you'd like to know," he said, "that orders have gone out to leave you alone. Those guys that chased you down the river were acting on their own initiative. When the big boys heard about it, they called a meeting in Sleepout's office above the Flamingo. The younger men wanted you hit but the older ones argued that it would create too much heat. One guy told about what happened to Jerry Buckley in 1930."

"Who is Jerry Buckley?" I asked.

"He was a radio newsman who led a drive to recall the mayor of Detroit. On election night he was shot eleven times while sitting in a hotel lobby. The heat that resulted caused the Purple Gang to scatter and the word went out that it doesn't pay to kill a newsman."

I digested this for a few seconds and then asked why he was talking. He laughed.

"I was in Newport back in the Twenties. Things were really wild then. Somebody wanted my joint so they framed me. I bribed my way out of jail and left town for awhile. I'm a farmer now but I still hear things."

He told me how I could reach him and left abruptly as Bernardini and Chris walked over. We all shook hands. Vance agreed to drop me at the airport before going back to Frankfort.

"I'm glad to go back to a place that has some rules," he said.

I felt a little sorry for him.

A week later, the trial of Vivian Schultz, the real owner of the Fourth Street Grill, was held. This time around Davies contended that Bernardini and I had crashed a birthday party for Alice and were told to leave. The jury believed us, however, despite the attorney's efforts to make us look like liars and fools. Yet Davies won his real goal — Vivian escaped a jail sentence and paid a two hundred dollar fine. The third defendant, Emil Bridewell of the 345 Club, had his trial postponed indefinitely. According to Wise, Bridewell had an infected big toe and was going to die so there was no point in wasting time with him. Somehow, the man survived, pleaded guilty, and accepted a two hundred dollar fine.

By then I was something of a local celebrity. A Cincinnati newspaper ran a story under an eight column banner:

GIRLS "IN BACK ROOM" MESSICK SAYS

And at the *C-J*, nimble fingered comedians began producing cartoons depicting me cavorting in the brothels of Newport. Some of my younger colleagues actually expressed envy but, I noticed, none volunteered to accompany me on my next expedition.

SEVEN
12 September '60

The Reverend Dudley Pomeroy invited me to a crucial meeting of the Newport Ministerial Association on condition I would keep secret any decisions reached. Reluctantly, I agreed, and on a pleasant afternoon I returned to a divided city.

At issue was whether to continue fighting and, if so, what to do next. Pomeroy wanted to continue. He told his colleagues that great progress had been made and the stage was set for a showdown in 1961. After debate, they voted to continue for one year and then quit if no progress occurred.

"There are more churches needing preachers than preachers needing churches," said one man. "We won't starve."

"They need ministers in Las Vegas," said another. "We'll all feel at home there."

They moved to the next question and a motion was made to hire Attorney Jesse K. Lewis to begin ouster proceedings against top local law enforcement officials.

Lewis was a former assistant attorney general of Kentucky who had won fame in 1947 when he led a successful move in Federal Court to disbar Kenton County's commonwealth's attorney, a victory that was decisive in the cleanup there. He added to his reputation in 1951 when he filed ouster charges against the Henderson County sheriff, forcing that official to resign. Since those glory days he had been labeled a champion of causes no one else would touch.

Pomeroy permitted me to listen in when, after the meeting, he called Lewis in Lexington.

"You will be fighting some of the strongest forces in America today," said Lewis.

The old crusader suggested his appointment be kept secret until the Social Action Committee could visit the major vice spots and collect fresh evidence. Pomeroy assured me that when the time was ripe, I would break the story. That was all very well, I decided, but I needed a story today. I didn't want to go back empty handed. I recalled that during the vice trials, a spectator had been a tall, well muscled man with red hair who had given me a long, steady stare while I was in the witness chair. Someone told me the man was Albert "Red" Masterson, and that he was considered to be "the enforcer" for the Cleveland Syndicate. I decided to give him a visit.

Masterson's joint was The Merchant's Club and it was just up Fourth Street from the courthouse. Many officials ate lunch there. It was a large rambling building in need of paint. I entered into a dining area and was immediately stopped by a well dressed man.

"I'm sorry, Mr. Messick." he said, "but you can't go into my back room."

"Are you Red Masterson?"

"Yes," he replied. "Won't you sit down and have a drink?"

"Thanks," I said. "I'd like to interview you."

"No reporter ever wanted to interview me before," said Masterson, and he led me to an isolated table. We sat facing each other. A waiter appeared. I hesitated and then ordered a coke. When it arrived, I took a sip and felt brave. This was living dangerously.

"How many men have you killed?" I asked.

"I never killed anybody that didn't need killing," he replied. "I've had a little trouble from time to time, that's all. I just won't take anything off anybody. You wouldn't either, would you?"

This little speech was delivered with a straight face. He seemed friendly enough.

"What do you think of the cleanup drive?" I asked.

Newport, he said, would never be cleaned up. The town would die. The syndicate — he used the word — was opposed to prostitution and bust-out gambling. Honest gambling was all right. After all, the farmer gambles everytime he plants a crop.

"Why won't you let me go into your back room?"

"Why do you want to go?" he countered. "You know what's back there as well as I do."

"I gotta see it before I can report it. By the way, why did you attend the vice trials?"

"To see the witnesses."

"Prosecution or defense witnesses?"

"Both."

We looked at each other. His lined face was expressionless. According to old newspaper clips, this man had at least four killings on his record. He'd pleaded self-defense and been acquitted. If some of my sources — and by now I had plenty — were correct, he had helped burn the first Beverly Hills Country Club. Peter Schmidt had rebuilt it on a more lavish scale before surrendering it to the syndicate. A child had died in that long ago fire.

I stood up. Masterson also rose.

"You're always welcome. No one will hurt you or humiliate you, but they won't let you into the back room."

I wandered down to the courthouse. City Manager Hesch refused to see me. "Too busy." Chief Gugel was also busy. The old man was approaching mandatory retirement age and I wanted to ask him about his successor. Rumor had it that the two candidates were Detectives Pat Ciafardini and Upshire White. Judge Paul Stapleton was available, however, and willing to talk off the record.

Stapleton handled civil matters for the circuit court and until recently his major gripe had been his inability to wear a black robe. Senior Circuit Judge Ray Murphy refused to wear a robe on the grounds the citizens would think him pretentious so Stapleton felt compelled to do likewise. A few days ago, however, the judge found something else to worry about. During a divorce hearing, the aggrieved wife testified her husband was "a dealer of craps" at the Snax Bar. Immediately

Stapleton summoned Sheriff Norbert Roll and ordered him to go to the Snax Bar "and arrest anyone connected with it if there is evidence of gambling."

The sheriff, an aging party hack, reported back that he'd found no evidence. Cincinnati newspaper reporters visited the casino an hour after the sheriff and found everything wide open as usual. Moreover, they had reported their findings on the front page. Apparently it was a slow news day. The judge sent the sheriff back again. Two minutes later Attorney Lester appeared and asked:

"How long are you going to keep annoying my clients?"

"As long as I consider it necessary," said Judge Stapleton.

Lester picked up the telephone in the judge's chambers and called the Snax Bar. He hung up laughing.

"They already know about it."

I told the judge I visited the Snax Bar upon arriving in town that day and found the casino doing a big business. Stapleton said I could quote him as saying the matter "might receive additional consideration."

It wasn't much of a quote but I jotted it down. The judge asked if I was going to stay over and see Bobby Kennedy. It was news to me that the brother of the Democratic candidate for president was coming to town. I made some phone calls and got myself invited to a press conference next day. James Lukens, a Cincinnati Teamster official who had defied Jimmy Hoffa, was in charge of the arrangements.

That evening in Houston, Senator John F. Kennedy faced a group of Protestant ministers and declared:

"Whatever issue may come before me as President, if I should be elected, I will make my decisions in accordance with what my conscience tells me to be in the national interest and without regard to outside religious pressure or dictate."

This so-called "Catholic question" had defeated Al Smith in 1928 and had become the burning issue in the 1960 campaign. Bobby Kennedy had been asked about it at each stop of his current tour.

Next morning a conference room atop one of Cincinnati's tallest towers was full of reporters and photographers. As had become the practice, television crews outnumbered the print media and tried to dominate the proceedings. Lukens, a bit harried, confided that Kennedy had arrived in the early morning hours and was nearly exhausted. That fact was confirmed when Robert F. Kennedy at last entered the room. He seemed tiny somehow, his frailness accented by dark circles under his eyes and lines of strain. The former counsel of the Senate Rackets Committee seated himself in the middle of a large sofa and forced a smile. The first question was about religion.

At times Kennedy seemed to be talking in his sleep as he repeated the answers he had given many times before. When the print reporters finished, he had to go over the routine again for the benefit of radio and television. Lukens flashed a glance of warning as the questions ceased, and the young man prepared to rise. I glanced above his head to the open window. Newport, bathed in morning sunshine, was visible. I plunged in with my first question.

Kennedy seemed startled, then pleased, at the abrupt change of subject. He sank back on the sofa.

Instead of worrying about the religion issue so much, the future Attorney General of the United States declared, the public should concern itself with such matters as organized crime.

"How can an administration handle Khrushchev and Castro when it can't handle Hoffa?" he asked.

Kennedy said he was familiar with crime conditions in Newport. He pledged that if his brother was elected a new anti-crime fighting unit would be established to deal with problem areas such as Newport.

I had my story, and, as I glanced around the room, I could believe I had it exclusively. Not one of the Cincinnati reporters was making notes. Well, perhaps they had what their editors told them to get. The Queen City press was avidly pro Richard Nixon.

Lukens reminded Kennedy that he was due at another meeting. As he walked by me he extended his hand. It was almost inert. I was afraid to squeeze it.

Back in Louisville I felt a bit frustrated. The Chief announced the paper was too tight for another Kennedy story. The *C-J*, for reasons none of its reporters understood, supported Lyndon Johnson and was not reconciled when the Texan took second place on the ticket. It was too much like the Combs-Wyatt fiasco of the year before.

I appealed to Pope on the grounds that Kennedy's promise to do something about Newport would help the reformers. He agreed and put the nine inches of space they allowed me on the front page. It was a scoop, Pope said. Where were the Cincinnati reporters?

"They weren't interested in crime," I replied.

Of such stuff are journalistic reputations made.

*****

"You get along with preachers," said City Editor Herchenroeder, "How about going out to Freedom Hall tonight and listen to Oral Roberts? Spaid went last night."

The man who was later to become famous as a TV evangelist was in 1960 chiefly known as a faith healer. Currently he was practicing his craft at the state fair grounds in a huge barn big enough for a football game. *The Courier-Journal* was not covering the event as such, but since several thousand people were there each night, it was felt wise to have a reporter on hand in case the roof fell in. Since Freedom Hall was on my way home, and I wouldn't have a story to write, I accepted the assignment. Not that I had much choice.

Upon entering the vast building, I found only about half of it in use. Thousands of metal chairs had been placed in front of a platform, behind which a curtain rose fifty feet high. As I crossed the empty floor towards the seats, a gaunt young man who looked like an undertaker in his black suit walked up to me and said: "Please don't smoke. This is God's house."

"I thought it was Freedom Hall," I said, but I knocked out my pipe and put it away.

The seats were full of men and women dressed in their Sunday best. Their faces were serious, their eyes intent. I thought of revival times in Happy Valley. One could not mock such people, but it was possible to feel sorry for them.

RAZZLE DAZZLE

The program was as orchestrated as a Broadway play. Roberts alternately preached and prayed over the blind, the crippled, and the mute. One could feel excitement mount. At intervals buckets were circulated by black clad young men and returned filled with cash. The climax came when all who felt possessed by devils were taken behind the curtain to receive individual attention. Apparently others who had been too possessed to attend the sermon were already back there. The audience began singing hymns to provide moral support, and I slipped behind the curtain.

Canvas cots were stretched in rows and on each a man or woman lay. Over each bent one of the black suited men who sternly, and repeatedly, ordered the demon to depart in the name of Jesus. A bluish smoke filled the area, lights were dim, an acrid smell hung. Every minute or so one of the recumbent figures would rise to a sitting position, hold up his arms, and scream in exultation:

"I'm free. Praise God, I'm free."

And somehow an eerie light would flicker through the gloom as if a demon was fleeing in great haste. I wondered how it was done. The entire scene reminded me of what I'd read about the Dark Ages, and the sound of people singing familiar hymns on the other side of the curtain only made the affair seem more bizarre.

Ultimately, one of the young men noticed me and politely but firmly explained the area was out of bounds to reporters. My presence, he said, gave aid and comfort to the Devil. I'd seen enough so I returned to the better lighted area where buckets of cash were still being collected.

When the service ended and the crowd began to disperse, I called the city desk to say that the roof hadn't fallen in but a lot of demons were apparently homeless and looking about for new quarters.

"Don't bring any to the office. Go home," was the reply.

On the way I compared the spectacle I'd just witnessed with the Newport ministers I'd come to know. They too fought devils but their foes were visible and dangerous. I rated them far above Oral Roberts and all his grim young men.

The uneasy calm that settled over Newport was broken on October 20 when news came in from New York that the FBI had seized four hundred and twenty slot machines en route from Newport to England where gambling had recently been legalized. The machines were old and some of them were unworkable. Lester had made a trip to London to arrange the deal.

Newport took a back seat, however, as election day arrived. Early returns indicated a sweep by Kennedy. Faye and I went to bed happy only to arise next morning to discover that Nixon had made it close, at least insofar as the popular vote was concerned. In this case a miss was as good as a mile — the man Duke University faculty had rejected for an honorary degree had now been rejected by the people. Hopefully, Robert Kennedy's promise of a drive on organized crime would be realized and Newport would get help on the federal level.

Campbell County voted for Nixon by a narrow margin, the first time it had gone with a loser in history, but hardly had the election passed when a new problem developed. The regular fall grand jury was ready to report and Judge Murphy was too ill to appear. The Kentucky Court of Appeals stepped in and — call it divine intervention as did Chris Seifried, or just plain luck — selected Judge Edward G. Hill to sit until Murphy could return.

Hill, at fifty years, was a legend. Born in Harlan County, home of mountain feuds, he worked his way through high school and college by loading coal. Winning a scholarship, he studied law at the University of Cincinnati — where he became acquainted with Newport — and was admitted to the Kentucky Bar in 1937. During World War II he had served as a gunnery officer on merchant ships in the North Atlantic. Upon resuming his law practice in Harlan, he was appointed Circuit Judge to fill a vacancy. Quickly he won a reputation as "the tamer of Bloody Harlan." Mountaineers were taught respect for law and order by vigorous attention to legal forms and an understanding of human problems. The natives identified him as one of their own and were proud of his achievements.

I was on hand on the day the grand jury reported. Hill was handsome, I decided, his curly black hair matching his black robe which he wore in complete confidence. The jury, a non-descript collection of men and women, filed in and presented its report. It had returned 71 routine indictments and had "dismissed two homicides which resulted from shooting, which upon mature evaluation of the evidence, appeared as manifest cases of justifiable homicide by reason of self-defense." It was the code of the Old West, of Little Mexico.

Judge Hill accepted the report without comment, dismissed the jury, and announced he was entering an order for a special grand jury to convene on November 10. As an afterthought, he ordered some long confiscated slot machines destroyed on the steps of the courthouse.

It was all quite shocking.

The ministers recovered first and authorized Chris to appear before the special grand jury to ask for the indictment of various officials for failure to enforce criminal laws. Chris was also given permission to use some of the new evidence collected by the Social Action Committee at the request of Jesse Lewis. Hill had provided an unplanned opportunity.

Danny Davies regained his poise and filed an objection to the manner in which the special grand jury had been called. Wise agreed the rules of Campbell County had been violated but legal technicalities seemed too weak to stand up in the face of a hurricane of public approval aroused by the sight of an honest judge trying to do his duty.

On the day the grand jury was to be impaneled, Judge Murphy climbed out of his sick bed. Pale and drawn, he pulled himself up the stairs past the mural of civic virtue to resume his duties. The assembled jurors were told he had "no idea" as to why they had been called, but he gave what he called "my usual admonitions." He even noted that, "according to the press," the ministers wanted to present evidence.

Just in case the new grand jurors were curious as to what Judge Hill had planned, I called the judge and asked him. He'd intended to ask for an investigation of vice and gambling, and so I quoted him in the *C-J* next day.

Carl A. Giancola, a retired druggist, was selected foreman. In later sworn testimony he described what happened. The first item of business was to tell Commonwealth's Attorney Wise to get lost — after all, he'd said they were sitting illegally. Four members of the Social Action Committee appeared to give up-to-date testimony about local conditions. The jury called County Judge Jolly, County Attorney George

Muehlenkamp, and Sheriff Roll. The first two men "cleared themselves of responsibility" but Roll denied the existence of gambling.

"We were all sitting on the edge of our chairs," according to Giancola, "and when he said there was no gambling, you could just see the jurors flop back. That sunk them. When he said there was no gambling, that was it. We had no alternative but to indict the sheriff."

Everyone remembered Roll's fiasco at the Snax Bar.

"After we indicted the sheriff," Giancola related, "Wise came in and tried to talk us out of it by telling us the trouble it would cause, the hurt to his family, and things of that sort. But the jury was pretty well set on it."

While Wise was trying to save Roll, I waited outside the jury room with other reporters. Chief of Detectives Fredericks wandered by. I told him the Snax Bar casino was operating despite the special grand jury. Apparently the gamblers didn't consider an extra grand jury worthy of respect. Fredericks clicked his tongue against his teeth and commented:

"I think I'll go get a sandwich and a bowl of soup."

It was mid afternoon before Wise abandoned his efforts. Unrobed, Judge Murphy ascended the bench and the jurors were allowed to enter. Giancola, a little man with a bow tie and a poker face, handed over a list of indictments. The clerk read them off rapidly. In addition to Roll, four of the indictees were gamblers, three from the Snax Bar and one from the old Glenn Rendezvous which had recently changed its name to the Tropicana.

Curtly and without thanks, Murphy dismissed the special grand jury. He adjourned court. As reporters crowded around, he reminded them that Police Chief Gugel had once been indicted for nonfeasance and acquitted. Obviously, he expected Roll to have the same good fortune.

The trial of the sheriff was scheduled for December 6. In an effort to increase the heat, the ministers allowed me to break the story about plans for Jesse Lewis to file ouster charges against top officials. Pope gave it a good play. Next day a stranger walked into the newsroom and handed me a piece of paper. Signed by Sheriff Norbert Roll, it was a subpoena commanding me to testify at the trial of Norbert Roll. Late in the afternoon of December 5, I flew up to Cincinnati.

The afternoon newspapers headlined a story about a motion by Roll's attorney to set aside the indictment. Allegedly, Judge Murphy had the motion under consideration and would rule that night.

The Reverend George Bennett was no longer in Newport. For the sake of his family which had repeatedly been threatened, he had resigned his post. Donald Witzl, his successor, let me buy him dinner in Covington and then took me on a tour of Newport. About 8:30 p.m. we drove by the courthouse. I noticed that lights were burning in the judge's chambers. Up ahead on York Street we could see a large crowd in the vicinity of the Yorkshire Club. The minister parked and we proceeded on foot.

At least fifty men, most of them in business suits, milled aimlessly on the sidewalk in front of the casino. Some were angry, others bewildered. From snatches of conversation, it was evident they had abruptly been evicted. One man announced he was in the middle of dinner. Another man chimed in:

"Brother, I was in the middle of a winning streak."

Witzl, a newcomer, was astonished by the scene, but he followed me through the door. A man in evening clothes stopped us short.

"Sorry, bub, the joint is closed."

Up the street on the other side a similar crowd was standing in front of the Flamingo. We approached, walked through complaining men and a few women to the door. No one was guarding it. Inside we went, by the unlicensed bar — no flowers on it this time — to the casino in the rear.

It was an incredible scene of confusion. Dice tables were being dismantled. Wallboards in the handbook were being taken down. The carpet on the floor was being rolled up. Men scurried about, oblivious to our presence. I stopped one long enough to ask what was happening.

"The Sheriff's in trouble," said the man hurriedly. "We hope it's only temporary."

Witzl and I watched the stripping of the casino for a few minutes, then went outside and walked around to the Snax Bar. Enroute we met unhappy patrons. No one barred the door so we went through the lunch room and into the casino. It was the same scene of organized confusion — gaming tables being taken apart, wallboards taken down and erased before being carried out through a rear door, the carpet being rolled up, and finally, amazing as it seemed, golden sheets of wallpaper were being taken down one by one.

In the midst of the activity, two men sat at a little table playing cards and ignoring repeated requests to hurry up. Again we got the message from a casino supervisor:

"The sheriff"'s in trouble."

We walked back to York Street. It looked as if every cab in the greater Cincinnati area had arrived to pick up the disappointed customers. Some of the cabbies offered alternate entertainment.

"Here for women," shouted one driver. "Here for the prettiest girls in town."

A taxi slowed beside us. "I can take you to where the girls are real pretty," said the cabbie.

I had more urgent business at the nearest telephone booth. A call to the city desk in Louisville got me Dick Hunter on rewrite. I dictated a story, composing it as I went along...

"Newport, Dec. 5 — The lid went on Newport gambling joints Monday night on the eve of the scheduled trial of Sheriff Norbert Roll..."

When I finished, Witzl commented. "I guess Judge Murphy has decided to go on with the trial and he wants Roll to be able to swear there's no gambling in Newport."

"You catch on real fast," I told him.

I went back to the phone booth, dialed the *Cincinnati Enquirer* and asked for the City Desk. A man answered. I identified myself and told him what was going on in Newport.

"The Kentucky page has gone to bed, " he replied in a bored voice. I hung up.

In court next morning, Defense Attorney Otis Bertelsman told the judge that "Mr. Roll prefers to have his case decided by a jury rather than a technicality." He asked Judge Murphy to withhold a ruling on the motion to dismiss until the end of the trial. That made the outcome of the trial rather obvious: if the trial jury crossed him up, Roll could fall back on a ruling from the judge.

Instead of a legal contest, the proceeding had become a battle for public opinion. It was interesting for the opportunity it provided to observe Judge Murphy and Wise. Of the two, Wise had the more difficult task — he had to go through the motions of prosecuting and try to make it convincing. Murphy could be impartial, unless of course, he was forced to rule on the motion to dismiss. In fact, while Seifried was under cross examination, Murphy found it necessary to rebuke Wise for not objecting to the defense attorney's questions.

Jack Steinman, a Social Action Committee witness, testified later that "I felt as if I were on trial."

When I took the stand, Wise asked only the most general of questions and, apparently satisfied, Bertelsman quickly excused me. My disgust was evidently plain on my face for as I stood up, Wise asked:

"Did you have something more?"

There had been no pre-trial interview so Wise really didn't know what I had to say.

I told him I had a lot more, so he began to question me in rebuttal and allowed me to introduce various bet tickets, casino gambling chips, and the matchbook advertising the Spotted Calf Cafe. This time I was cross examined more sharply.

Roll's defense was based on two contentions — there wasn't any gambling in the first place and, if there were, it was unfair to single him out for blame. His attorney introduced hundreds of reports of monthly inspections made by Roll and his deputies as required by law. In none of the inspections had gambling been found.

Ironically, some of those same reports would later be used as evidence against Roll.

The trial concluded the following day and by its end Wise was showing the strain. His assistant, my former bodyguard, was kept busy refilling his "water" glass. When the jury retired, I leaned forward from my seat behind the Commonwealth's Attorney and asked if he thought there was any chance of a guilty verdict.

Wise replied:

"I'll tell you one thing — if they find him guilty, you can write my obituary."

The man was serious; half drunk, perhaps, but serious.

He had no reason for worry. Twelve minutes after the jury retired, it returned to announce Roll was innocent. It would have been back sooner but several minutes were wasted finding the judge. Chris Seifried issued this statement:

"I think it is possible the gamblers have won a victory today and lost the war."

The verdict fooled no one and made a lot of good citizens angry. The year ahead promised to be an exciting one.

Meanwhile, back at the office, rumors were again circulating. The Ethridge Era was nearing its end. Word was that Executive Editor James Pope would retire first and be replaced by Norman Isaacs. During coffee breaks, in "Mama Bingham's kitchen, "we speculated as to who would leave and who would stay. There was general agreement the shift in command would bring an exodus of veteran reporters.

In this atmosphere of speculation, I was approached by James Pope, Jr.

He had worked for years on *The Louisville Times* but after a crippling illness, had been made assistant city editor of the *C-J*. Never before had he shown much interest in the Newport story so I was rather curious when he took me aside one evening and asked about the status of the reform drive. Was young Pope's interest connected with the rumors about his father? Perhaps it was beneath the Editor's dignity to ask me directly.

"Things have been building up to an explosion," I said. "The lid will blow off next year."

Pope did not retire at year's end. Apparently he decided to try to win a big one before quitting, knowing well that Isaacs would not continue the fight in Newport. For that decision I was very grateful. It was my fight too. I still hadn't located Frank Andriola.

EIGHT
2 March '61

Action and reaction.

In Washington the Age of Camelot, with a young President and his lovely wife in the White House, began with a challenge: "Ask not what your country can do for you; ask what you can do for your country." The second United Effort Day in Newport brought a flood of cash contributions from congregations in Cincinnati and throughout Kentucky. The money didn't come in bucketfuls, as at an Oral Roberts revival, but it did come in sufficient quantity to pay legal fees in the drive to oust public officials.

In an attempt to counter the ministers' attack, the Campbell County grand jury issued a blast against reformers and *The Courier-Journal*. The grand jury's report, which was admittedly written by William Wise, maintained that Newport was no worse than any other city, and it noted:

"We are mindful of a continuing campaign being carried on by a reform group which has enjoyed the active assistance of newspapers published in Louisville. As representative citizens who consider ourselves decent, law-abiding people, we feel impelled to assert that this group, essentially devoted to reform, has caused a grossly distorted picture of our community to be presented to the various news media. Those who manufacture news through public pontifications likewise thrive on the publicity that they thus enjoy."

"A community in many ways chooses its way of life as do

individuals. Its choice is reflected in the voice of the electorate. If that way of life be distasteful to some, let it be submitted to a plebicite. Some, of course, will find any way of life distasteful."

Action and reaction.

The grand jury's diatribe was answered by a lead editorial in the *C-J*.

For thirty months the newspaper had printed my stories but its editorial pages had been silent about Newport. Now, abruptly, it had launched a crusade. Cynically, I understood the sudden outburst. The Combs-Wyatt team had been wracked by an unusually messy scandal which tarnished Lieutenant Governor Wilson Wyatt's political hopes. To counteract this, the editorial board had obviously decided to push the administration into a crusading mode. The editorial urged the state government to crack down on the "vice capital of Kentucky."

Accompanying the editorial was one of Hugh Haynie's most inspired cartoons. It depicted a painted lady, gaudy fur draped about her, hand outstretched in welcome. A bare light bulb glowed. The caption read, "Green Light District," and on the wall was a sign reading "Campbell County Grand Jury BILL OF HEALTH." Another sign said, "If you don't see the vice you want, ask for it." There was a blank sign. On it Haynie had originally written, "Messick Wuz Here," but the editors made him erase it. He restored the message on the original mat and autographed it. I had it framed and we hung it in the family room. My sons called the cartoon figure "Cruella."

Action and reaction.

"The preachers are coming. Run for the hills."

That was my greeting when I walked into the Frankfort Bureau. Kyle Vance and his associates were happy enough to have me come from Louisville when the story concerned an attempt by Newport ministers to force Governor Combs to do something he really didn't want to do.

The delegation of ministers was accompanied by Attorney Jesse K. Lewis and his associate, John Anggelis, a younger and less grumpy attorney. Combs was said to be absent but his secretary accepted a thirty-one page affidavit which asked that eight officials be ousted on the charge they had failed to do their sworn duty in suppressing gambling, prostitution, and illegal liquor sales.

"This is what we have been working towards for four years," said Dudley Pomeroy.

The affidavit cited statutes empowering the Governor to remove from office any "peace officer" found derelict in his duties. Circuit Judge Ray Murphy, County Judge Andrew Jolly, and Newport Mayor Ralph Mussman were included in the "hit list" on the grounds their duties included those of a "conservator of the peace." The Governor would ultimately strike them from the list, ruling that conservators were not peace officers. Remaining were Police Chief George Gugel, Chief of Detectives Leroy Fredericks, Campbell County Police Chief Harry Stuart, and Sheriff Norbert Roll.

I located the Governor that night at a country club near Louisville. He had no comment on the ministers' action, but did recall when questioned that he'd encouraged the ministers at an earlier meeting.

The Courier-Journal responded with another biting editorial demanding action. Executive Editor Pope, elated at having editorial support, hired two private detectives from out of state to visit Newport and compare conditions there with what they had seen elsewhere. Just in case the private eyes couldn't find their way to York Street, Pope told me to give them a guide listing the major joints and their locations. The detectives after their visit signed a long affidavit. Their spokesman declared:

"I never in my life saw anything like it. I've done the same type of work in New York, Baltimore, Washington, New Orleans, and I've never seen anything so wide open as in the Newport area."

Pope devoted almost a full page in the Sunday edition to the affidavit. The story bore this headline, an obvious answer to the grand jury's blast:

IT'S REALLY TRUE WHAT THEY SAY ABOUT NEWPORT

I wondered why I didn't feel vindicated.
Action and reaction. Enter George Ratterman.

A meeting of Social Action Committee members was being held in Ft. Thomas — a wealthy suburb on the bluffs above Newport — when in walked Ratterman. As he told it later:

"It had been somewhat embarrassing to me as a Catholic in Campbell County to find that most of the reform activities had originated by some Protestant group. A bunch of them were sitting around and I came in late. I told them the reason I was there was to show Catholics were interested."

Ratterman was four years younger than me, a native of Cincinnati. Coach Frank Leahy called him "the greatest all around athlete in the history of Notre Dame." And he had brains as well. He was permitted to enter law school although lacking an undergraduate degree. After a semester, professional football wanted him. He returned to college during the spring semesters and in 1947 married Ann Hinglebrok, a native of Newport. By 1961 the couple had eight children.

A quarterback who won the nickname "Snake" for the way he could send a team slithering down the field, Ratterman played pro ball in various cities before ending as backup to Otto Graham at the Cleveland Browns. In Cleveland and later in Cincinnati he continued his law education and received his degree in 1956. That year injuries forced his retirement from football. He settled down in Fort Thomas and became an investment broker in Cincinnati.

Not only did Ratterman interest other Catholics in joining the reform movement, he persuaded the Bishop of Covington, Richard H. Ackerman, to issue a statement. Released on March 10, it came as a stunning blow to the politicians of Campbell County.

The bishop said he had been asked to comment on the church's stand in regard to public officials who failed to fulfill their oaths of office.

"That is easy. Turn them out if it is proven they are dishonest, capricious — turn them out. They are useless, dishonorable servants."

The Bishop went on to condemn prostitution and drunkenness. He said that to make gambling "morally permissible" it must be, among other things, "decent". Gambling that takes place "in defiance of the law" is not "decent."

This statement ended the stalemate that had long prevented united action against vice. Many Catholics now came forward. The Committee of Five Hundred was formed. It described itself as "religiously non-sectarian and politically non-partisan." Its purpose was to find and support for public office "men and women of unquestioned honesty and integrity." The search began.

These developments kept me busy. On March 18, however, I was asked to cover Louisville Police Court. It was a routine Saturday assignment that sometimes provided a human interest story such as the time I found Cassius Clay listed on the blotter. On this occasion a bondsman, Lawrence "the Barber" Detroy, walked up and fingered the lapel of my rather worn sports jacket.

"You can do better than this," he said. "I want to talk to you after court."

A couple of hours later, with court adjourned, Detroy called me to the center of the empty courtroom. He frisked me expertly, muttering, "They tell me you sometimes carry a recorder."

I had done so once while buying drugs from a character who was selling them to prisoners in the State Reformatory.

Detroy had connections in Newport and had served time in federal prison. In Louisville he'd achieved a degree of respectability despite the time he was arrested for chaining his wife and cutting off her hair. In fact he had lunch every Friday with Commonwealth's Attorney Lawrence Higgins, the man who had succeeded the great spy hunter.

After shaking me down, Detroy said he'd been in Newport the day before and the big boys up there wanted to do something for me. He had volunteered to approach me. The boys wanted to take care of me on a regular basis. All I had to do was stay away from Newport.

"How much?" I asked.

"Anything that's reasonable."

"How about one thousand dollars a month?"

"Sounds reasonable to me. I'll set it up."

When I reported this to Pope, he took me to Mark Ethridge. There was some discussion about the possibility of photographing a money exchange, but it was decided to drop the matter. Ethridge had some doubts for my life expectancy if we should try a double-cross.

A few days later I met Detroy. He produced a wad of one hundred dollar bills. I told him I wasn't interested. He turned on his heels and walked away.

Next day I went back to Newport. The search for a candidate to run for sheriff in that fall's election had ended. A special meeting of the Committee of 500 at the Newport Public Library had been advertised in the Cincinnati newspapers. City commissioners meeting that afternoon had laughingly suggested a special police detail would be necessary to handle the crowds.

When I arrived the meeting hall on the second floor was overflowing. Among those with a seat was Red "the Enforcer" Masterson. Unexpectedly, I was introduced, to loud applause.

Ratterman, tall and lithe in a well fitting business suit, got a standing ovation. The only man who remained sitting was Masterson. His face expressionless, his eyes shifted from person to person as if trying to understand what all the noise was about. Ratterman began to talk:

"I am willing to run for office if you people are really serious. I am not willing to sacrifice four years of my life if this is to be but a temporary clamor. There have been reform movements in our county before. They did not last. That is the reason this county is in the mess which we all know exists today. We must not let that happen again.

"I have eight children. I don't want them to grow up in a community where syndicated gambling finds a home, where prostitution flourishes, where officials are known to be corrupt, and where now the illegal narcotics industry has found a home."

"I'm told that if I run for sheriff, I will probably be the victim of all sorts of slanderous attacks. If this is the price which one must pay to run for office as your candidate, so be it. But I say to our opponents, let the battle be joined now, for I shall not accept one penny of their foul money nor shall I be influenced by any of their cheap threats..."

"I ask you to prove that democracy will work in Campbell County. I ask you to vote for a candidate who swears that he will not only take an oath of office, but that he will keep his oath: who swears that he will enforce the laws fearlessly and relentlessly until those who have polluted this community are driven from our midst. This is what I swear to do, ladies and gentlemen. I swear to you and to God Almighty that I shall be your honest servant to the utmost of my abilities."

Confusion. Screaming men and women fought to shake the candidate's hand. Chris Seifried was there, looking as if God had just answered another of his prayers. Protestant ministers pushed forward to embrace a Catholic.

Red Masterson, who had boasted to me that he got his first square meal in a Newport whorehouse, sat as if stunned. I asked if he still believed Newport could never be cleaned up.

"I'm still waiting to see it," said Masterson slowly.

On the street below, uniformed policemen looked curiously upward towards the windows from which the cheering came. A large crowd of citizens had gathered. Cars were stopping, and the policemen who'd been sent there as a gesture of derision by the mayor found themselves with a traffic jam.

Next day Ratterman and a delegation of supporters flew to Frankfort to confer with Governor Combs. The Governor promised to help "provided the people of Newport show good faith and willingness to cooperate with me."

Combs announced he was sending Alcoholic Beverage Control agents into Newport to look for gambling on premises holding a liquor license. The reformers said they were very disappointed. The Governor had promised privately a year before to hold ouster hearings if proper affidavits were presented. Combs responded:

"I shall do my duty as I see it. I will not be swayed from my duty either by the gamblers or the zealots."

A tour of Newport uncovered an ironic situation — gambling casinos which for years had sold liquor without a license were continuing to offer gambling and liquor, but the smaller places whose owners had been unable to operate without a license were afraid to pay off even on a pinball machine. The Beverly Hills Country Club, however, currently starring Jimmy Durante, had a license and closed its casino. Durante professed indifference. "I don't go near the tables," he said when I called him.

"People wave at us as we drive by," complained one ABC agent.

"They've sure got an alarm system in this town."

Another man who could testify about the Newport warning system was Arthur Helliwell, correspondent for a string of British newspapers. Arriving in town, he did what he would have done in London — he went to the police station and introduced himself "to the Bobbies." Following dinner he decided to make the rounds of "the pubs." Everywhere he was refused entrance. Doormen knew his name, the name of his newspapers, and his purpose.

I happened to run into Helliwell next day. In a thick British accent, he asked for aid. I introduced him to the "American way" of investigating vice. Some Social Action Committee members gave him a new hat to replace his Homburg, told him to keep his mouth shut, and visited several casinos without difficulty. Later, Helliwell wrote:

"After three astonishing days in this wild and wicked little border town, I still have the feeling I got mixed up with a Hollywood film on location."

I was in Newport at the time to check on the price of eggs. An egg salesman, who got fifty dollars a dozen, had disappeared four weeks before. He was a Campbell County constable with arrest powers, and his customers were Newport casinos. Allegedly, he had tried to increase the price of eggs after the ABC men came to town. His car had been found near the Ohio. I had information that he'd gone to Arizona but it gave me an excuse to question his attorney, Charles E. Lester.

A small, white haired man with a pale face, Lester was the evil genius of Newport politics. Originally he played the role of reformer, but his halo vanished when it was discovered the brothels he had closed had reopened at other locations he had provided. For twenty years thereafter he had schemed to win political control of Campbell County and he had made the frameup into an art form. While he had been much mentioned, this was my first conversation with him. The constable, Lester said, had probably been killed and thrown in the river encased in a "Newport Nightgown" of concrete.

The attorney was more concerned with the living than with the alleged dead. He went down the list of Committee of 500 officers, giving me the dirt on each. This one was a drunk, that one beat his wife, et cetera, et cetera. For George Ratterman, however, he reserved his foulest language and wildest charges.

Ratterman, said the attorney, practically lived at the Glenn Rendezvous — it recently had become the Tropicana where three neon nudes danced above its marquee — and engaged in unnatural sex orgies there. He'd been booted out of Notre Dame, fired off the Cleveland Browns, and was in general a liar and a hypocrite.

The man followed me to the door of his second floor office and continued to describe the candidate in obscene terms as I descended the stairs.

The constable was never found, but he was reelected that fall, having filed for reelection before he vanished. Election night coverage paired him with another Kentucky official who won reelection while serving life for murder.

Somewhat shaken by the intensity of Lester's hatred of reformers, I returned to Louisville to be shaken yet again. In my absence, Ben Reeves had been appointed Assistant Managing Editor and moved into the long vacant office next to Pope. Scuttlebutt had it Pope hoped to prevent Isaacs from ultimately taking over by grooming Reeves as a possible successor.

Reeves was a young man of stocky build with a ruddy face and a great interest in politics. He'd served tours in the Frankfort and Washington bureaus in preparation for an executive job. I was not impressed when he took me to dinner at the Pendennis Club, Louisville's elitist establishment where black waiters served WASPS only, and commented:

"I want you to regard everybody in Newport as if they'd just crawled out from under a rock."

After three years, I thought I knew the good guys from the bad without any editorial direction.

May 8 arrived. I was at home getting ready for bed when at 11:38 p.m. the telephone rang. A rough voice ordered me to come at once to a night club near Churchill Downs if I wanted some confidential information. I hung up and went to bed. The next thing I knew, it was early morning and the telephone was ringing again. Claude Johnson,

Publicity Chairman of the Committee of 500, was calling from Newport.

"All hell's broken loose up here," he said. "Ratterman has been arrested with a woman."

I called Ben Reeves at his home to tell him I was catching the next plane to Cincinnati.

*****

The police report was number 59401. It listed the complaint as having been received at 2:32 a.m., May 9, 1961.

Upon arriving at the airport, I'd gone by cab to the law office of Henry Cook. A former United States Attorney for the Eastern District of Kentucky, he was counsel to the Committee of 500 and was George Ratterman's attorney. I'd met the man only briefly. He promised an interview with his client later in the day, so I had walked the half block to the police station where, for once, I was welcome. All reporters were welcome on this day. I was handed a copy of the police report and quickly scanned the three pages.

The report said someone had called the police station and asked to talk to Detective Ciafardini who, although off duty, just happened to be there. He took the call and informed the officer in charge that prostitution was going on at the Glenn Hotel (the old name of the Tropicana Club).

Ciafardini called in the patrol car containing Detectives Upshire White and Joseph Quitter and "they in company with Detective Pat Ciafardini went to the Glenn Hotel to investigate the complaint."

I had to laugh at this point. The idea of three Newport detectives going to investigate prostitution on the basis of an anonymous call was actually funny. At the same time, I credited Ciafardini with a certain shrewdness. White was his rival for the job of police chief so he had been careful to involve him in the caper.

According to the report, the detectives entered the lobby only to have Tito Carinci attempt to stop them. They placed Carinci under arrest and took him along to the third floor where they entered Room 314. There they found "one April Flowers, female, white, age 26 years, alias Juanita Jean Hodges, particularly (cq) clothes seated on a bed in the room, a robe pulled up around her waist and one George William Ratterman, age 38 years..."

Ratterman was said to be wearing only a white shirt and a pair of socks. He jumped up from the bed, the report continued, and shoved Ciafardini who in turn shoved him back onto the bed. He then "donned a light blue-green Chinelle (cq) bed spread and he, Flowers, and Carinci were brought to this office." Flowers was charged with engaging in prostitution, Carinci with breach of the peace, and Ratterman with breach of the peace, disorderly conduct, and resisting arrest. Bond for each was fixed at $5,000.

The report noted that Carinci and Flowers were released on bond at 3:25 a.m. Ratterman was held until 3:50 a.m. when Cook appeared. "At the time of bringing Carinci, Flowers, and Ratterman to this office, the Detectives brought a gray flannel suit to this office which they had found in Room 314 of the Glenn Hotel with identification papers of George William Ratterman in same... Upon Ratterman executing bond, he donned the gray flannel suit and wore same from Police Headquarters."

Reporters thronged the police station, most of them from Cincinnati. Television cameras were rolling. Ciafardini was the star, repeating over and over his version of the events of the night before. I got tired of listening to the plump, greasy detective and went out to check other sources.

It was quickly apparent that someone had miscalculated. Over the years Newport had become sophisticated: it recognized a frameup when it saw one. Instead of disgust on the part of reformers, there was sympathy for Ratterman's family and the conviction that this was the last straw.

Chris Seifried told of delivering the mail and having women with tears in their eyes come to the door to shake his hand. Don Baker said he was downtown when the news broke and in one, two order, the word came down the street:

"Ratterman is arrested. It's a frame.

I went back to the police station. Ciafardini was still talking but by now he had improved on his story considerably. Fredericks told him to shut up. The contradictions between the story and the police report were becoming apparent to all.

Baker and I ate a late lunch and he tipped me that the ministerial association would be meeting at Ratterman's home. We drove out to Fort Thomas, the bedroom community where no vice existed, and found the streets clogged with cars near Ratterman's house. Don managed to park his little foreign job two blocks away, and we walked. A guard screened visitors. When I introduced Baker as a minister, he was admitted. A press conference was scheduled for 5:00 p.m. Other reporters began arriving. Television cameramen brought up equipment. A sense of tension gripped us, the feeling that something big was beginning.

Father P.H. Ratterman, Dean of Men at Xavier University, gave me a statement:

"I thank God that my brother, George, is alive. Threats of violence have been communicated to George through others and through me. We did not know exactly what form of foul play was to be expected. We are not surprised by what has been done."

Claude Johnson, the man who had called me that morning, handed out a prepared statement.

"With deadly efficiency our opponents have executed a vicious frame. Had George Ratterman not been an independent candidate for sheriff, it would never have happened. George has been under observation this morning at St. Luke Hospital. We believe there is absolutely no doubt that our candidate was drugged.

At last we were admitted to the large house and ushered into a spacious sitting room on the left. Across the hall the ministerial association members were meeting. Photographers adjusted cameras, television and radio reporters jiggled wires, print reporters checked their pencils. Everyone joggled for position. Ratterman entered, walking stiffly as if very tired. His ready grin flashed, however.

"A funny thing happened to me yesterday on the way home from the office," he said.

He read a prepared statement. It began:

"I was drugged last night and awakened in the bedroom of the apartment of Tito Carinci at the Glenn Hotel in Newport. I was awakened by a commotion in the room. Several people had entered and were tearing at my shirt and trousers. Several men, who I was informed were police officers, tore off my trousers and shorts. I was so groggy and weak I could hardly lift my arms. I was pushed to the floor several times. I recall seeing a woman with the men in the room when I was awakened. I have no idea who she was and had never seen her before. The officers refused several requests to return my trousers and I was taken to the police station wrapped in bed covering..."

The statement described how a friend had been approached by Carinci to arrange a meeting with Ratterman and how the friend took Ratterman to Cincinnati to meet the nightclub operator. After drinks, Carinci returned them to Newport where Ratterman passed out on a bed.

At this point Father Ratterman read the results of a blood test conducted earlier that day by Dr. Frank Cleveland of the Kettering Laboratories in Cincinnati. The test showed the presence in Ratterman's blood of a massive dose of chloral hydrate, commonly known as knockout drops.

The announcement caused a sensation. Reporters rushed for the door. The appearance in a body at that moment of most of the members of the ministerial association was something of an anti-climax. The Reverend Pomeroy read aloud this statement:

"We, the Newport Ministerial Association, believe that George Ratterman was framed, the victim of a malicious plot, by members of the local underworld who were seeking to defame his reputation and discredit the movement to clean up Newport and Campbell County. In light of this development, we unanimously affirm our intention to support George Ratterman's candidacy for Campbell County sheriff. We urge that all people who are interested in good government in Campbell County, and who deplore these tactics, rally to his support.'

Flashbulbs lighted the room as a Baptist minister shook hands with a Catholic layman. One of Ratterman's children, a pretty little girl, wandered in and hugged her Daddy. Mrs. Ratterman came in to recover her and gave me a statement as I followed her to the door. Petite and beautiful, despite the excitement of the day, Ann said:

"I wasn't too much in favor of him running, but I don't want him to get out now. I have no doubts as to what happened."

In the other room, George was displaying his gray trousers. The tab had been torn from the zipper and the cloth was ripped. But I was on deadline. All the telephones in the house were being used by Cincinnati reporters. A Committee of 500 member took me down the street to another house and upstairs to a bedroom with a telephone. I spread all the notes, statements, and reports I'd collected that day on the bed, then called the *C-J* collect and asked for rewrite.

Dick Hunter, much to my delight, answered. Although he called himself a veteran cub reporter, Dick was an excellent rewrite man. I told him:

"I've got a helluva story but I haven't had time to write it. I'll have to put it together as I go along so protect me, please."

He agreed and I began dictating.

"Newport, Ky. — May 9 — George Ratterman, reform candidate for sheriff of Campbell County, was drugged prior to his arrest here early Tuesday, according to a medical report from Dr. Frank Cleveland of the Kettering Laboratories..."

And on and on it went for three full columns. I moved slips of paper about the bed as if they were pieces on a chess board. When at last I finished, Dick, who had been writing in "takes," made a final check with the news editor.

"The chief says you'd better be right about the knock-out drops," Dick said.

I told him not to worry; the wire services would have confirmation of it eventually.

"Take care of yourself," said Dick, and, wearily, I hung up. Momentarily I was exhausted. Jack Cook, by now an old friend and brother of Ratterman's attorney, took me to his house where Edie plied me with black coffee. Soon I began to recover and began making plans.

April Flowers, the stage name of Juanita Hodges, had been identified as a stripper currently appearing in the Glenn Hotel where I had vainly sought a hotel room on my first visit to Newport. I decided to watch her act.

For the first time in my experience, I could get no one to accompany me. Even Jack, who was braver than many, agreed only to drop me off a block from the joint. He promised to call the FBI if I didn't report back by eleven o'clock.

I walked up Monmouth, admired the neon nudes dancing above the entrance, and walked in. No one was in the lobby. I turned right into the nightclub area and found a table. A table wasn't hard to find; only a handful of people were seated despite the free publicity on the front page of the Cincinnati newspaper. A waiter appeared and took my order of sirloin tips. Greatly daring, I also ordered a martini. It had been a long day.

The drink was good. While sipping it, I looked around the room. Four men sat in a booth against the wall and two men in an adjoining one. They all looked alike — big, short-haired, wearing dark clothing. The food was good also and I ate it with relish. Abruptly, a short, fat man in a tuxedo stood glaring down at me.

"How did you get in here?" he demanded.

I'd seen the man before. This was Marty Buccieri, partner of Tito Carinci. I looked up at him and grinned.

"It's a free country," I said cheerfully.

"I gave orders to keep you out," he replied.

"Things are a bit disorganized, maybe. Where's April?"

"Nobody tells me nothing," he said in disgust and walked out of the nightclub. I wondered if he was going to look for a bouncer.

One of the two men in the booth against the wall caught my eye and gestured. I went over.

"Perhaps you'd better sit with us," he said, holding out his hand. "I'm Frank Staab, FBI."

I shook his hand. The other man moved over and made room for me. I pointed to the four men in the adjoining booth.

"FBI?"

Staab nodded. "The Attorney General ordered us to make a

preliminary investigation this morning. That's off the record, of course."

The Attorney General of the United States was Robert F. Kennedy, brother of the President and the man I had interviewed last September.

Staab, it developed, was stationed in Louisville. A tall, rangy man with gray in his hair, he had been waiting a long time for a handle to investigate Newport. He had read my stories, of course, and we established an instant rapport despite the fact that the *C-J* and the FBI had been at odds since the Great Red Scare centering on the newspaper's copy editor. We chatted about an FBI probe of the Ratterman case and I knew I had the lead for next day's story. Finally, almost idly, I asked:

"Did you ever hear of a Newport character named Frank Andriola?"

"That's Screw Andrews," said Staab.

In a day of surprises, this was the biggest jolt of all. My mind went back to Waynesville. The old pain had lessened over the years and the recollection of my father's death brought no surge of anger. It had long been obvious Waynesville was not unique in its corruption, and my personal vendetta had been transformed into a deeper compulsion. Yet it was chilling to know the man I'd targeted so long ago was still alive and active on the mean streets of Newport.

Staab stared at me. "You got a problem with Andrews? No need to worry about him. IRS Intelligence is saving string on Screw."

I shrugged. The house lights dimmed and a spotlight illuminated a stage at the end of the room. A man in a tuxedo appeared and began telling jokes. He drew one laugh when he told of Newport firing a Negro into space aboard a rocket.

"The headline," he said, "was 'The jig is up.'"

Whether the laughter was racist or just anti-Newport, I couldn't be sure. He tried again:

"Know what a Ratterman Cocktail will do? One drink in May and you wake up in April."

No one laughed.

Several strippers followed. Then came the star, April Flowers, wearing a red robe and beneath it a costume covered with tiny reflecting mirrors. She began to wiggle and dots of light wiggled with her on the ceiling and the walls. Dark haired and tall, almost skinny, April slowly stripped, the dots of light disappearing until only a cluster in her groin remained. She wiggled some more. The last dots vanished, and she darted behind the curtain. The show was over. The applause was polite.

I shook hands with Staab and his associates outside the building. Then I headed for a telephone booth. Newport had lots of public phones and they all worked — after all, one never knew when a hot tip would necessitate a call to one's bookie. Dick Hunter was still on duty. I dictated a paragraph about April's performance. It would go on the end of my story in the final edition. Then I called Jack Cook.

Jack took me to a motel in Covington. It was owned by gangsters, he said, but it was convenient to a cab stand. Naturally.

NINE
16 May '61

Two cops in uniform were waiting on the steps of the court house. They handed me a subpoena. In an instant I was transformed from a working reporter into a witness for the city. It was as unreal as other aspects of the case against Ratterman. I had not been present when the candidate was arrested. In fact, a call to my home the night before had ascertained I was not in Newport. Obviously, someone didn't want me to report the trial. Well, the *C-J* had other reporters even if they didn't want the assignment.

Crowds started gathering before the doors opened at 8:00 a.m. They reached such proportions the proceedings were moved from the small police courtroom above the jail to the main building and its larger circuit courtroom. Even its capacity was insufficient. People were left standing in the hall and on the stairs. Since it was to be a trial without a jury, the press annexed the jury box where seats had cushions and the view was better. Newport was national news now. *Time* was represented. I recognized Bill Rollins, a former Louisville reporter now with *The New York Herald-Tribune*. The wire services had staff men present. A television camera was set up at the rear of the courtroom. Other cameras were in the hall. Live coverage was to be provided at every recess.

The story of the reformer caught with his pants off — framed or not — had piqued the public's fancy around the world. Newport, as I had already reported, had become a primary target of Robert Kennedy's "coordinated war on crime." Several federal agencies were investigating.

To the left of the judge's bench was a table for Lester, Carinci, April, and a second stripper later identified at Rita Desmond. At a center table, Ratterman, his wife, and Henry Cook had seats. To the right of the judge were Newport Special Counsel Thomas Hirschfeld — partner of Danny Davies — and Mayor Mussman. A brass rail separated the spectators from the principals. Red Masterson sat in the front row.

Ann Ratterman was composed. She wore a string of pearls against a dark dress and, somehow, without any effort, made the strippers look trashy by comparison. Carinci blew a great balloon of bubble gum. Mayor Mussman spoke to the press: "This is only a ten dollar police court case."

Tension grew until Police Court Judge Joseph Rolf ascended the bench. He wore a candy-striped bowtie and was plainly nervous. A bailiff announced that court was in session.

Cook moved the three cases be separated. Rolf granted the motion. Cook asked that Ratterman be tried first. Special Counsel Hirschfeld objected. The charges against April were more serious, he said, so she should be tried first. Rolf agreed.

"I call George Ratterman to testify," said Hirschfeld.

Cook objected. Defense Attorney Lester arose.

"Who is this gentleman, your Honor? He doesn't represent the defendant in this case."

"Proceed," said Judge Rolf.

Margaret Josten, one of the better Cincinnati reporters, was to write next day:

"George Ratterman, anti-vice candidate for sheriff of Campbell County, went on trial immediately. Not per se, maybe. But on trial nonetheless... Cook had been maneuvered into a position where he could not effectively defend his client. For how can you defend a client who is not on trial?"

Ratterman took the stand to be questioned at great length by Hirschfeld and cross examined at even greater length by Lester.

Cook interrupted the examination several times. At one point he shouted:

"I can't see how this has anything to do with trying a girl for prostitution. He's trying to discredit this witness. Why don't you go out and get a camera, Mr. Lester? That's your specialty, cameras."

Cook was overruled. No one attached any special significance to his mention of cameras.

The grilling of Ratterman continued until lunch break. I took Rollins over to the Playtorium. Along the route people came to doors and windows and screeched insults. Rollins wondered why I was so unpopular. I told him I had a few friends in town.

Elmer Hall arrived from Louisville. He'd joined the newspaper after I was hired and spent a long time on the copy desk. About forty, he quickly sensed the way to get ahead at the *C-J* was to be cautious in both reporting and editing. As far as I could recall, he had never written anything in any way controversial or distinguished. I filled him in on events of the morning and introduced him to the proper people. To my surprise he said he planned to drive back to Louisville that evening and return next morning.

"I'm not spending the night in this shithole," he explained.

The man was willing to spend six hours daily on the road just to avoid what he conceived to be personal danger. I thought it a little ridiculous given the circumstances.

The farce continued. April lied, Carinci lied, Ciafardini lied. Seven major witnesses perjured themselves and later, in federal court, admitted it. There were histrionics as well. At the conclusion of his testimony, Carinci asked:

"May I say something, Judge?"

"No, you may not."

"Do you have something else you wanted to add, Mr. Carinci?" asked Lester.

"Objection," said Hirschfeld.

"Sustained," said the Judge.

"Well, let's hear what he says, Your Honor," said Lester.

Carinci rose to his feet, pointed his finger at Ratterman and shouted:

"I went to a Jesuit priest this morning and I knelt before the altar and swore that my statement is true. Could you do that, George?"

There was an outburst of cheers from Carinci's friends in the courtroom. They were treating the whole affair as if it were a sporting event. Carinci had played football for Xavier University and Ratterman, of course, had been a pro. The night before I had asked Ratterman if his sensations were in any way similar to what he had felt on the eve of an important football game. He replied:

"In football, there are rules."

Now he stared at Carinci in amazement and disgust. Their eyes met and slowly Carinci's pointing finger dropped.

Lester's version had it that Ratterman and a friend, Thomas J. Paisley of Medina, Ohio, met Carinci for drinks at a Cincinnati hotel. Ratterman became drunk and demanded some broads. In fact, according to Carinci, he banged on the table with his fists and shouted:

"Bring on the broads."

Ever willing to be helpful, Carinci brought Paisley and Ratterman to Newport and to his private suite. He paired Paisley with Rita Desmond and sent the star up to Ratterman. Then police arrived.

The story went unchallenged. Cook could only sputter in helpless rage as the alleged facts were confirmed by various witnesses. Rita drew a laugh when she testified that she and Paisley had gone elsewhere, thus avoiding arrest, because the sofa in Tito's sitting room was "too narrow to make love." April sounded most convincing when she produced a ballpoint pen bearing Ratterman's name, business address, and telephone number. He'd given it to her, she explained, and told her to call him up sometime.

Elmer Hall wrote stories that reflected the testimony despite my efforts to provide balance. He was very impressed with the ballpoint pen and gave it a good play. I decided to call Ben Reeves and tell him some surprises were coming.

The basis of my confidence was a whispered word from Jack Cook:

"We're going to prove the frame; we've got three witnesses. I'm baby-sitting them."

At the end of a long day, with the hapless Ratterman thoroughly smeared, Hirschfeld announced:

"Your Honor, at this time we move for the reduction of the charge against the defendant to breach of the peace."

Lester responded:

"Defendant moves to dismiss the charge. There's no showing of any offense here on the part of this defendant. It's resolved itself into a case of the testing of the veracity of Mr. Ratterman upon one side and Mr. Carinci upon the other. But I see no reason why this young woman, in order to satisfy the political ambitions of anyone on either side, particularly this high noon Dr. Jekyll and midnight Mr. Hyde — Mr. Ratterman — should be compelled to be put upon her proof."

"I'll submit the matter," said the Judge. "Court is going to adjourn until ten o'clock in the morning."

The prosecution of Ratterman lasted for three days. Witnesses repeated their lies but this time they were subjected to a stern cross examination by Cook who reduced the burly Ciafardini to tears. The detective screamed:

"May God strike me dead if I'm not telling the truth."

Almost every head in the room turned expectantly towards the ceiling.

"Tomorrow we hear the truth," I told Hall.

There was contempt in the glance he gave me as he got in his car. I was not as confident as I sounded. Lester had woven a complex web and the hopes of the reform drive were at stake. My standing at the *C-J* might also be at risk. Elmer Hall was not alone in his skepticism. I spent a restless night wondering if Cook's defense could rescue Ratterman.

Saturday dawned in sunshine. The crowd in the courtroom consisted almost entirely of reformers, most of them women. They learned after the first day to bring their lunches to court in order to keep their seats, and had gradually ousted the opposition. The gamblers and prostitutes had apparently decided the fun was over. Only Red Masterson remained. When the reporters assembled in the jury box, I noticed *Time* was missing. Its representative had been an apple-cheeked kid who had apparently enjoyed a welcome at various casinos and had laughed openly at my suggestion he had not heard the full story. Bill Rollins, however, was still present. His stories had been more restrained than those in the *C-J*. Even Lester, no longer having an official role, was absent, but Carinci was still blowing bubble gum beside April and Rita. Mayor Mussman again joked that it was only a ten dollar police court case and not worth all the attention it was receiving.

Cook put Ratterman on the stand and drew from him a straightforward account of events before and after his arrest. The candidate testified he met with Carinci because the gambler wanted his help in getting out of the rackets. Paisley had arranged the meeting in Cincinnati at Carinci's request. He'd been drugged there, he said, for he had only vague memories of being taken back to Newport.

As to the ballpoint pen, Ratterman testified he had distributed such pens to professional people in Newport and Cincinnati when he opened his brokerage business. He had given a pen to Lester. Since then he had moved his office and both the address and phone number on the pen April produced were incorrect. If she tried to call him at that number, she would have no luck.

Cross examination was casual. Hirschfeld seemed almost bored. Ratterman stepped down and Cook, slowly and dramatically, said:

"Call Mrs. Nancy Hay."

"Here it comes," I told Hall.

A tall, spare woman in a plain dress entered from the door behind the bench. She had alert blue eyes and gray hair. In a calm, clear voice she swore to tell the truth and took her seat in the witness chair. A hush settled over the courtroom. Under Cook's questioning she said she lived with her granddaughter who was married to Thomas Withrow, a commercial photographer. On April 14 she got a call from a man identifying himself as Charles Lester. He wanted to speak to Withrow. She told him Withrow was not at home. He left a number. When her son-in-law returned, she gave him the number and heard him call it back. She tried to tell of another call that came later but Hirschfeld asked:

"Why did you come forward to tell this story?"

"Because I pride myself on being a good Christian and a good citizen," she said evenly.

"No more questions," said Hirschfeld.

"Call Thomas Withrow," ordered Cook.

A short, stocky and very defiant Withrow came in, took the oath, and told his story.

He'd returned Lester's call and been told to go to the Glenn Hotel and see Marty Buccieri, a partner of Carinci.

"What for?" Withrow said he asked.

"'To take some pictures. You will be paid very well. I got your name from Bill Wise.'"

A sigh went around the room at the mention of the Commonwealth's Attorney.

The meeting with Buccieri, Withrow testified, took place in what he called "the old casino. Marty started talking like I knew exactly what was going on. I guess he figured Lester had set it up."

"What did he say?" asked Cook.

"He said, 'We want you to take this picture. It'll be of a man and a woman. It'll be in a room. We'll open the door and you take a picture. We'll protect you.'"

"What in the hell am I getting myself into here?" Withrow said he asked himself at the time.

Buccieri wanted his phone number so he gave him a card with his home number on it. When he got home, however, he told his wife:

"If Marty calls, tell him I'm not here."

Hirschfeld began his cross examination, then broke off abruptly. He was obviously in deep water and knew it. Withrow had been around Newport a long time and perhaps knew where other bodies were buried. In fact, as I discovered later, he's testified against a Newport cop who had developed ambitions several years before. Since then, he had married and acquired a strong willed grandmother-in-law.

Cook had one more question.

"Are you under subpoena in another jurisdiction?"

"Yes," said Withrow. "On Monday before the federal grand jury in Lexington."

There was a ripple of excitement which died quickly as Cook called Mrs. Thomas Withrow to the stand.

An attractive woman who held her head proudly, she told of being awakened by a telephone call at 1:35 a.m. on the night of May 9. This, according to earlier testimony, was five minutes after Ratterman reached the Tropicana. She said the caller asked for him.

"Tom isn't here," she replied.

"How soon can you reach him?"

"In ten minutes."

"Have him call Marty at the Glenn Hotel."

She remembered her husband's instructions and made no effort to find him. At 2:00 a.m. the telephone rang again. She looked at her grandmother who was also awake. They ignored the phone. It continued to ring at intervals until 3:00 a.m.

Hirschfeld had no questions on cross examination. He sat as if stunned. Mussman was frowning. The room was strangely silent until Cook suggested a pause for lunch. The Judge quickly agreed. Carinci lowered his head and plunged through the crowd. In his days at Xavier it would have meant a touchdown.

What happened during that lunch hour later became a matter of record. Hirschfeld called Lester from the Yorkshire Club and asked for information to counter Withrow's statement. Lester promised to "think of something" and told him to delay the trial until Monday.

Reporters hastened back to the courtroom after lunch at the Playtorium. Speculation centered on the next witness. Would Cook drop another bomb? The crowd was building. Word had spread and reform minded citizens were rushing in from all over town. Again the crowd overflowed the courtroom and spilled down to the first level.

Bill Rollins, writing in *The New York Herald-Tribune*, put it this way:

"The corridors of the grimy old courthouse resounded with dark whispers. When the trial was resumed, Mr. Hirschfeld entered the court and beckoned to Mr. Cook. They looked like a pair of masks representing Greek drama."

The two men conferred briefly. Hirschfeld turned to the Judge whose face wore a worried frown.

"I've known Thomas Withrow for a number of years," Hirschfeld said, "and I'm inclined to believe his testimony. This is not a police court case. I think it should be investigated by the grand jury."

"I agree," said Judge Rolf. He tapped his gavel. "Case dismissed. Court's adjourned."

And he scurried quickly from the courtroom.

With the tap of the gavel, I was once more a reporter. "Get the color," shouted Hall. "I'm going after Grandma."

The crowd broke into no wild cheer. It was a quieter kind of exultation. Men shook hands solemnly. Tearful women kissed everyone they could reach. Ann Ratterman kissed her husband as flashbulbs flickered like heat lightning. The television camera was grinding from the rear of the room, providing live coverage. I asked Mrs. Ratterman for a comment.

"I've always been proud of my husband," she responded, "and I have always considered it an honor to be his wife."

Ratterman commented:

"I consider it a full vindication."

Then Ratterman and Cook disappeared into the office behind the bench. The crowd surged out into the hall. When the reform candidate appeared after a short wait, the applause began. It came in waves, louder and louder. It followed Ratterman down the stairs, past the mural of civic virtue, to the first level of the courthouse. Ratterman moved slowly, returning hand shakes, accepting kisses. And still the applause continued.

Bill Rollins and I exchanged glances. He shook his head in awe. As a spontaneous demonstration of respect and affection it surpassed anything he or I had ever seen.

Finally, out the door and into the bright May sunshine went the procession. Applause echoed down the street. A block away Lester could see and hear it. So impressive was the enthusiasm, the tremendous outburst of happiness, that Rollins began his *Herald-Tribune* story with this lead:

"Newport, Ky., May 20 — George Ratterman won his case today and Newport may never be the same."

Elmer Hall and I rode back to Louisville in Hall's car. I was excited, somewhat triumphant, joyfully aware of the many components that had made this day possible. Mrs. Withrow, for example, called her minister on May 9 as soon as she heard of Ratterman's arrest. The minister called Henry Cook who interviewed the witnesses minutes later. Hall was silent, responding to my comments with an occasional grunt. Apparently he was worried about something. Finally, he announced:

"I don't think I'll say anything about the ballpoint pen."

He had decided to take the easy way out of the predicament he had created for himself and let the smear stand uncorrected. After a silence. I asked:

"Do you realize that the arrests were illegal in the first place? The cops had no warrant. I can remember taking Chandler's ABC man in there and being stopped by Lester because we didn't have a warrant. All Cook had to do was to move for a dismissal on those grounds and the case would have been over."

"Why didn't he?"

"Because he had to prove that Ratterman was framed. Getting him off on a technicality wouldn't restore his reputation."

Elmer grunted something and relapsed into silence. Word had come in via teletype about the verdict before we reached the newsroom. Everyone there appeared astonished, apparently convinced on the basis of Hall's stories that Ratterman was guilty. Hall's first action upon arrival was to pick up a telephone and call his wife.

"I'm back," he said.

John Meehan expressed the general cynicism when he told me:

"Only yesterday I was predicting that Ratterman would be found guilty and you would cut your throat on the courthouse steps."

"Why would I do that?" I asked.

Meehan laughed. "We thought you were too personally involved. Maybe you were more objective than we thought."

"Being involved and being objective are not necessarily incompatible," I said sourly.

When the first edition came out carrying our stories, I went home to my family. It had been a long week. Ratterman's victory was a triumph for Faye as well. For several weeks we'd been receiving anonymous calls at all hours of the day and night. If I answered, there were curses and threats. If Faye answered, there was only deep breathing. We told our daughter not to answer and Faye placed a small radio on the counter near the phone. When the deep breathing started, she turned the volume up and placed the phone in front of it. When she returned, the deep breathing had been replaced by a dial tone.

Faye, I decided, needed a reward for her courage and faith. Our fourteenth anniversary was coming up soon. Perhaps dinner at the Beverly Hills Country Club was in order. If, of course, that rug joint was still open. Meanwhile, we ate hamburgers. Later, after the children went to bed, I found some bourbon and we drank a toast to Ratterman.

I read Faye a poem I had taken from a bulletin board at the *C-J*. Actually, it was supposed to be sung to the tune of the Notre Dame Victory March:

> Let's drink a toast to Ratterman's name
> He got a Mickey, he's not to blame
> April Flowers stripped to her shoes
> Helped our George make Newport news.
> Courageous and brave like Notre Dame men,
> Armed only with a ballpoint pen,
> George made history, women, and wine,
> And taught us how to hit the line.

TEN
2 June '61

The atmosphere was tense as we waited for the governor's decision on the ouster hearings. I was writing an obituary one afternoon when I received a call from John Anggelis in Lexington.

Anggelis was the young attorney acting as aide to Jesse K. Lewis, the aging crusader hired by the ministerial association. Ambitious in his own right, Anggelis brought his troubles to me. Lewis, he said, had become impatient with the delay in calling ouster hearings and was now planning to hold a press conference to denounce the governor.

"What does he hope to achieve by that?"

"He'll get his name in the headlines one more time," replied the lawyer. "At his age he wants one last hurrah."

"Can't you stop him?"

"'Fraid not. He hates Combs and he's determined to go down in flames."

"Let me think about it," I said and hung up.

The Chief was close enough to hear the conversation but his face remained expressionless. Did he think I was exceeding my role as reporter? Somehow I had achieved a unique position in the Newport drama where people felt free to tell me their troubles and let me find a solution when all I wanted, yes, really and truly, was to report the facts as they occurred. Feeling somewhat put upon, I dialed the Reverend Pomeroy in Newport.

"Call your man off," I told him. "According to my information, the

Governor is about to act. An outburst from Lewis right now could ruin things."

Actually, I had no inside information. The newspaper had continued its editorial pressure and demands had arisen all around the state from churches and civic groups. There seemed no real reason for Combs to resist.

Pomeroy accepted my advice and Lewis kept silent. A few days later the Governor charged Sheriff Roll, Newport Police Chief Gugel, Newport Detective Chief Fredericks, and Campbell County Police Chief Stuart with neglect of duty. Lexington attorney, John L. Davis, was appointed to conduct the ouster hearings. Attorney General John Breckinridge agreed to represent the Commonwealth in prosecuting the allegations.

*****

It was a warm night. Faye looked lovely in a wine colored velveteen suit. She'd had her hair fixed in loose curls that exposed her broad forehead and heavy eyebrows. I wore my usual sports coat and slacks, but I did have a new shirt for the occasion. The doorman whistled over a cab and told the driver to take us to the Beverly Hills.

It was June 9th. Fourteen years earlier we'd been married in Atlanta and spent our wedding night in a downtown hotel. (I'd tipped the bellboy two cents.) The day after had been Faye's birthday and I had joked that she aged a year on our wedding night. Well, she'd be a year older tomorrow if we lived that long. Already I was wondering why I had brought my wife to Cincinnati. She didn't seem frightened, however, just mildly excited at the prospect of a night out.

We rode over the Ohio, down York Street past the courthouse, the casinos, the brothels, and the bustout joints. Lights were on: it was business as usual. The world might end tomorrow but until it did the suckers would continue to be fleeced. The Beverly Hills Country Club glowed like a magic castle on its hill and its parking lots were full. A doorman in uniform helped Faye out of the cab, another one held open the doors. We walked by the circular bar to the amphitheater where our reservations were checked and we were escorted to a table near the top level. There was a linen tablecloth, gleaming silver, a lot of happy people, laughter and talk. All very reassuring.

We ate filet mignon and drank a bottle of red wine. A pretty young lady with a top hat and short shorts wanted to take our picture. She was a house photographer, she explained, and would develop the pix and deliver them later in the Blue Room. Would she take our picture in the Blue Room? It would impress our friends back home in Podunk if we were posed before a roulette wheel. No, unfortunately, she wasn't permitted to take pictures in the Blue Room.

Fire away, I told her and we smiled sweetly at the camera.

The floor show began below us. It was equal, I discovered later, and very similar to the best Las Vegas produced. There were a lot of high-kicking naked legs, sequin covered breasts, and high headdresses with feathers. The stars were a rather well known singing team, Gordon and Sheila McRae, and there were music, jokes, and general confusion. Faye seemed to enjoy the affair but I was nervous. When the lights came up, tuxedoed men began distributing large bingo boards while the stars made a slow procession through the amphitheater and down the corridor that led to the casino. About half the audience followed immediately, the remainder rented the bingo boards.

"Look," said Faye, "behind you."

I turned. A tall man in a tuxedo stood looking across the room. He held stacks of bills, each secured by a rubber band. The casino bankroll, I guessed, as the man turned and vanished down the corridor toward the Blue Room. A waiter brought my check. The two meals and wine cost less than eighteen dollars. I dropped a twenty on the table and we started for the Blue Room. En route I passed a table piled with bingo boards. I picked one up. On the back, stamped in red letters, were the words:
PROPERTY OF THE DESERT INN
LAS VEGAS, NEVADA

The Desert Inn was the first property developed by the Cleveland Syndicate when it moved to Nevada from Ohio and Kentucky. I tried to find a place to hide the board, but it was too large to fit under my coat or in Faye's purse.

The casino was as I remembered it: plush, decorous, and efficient. We wandered around observing the crowds and the action. At one roulette wheel I noticed a bald headed business type putting fifty dollar chips on red. I began playing the black with one dollar chips. After I'd won ten times the business man got the message and moved on. There's always an angle.

Our pictures were delivered on schedule by the girl photographer. Faye looked lovely but as usual, my weak chin was all too prominent in profile. The crowd swelled and by midnight the action was heavy. We accepted free drinks from another pretty girl and decided to adjourn. Downtown Newport was full of cars. The cab took us back to the Terrace Hilton where I proceeded about the business of making Faye age a year in a single night. It was more fun than gambling.

*****

"Out...out...out," shouted a voice within the office. A short, sharply dressed young man backed out the door. I recognized him as a Cincinnati reporter, who, at Ratterman's trial, had posed as a cynical sophisticate. Now his face was red and he was sputtering helplessly. The door slammed and he walked away muttering to himself.

I opened the door on the second floor of Covington's federal building and walked in. A tall, rangy man with dark hair wheeled around to face me.

"I'm Hank Messick. Does that 'out...out...out' apply to the press in general?"

The hard face melted into a smile. He held out his hand.

"It doesn't apply to you," he said. "I'm Bob Peloquin. Did you know they call you 'the agent without a badge'?"

I shook hands with him and he motioned me to the seat in front of a desk that looked like it had just been brought out of storage. The office, obviously, had been hastily assembled. Peloquin was a Justice Department attorney assigned to coordinate the varied investigations growing out of the Ratterman case. He was younger than me but there was an air of confidence, almost arrogance, about him.

"I was told you'd have something for me," I said.

He laughed. "The word came from Bobby himself. How did you manage that?"

"I called him," I said, "and reminded him we had met before the election."

Peloquin produced a large manila envelope from within his desk. "This is not for attribution, you understand, but it's all we know about Frank Andriola, a.k.a. Screw Andrews."

I slipped the envelope into my briefcase.

"Andriola is quite a character," said Peloquin. "He's tied into what the FBI calls the Italian mob. In short, the Mafia. Trigger Mike Coppola is his boss. The IRS got an indictment against Mike in Miami last April. His wife squealed on him. She came from around here and knew about the Andrews-Andriola connection."

So the trail I'd picked up in Waynesville led on from Newport to New York and Miami. Well, maybe I would follow it later. Right now, I had enough to do.

"Is the Mob mixed up in moonshining on a big scale?" I asked.

Peloquin glanced at me with curious eyes. "Matter of fact, the boys got back into the business during the war. Black market liquor was in demand and some southerners brought a taste for white lightning when they moved north to work in defense plants. Screw Andrews got his start selling moonshine in the black districts of Cincinnati. From there it was an easy step to numbers. He makes millions."

"Does he pay taxes?"

Peloquin grinned wolfishly. "IRS Intelligence is on his tail, but that's off the record."

"I'd like to be in on the finish," I commented.

"Perhaps that can be arranged," said Peloquin. "For a friend of Bobby Kennedy, anything is possible."

"Why did you throw that Cincinnati reporter out?"

"He's a jerk. More than that he's a stupid jerk."

Frank Staab entered the office. I'd not seen him since we watched April Flowers strip. We shook hands and he took his seat at a second desk. Peloquin excused himself and left. Staab stared after him.

"A nice guy," he remarked, "but rather strong willed. He and Ratterman aren't getting along."

"Why not?" I asked.

"He's too cynical. He thinks George is too good to be true."

"What do you think?"

Staab shrugged. "I've had special agents working in twenty five states to check out Lester's allegations against Ratterman. Obviously, when you have a complaining witness in a civil rights matter you have to be sure of the quality of your witness. We've conducted more than five hundred interviews. We found that Lester's stories were all cockeyed. There's no problem about Ratterman's character."

"Yet Peloquin can't accept that?"

Staab leaned back in his chair. "Let's say he prefers to consider Ratterman's character irrelevant. Ratterman doesn't like that attitude. I think Bob will be transferred before long."

Staab's prediction came true within a week. I would meet Peloquin again during an investigation into Teamster President Jimmy Hoffa and we would fashion a friendship that would endure until people started taking Nixon's advice and stopped asking what they could do for their country and inquired instead what they could do for themselves.

*****

For Charles Lester it was a season for fun and games. The patient old lawyer moved first to give Ratterman opposition in his race for sheriff. In primary elections on May 22, he picked the candidates for both parties. A former sheriff got the Republican nomination but would do no campaigning. Johnny "TV" Peluso, operator of a television repair store, won the Democratic nomination. He was Lester's main man and campaigned loudly.

Back when the charges against Ratterman were about to be dismissed, Lester had asked time to think of something. His counter move became apparent when the Campbell County Grand Jury — the same Grand Jury which in February had blasted reformers and the meddling press — was called back into session. Guided by Wise, the jurors, on May 26, only six days after Ratterman's victory, indicted Tito Carinci and Thomas Paisley on charges of conspiring to carry on a false prosecution against Ratterman.

In the bustout joints and casinos, the Grand Jury action was considered a master stroke. Ratterman would once more be forced to testify and be subjected to cross examination by Lester, who, of course, remained Carinci's attorney. Inevitably, the defendants would be acquitted and with the verdict would go the theory that Ratterman had been framed. Or so went the logic of the "liberals."

On June 12, three days after my anniversary dinner at the Beverly Hills, Lester struck again. The Federal Grand Jury met in Lexington. Delayed by the necessity of checking out Lester allegations, the jury was unprepared to hear April Flowers. I did not cover the proceedings assuming there would be little to report. I was wrong. April, acting on Lester's orders, produced a copy of a commission as a Kentucky Colonel. The press was delighted. Asserting the commission proved her a good citizen, April let reporters examine the document. It had been issued on September 6, 1960 and was signed by Acting Governor Wilson W. Wyatt. Combs had been out of the state that day.

Wyatt was instantly embarrassed. He'd been cast in the role of a white knight by the *Courier-Journal* too many times and April Flowers didn't fit into that picture. Acting swiftly, Wyatt "decommissioned" April, although there were doubts as to whether such action was legal.

Happy Chandler had a public laugh about the episode and reaffirmed his decision to run in 1963 on a "home rule" platform.

I went over to Frankfort and scratched around in the Secretary of State's office long enough to find that Albert "the Enforcer" Masterson had been made a Kentucky Colonel some years earlier by then Governor Chandler. Masterson's qualifications for the honor were listed in a handwritten scrawl as "Helps in the fire fighting field." Well, allegedly he helped burn the old Beverly Hills for the syndicate.

On June 20 the Circuit Court trial of Carinci and Paisley began before Judge Murphy. Henry Cook defended Paisley, the businessman from Medina, Ohio, who had talked Ratterman into meeting Carinci. That made him on the surface at least an ally of Lester, a fact the gamblers, prostitutes, and bustout sharpers found amusing. Paisley was the classic example of the innocent third party, yet if he were acquitted, it would also be necessary to find Carinci innocent. A man cannot conspire with himself alone.

None of the proceedings made much sense, and for once no one disagreed when, after the prosecution rested, Judge Murphy dismissed the indictments. Wise, he declared, had not produced "one iota of evidence."

Lester was well satisfied, however, and soon word spread that he was leaving for Europe on a combination business-vacation jaunt to Spain and Switzerland. Rumor had it that a large sum of money, several million dollars, would be transported to Swiss banks. The informed recalled that after a visit by Lester to London the year before, the slot machine shipment had taken place.

It was all fuel for Lester's ego. The pallid little attorney seemed on the verge of achieving his career goal. If, as expected, Pat Ciafardini became Police Chief, and Ratterman lost his bid for sheriff, Lester would emerge as the undisputed boss of Campbell County. All of which simply goes to prove that even clever men can lose touch with reality when they become too cynical.

I decided that I too needed a vacation. If I was to have one that crowded battle summer, the interval between the end of the Carinci-Paisley trial and the beginning of the ouster hearings seemed to be the only opportunity. Faye and I loaded the children into the Nova stationwagon and headed for Cumberland Falls State Park in southeastern Kentucky.

The park, located on the Cumberland River amid rolling hills, seemed an island of quiétude. Our cabin was some distance from the main lodge in a grove of pine trees. As I unloaded the bags, I took deep breaths of the clean mountain air and told myself I'd escaped at least momentarily from the shabby streets of Newport. At that moment, a park ranger dashed up in a pickup.

"Mister Messick," he said in an excited voice, "the Attorney General is calling."

I stared at him rather blankly.

"You can take it right over there," he said.

Sure enough, mounted on a large pine tree was a telephone. I picked up the receiver, spoke to Attorney General Breckinridge, who had questions about prospective witnesses, and hung up with a sigh. The woods lay around me peaceful and quiet and the river shimmered in the distance, but the illusion of escape had vanished.

We had fun but after a few days I became restless. Wandering down to the Falls one day, I plucked a copy of *The Louisville Times* from a trash can. *The Times* did not circulate so far, apparently this one had been brought in by a tourist. On the front page was a headline about Newport above the byline of Dick Harwood. It was the last of a series. Harwood was the only decent reporter *The Times* boasted.

I took the crumpled newspaper over to a seat by the thundering waterfall and scanned it. Anger flooded my body. According to Harwood, Newport had little gambling, no prostitution, and one of the best police forces in the country. To prove it, he quoted such notables as City Manager Hesch and Police Chief Gugel. It was the propaganda officials had been handing out for years. Not a single reformer was quoted.

Obviously Norman Isaacs had sent Harwood to Newport to get "the other side of the story." At least that had been his pretext. I stared into the white water and let my anger subside.

Faye joined me, picked up the paper, glanced at the headline, and threw it down.

"Why?" she asked.

"Nine rocks clean," I replied.

"What do you mean?"

"Back in Happy Valley before we got electricity, we used an outdoor privy. It was mounted on locust logs jutting out over Warrior

Creek. One day I asked my Scotch-Irish grandmother if it was right to pollute the water. She told me that once the water passed over nine rocks it would be all clean again."

"She really didn't believe that, did she?"

"No. We used the creek to bathe in and to wash clothes, but we carried our drinking water from a spring. And we washed dishes in the spring water too."

"So what do you mean?"

"It's an attitude. When some people don't like a situation, they create new explanations. My grandmother invented new facts; Harwood accepted lies without checking them out. In both cases they created the version they wanted. We've encountered the same attitude in Waynesville, in Durham, and even in Raleigh where the *N & O* really didn't want quality reporting from *The Times*."

"It's not just in journalism," said my personal sociologist.

A couple of days later, we returned to Louisville. I discovered that Harwood's stories had done little other than to enrage Pope and puzzle the hell out of Newport officials. When next I returned to the city up the river, everyone wanted to know what was going on. Judge Stapleton commented:

"Harwood came in and said, 'Don't tell me anything bad about Newport.' What was he trying to do?"

"Make things nine rocks clean," I replied.

*****

It was hot in Frankfort. The city of 18,000, located in a ravine cut by the Kentucky River as it moved sluggishly to the northwest and its juncture with the Ohio, was like a furnace in the summer. Visitors approaching from the west could pause at an overlook and gaze down on the dome of the Capitol. It was under that dome on July 17 the ouster hearings began.

Presiding in the large conference room was Special Commissioner

John L. Davis. A tall, hefty man with short dark hair, Davis was a respected attorney who had never dabbled in politics.

Also present was Attorney General Breckinridge, representing the Commonwealth. Breckinridge was a good looking man about forty with acknowledged political ambitions. Seated nearby was the elderly Jesse K. Lewis and his associate, former state senator John Anggelis. Lewis had appeared only to assert his right to do so; following the first session he withdrew and left Anggelis to represent the Ministerial Association.

The two factions in Kentucky politics — and in Newport gambling — were illustrated by attorneys for the defense. Campbell County Police Chief Stuart was represented by Joseph Leary, former campaign manager of Happy Chandler. J.D. Buckman, political boss of Bullitt County and a former attorney general, represented Roll, Gugel, and Fredericks. He was considered a friend of the Cleveland Syndicate.

I was present under subpoena so Hugh Morris, chief of the Capital Bureau, had to do the reporting.

The first witness was Bernard Eismann, a CBS reporter who had brought a team to Newport to investigate one of my stories that made the wire. No problems developed until he tried to take his camera crew into one of the casinos. Eismann said he and his crew were chased to the airport by angry hoodlums.

Chris Seifried recounted the entire history of the Social Action Committee, describing in detail the repeated visits to illegal operations and the fruitless appeals for action to public officials such as Gugel, Roll, and Fredericks.

I described my experiences including the chase down the dark road along the river. It was the first time I'd ever related the incident. Morris reported it routinely and it caused no comment, as far as I could tell, although Norman Isaacs was to cite it later as an example of "Messick paranoia."

Next day I resumed my role as a reporter. Some excitement developed when Charles Hay, a resident of Covington, told of visiting Newport the night before. He'd found everything open, and reported it so at the police station. A cop told him to "go back to Covington before

I lock you up in the fucking jail."

Hay went back to the Yorkshire and waited. Gambling continued without interruption.

Breckinridge took advantage of the lunch break to confer with the Governor. He returned to tell me that Combs was furious. For years the casinos had closed during grand jury sessions. That the gamblers thought so little of the Governor to stay open during the ouster hearings was a personal insult.

Apparently the Governor let his rage be known. A telephone call went to the Flamingo Club in Newport. Within a few minutes of that call, the casinos closed. There was one exception, however: Screw Andrews continued to operate the numbers racket out of the Sportsmans Club.

The hearings continued as various ministers and church laymen described their experiences. Even George Bennett, my old friend who was now a graduate student at a seminary in Louisville, returned to testify. On the following day the witnesses included Dale Stevens, the amusement editor of *The Cincinnati Post and Times-Star*. He told of being called to the Beverly Hills Club in June following the Ratterman police court trial.

According to Stevens, John Croft, manager of the Club, told him the Beverly was an independent operation and had nothing to do with any syndicate. Moreover its gambling was honest. The Beverly, Croft added, was in no way connected with the attempt to frame Ratterman or with the bustout gambling at the Tropicana.

Under questioning, Stevens said he had been at the Beverly at least a hundred times in the course of his duties but had never been in the casino.

The life of an amusement editor can be amusing, but Stevens' effort at straight reporting proved even funnier. Back home in Cincinnati he wrote a story asserting the ouster hearings were "running out of steam." The story appeared on the day Hattie Jackson returned from the past.

Hattie Jackson, a former Newport madam, had testified before the Federal Grand Jury in Lexington. Handling her had been Assistant United States Attorney Mitchell Meade who owed his appointment to former U.S. Attorney Henry Cook. He called Cook and then Breckinridge about Hattie.

Tipped that sensational developments could be expected after lunch on Friday, I arranged to have a photographer standing by. Breckinridge had a sense of the dramatic. He waited until everyone was seated, then left the room and returned with a witness and her guard, Sgt. B.L. Sherrard, one of the largest men in the State Police.

Mrs. Jackson wore a black hat with a white brim and veil, a striped dress with wide collars which showed her neck and throat, and gloves of white lace. Trim and neat, with a thin intelligent face, she might have been a suburban housewife making an afternoon call.

Her voice was low, so low that Gugel and Fredericks used it as an excuse to move closer to her. And there they sat, giving her "the eye." She ignored them. Under questioning from Breckinridge, Mrs. Jackson told of being recruited in 1947 by Vivian Schultz to work at the 316 Club. Part of her duties was preparation of "the Payroll."

Working list of names provided, she put money in individual envelopes for officials and police officers. The list included Commonwealth's Attorney Wise, Judge Murphy, Chief Gugel, Leroy Fredericks, Pat Ciafardini, and many others.

There was complete silence in the room as she recounted the names. Word had spread and the conference room was suddenly full of people. I could read no expression on the faces of Gugel and Fredericks as they stared unblinkingly at the witness.

The envelopes containing money were given to Detectives Upshire White and Jack Thiem. The payoffs ranged from fifty to one hundred dollars a week.

After a year in Newport, Mrs. Jackson continued, "I got scared and left. Everybody was carrying pistols."

It was the period in which Screw Andrews and Red Masterson won their reputations as killers.

Mrs. Jackson returned to Newport in 1954. She checked in with Lester who set her up in business with the Bridewell brothers as a madam of her own house. Again, there were payoffs. Again she named officials who received them.

It was not a happy relationship, she testified. The Bridewells began overdoing the bustout business, putting knockout drops in customer's drinks and robbing them. When she objected, she was arrested and tossed into jail. Her conviction followed routinely and she was returned to jail to await sentencing. The grand jury came along on a tour of inspection. Such tours had become traditional, a means of giving the jurors something to do. They usually recommended the jail be painted. Hattie took advantage of the opportunity and told the jurors she wanted to testify about corruption.

Wise, in control as usual, promised to bring her before the jury later when she was scheduled to be sentenced. Satisfied, the grand jurors went on their way. As soon as they were gone, Gugel entered the cell and opened a sewer. A swarm of rats emerged. Hattie scrambled to the top of a table and sat there for five days and nights.

At this point, the witness broke into tears. Not a man spoke, not a man moved. Minutes passed. She wiped her eyes with a lace handkerchief, looked up at Gugel and in an angry voice said:

"For what I gave you, you should have put me in a penthouse."

Breckinridge commented later:

"There wasn't a man in that room that didn't know what she was talking about and didn't feel like beating that fellow to death."

When the witness regained her composure, she continued. Shortly before she was to appear before the grand jury, Gugel ordered the rats killed and the sewer closed. Taken before the jury, a chastened Hattie said only:

"I just don't feel like talking."

With that detail out of the way, Hattie was sentenced to five years in prison. She had never returned to Newport.

On cross examination Attorney Buckman sought to disassociate his client from the rat episode by asking if she had ever made payments to Sheriff Roll. She replied:

"I'd never seen Mr. Roll until a sheriff's convention last January in Louisville. I was working as a waitress. He recognized me and solicited me for prostitution."

The room exploded into laughter. Even Buckman grinned.

Mayor Mussman was the next witness and proved anti-climactic. He testified he'd been fired as city manager after ordering enforcement of the vice laws but he said that while he had been in most of the nightclubs, he'd never seen anyone gambling. There was another burst of laughter from the overflow crowd.

The hearings were recessed for thirty days to allow the defense to get ready and permit Commissioner Davis and his wife to take a long-planned cruise.

*****

Action and reaction. The Cleveland Syndicate flexed its muscles. With Lester on the high seas and the situation deteriorating rapidly, top Syndicate members came to Newport to confer with their lieutenants at the Beverly Hills. Present were Moe Dalitz, Sam Tucker, and Morris Kleinman, the three surviving charter members of the Syndicate.

Also attending the discussions were "Sleepout Louie" Levinson, Red Masterson, John Croft, Joe Berman, and Gilbert Beckley. The latter was considered one of the nation's top layoff bettors and with twelve other gamblers had just been indicted in New Orleans. Beckley had operated in the Finance Building for several years before moving around the corner to the second floor of the Glenn Hotel and, in fact, had dined with Tito Carinci at the Cincinnati hotel on the night George Ratterman downed a cocktail there.

The conferees adjourned next day to Miami where their arrival was duly noted by the FBI. Two days later Chief Gugel and Fredericks announced their resignations. Only a week before, Gugel had asked that his retirement be delayed so he could fight the ouster charges. Apparently the Syndicate had persuaded him to change his mind. After all, he had a retirement home waiting in Arizona. Fredericks was openly bitter and when I encountered him in front of the courthouse, he had a suggestion. Looking up York Street, he said:

"Tell you what, Hank. Let's me and you walk up the street. Every now and then I'll stop and point at something and you act like you're making notes. We'll scare the living shit out of them."

I was willing, but he backed out. Just for fun I walked down York to a street corner and leaned against a lamppost. Across the street was a typical handbook-tavern. A curtain at the front window moved and a face looked out. I glanced down at my watch as if checking the time and turned expectantly. The curtain closed. A side door opened and twenty-three men hurried out and up the street away from me.

Apparently I had scared the shit out of them all by myself. I decided to see what I could do with Judge Murphy.

ELEVEN
27 July '61

I knocked on the door of the judge's chambers, then pushed it open. Murphy was at his desk. Seated in front of him were Judge Stapleton and Circuit Court Clerk Virginia Drahmann.

Stapleton told me later that he and Mrs. Drahmann had just persuaded Murphy there was no need to probe Hattie Jackson's charges that Murphy had received payoffs when I appeared to ask:

"What are you going to do about Hattie Jackson's charges, Judge?"

Murphy stared at me. Color rose in his face. I noticed his large nose had a pimple on it.

"What would you do?" he asked.

He seemed serious. I paused a moment as if thinking and said slowly:

"If I were in your shoes and someone accused me of taking bribes, and I hadn't taken any, I'd call a special grand jury and bring out the truth."

He brought his fist down. "That's just what I'm going to do. I want that woman up here to testify."

I tried to manage a skeptical smile. "When?" I asked.

"Right now," said the Judge.

There was a warning cough from Stapleton. Mrs. Drahmann, an attractive woman in her forties, opened her mouth to speak, then closed it. Murphy had picked up the telephone

"Get me John Breckinridge in Frankfort," he barked.

I stood there — no one asked me to sit — as the call went through. After an exchange of curt greetings, Murphy announced:

"I'm calling a special grand jury to meet, let's see, August 14 is the soonest it can meet. I want Hattie Jackson up here to testify. Will you deliver her?"

Apparently Breckinridge promised to do so for Murphy seemed satisfied.

"I have assurance," Murphy said upon hanging up, "that Hattie Jackson will testify."

"May I quote you?" I asked. I intended to do so anyway since nothing had been off the record, but I wanted to see if he would give permission.

"Yes. You've got a story."

"What about Mr. Wise?" I asked. "He was on the payroll too, according to Hattie."

Murphy frowned. Wise, he said, would disqualify himself. Murphy himself would waive immunity and appear before the jury if it desired.

Stapleton and Mrs. Drahmann did not say a word. Murphy scribbled on a piece of paper and handed it to the Circuit Court Clerk.

"Enter it," he said.

"Thank you, Judge," I said politely and left the room. From Henry Cook's office I called the Attorney General and filled him in.

"I'll take it from there," said Breckinridge.

Breckinridge was as good as his word. As soon as he verified the official order had been entered on the records:

"I got on the phone and told Judge Murphy that in view of the fact that he was implicated in the testimony of Hattie Jackson, I felt that as a matter of judicial ethics, he should disqualify himself. He did disqualify himself and Judge Edward Hill was designated by the Kentucky Court of Appeals to serve as special judge."

For the reformers, it was an ironic jest indeed. In November, 1960, Judge Hill had called a special grand jury in Campbell County, but Judge Murphy had returned to the bench to direct it. Now, nine months later, Judge Murphy had called a special grand jury and Judge Hill would return to impanel it. And the gamblers of Newport feared no man more than the "Tamer of Bloody Harlan."

Breckinridge then asked Wise to disqualify himself and when he failed to do so, Breckinridge sought a Writ of Prohibition against his appearing before the grand jury. By a vote of four to three, the Court of Appeals refused on the grounds that Wise was not a judicial officer. But where Breckinridge had failed, Judge Hill was to succeed — with some help from the Social Action Committee. First, however, he had to get a jury.

On August 14th, potential grand jurors met in a town that was almost completely closed. A new order by Combs prohibited cab companies from transporting customers to gambling casinos. This rule knocked out the free limousine service from the airport to the Beverly Hills. Cincinnati cabbies were also grounded. Unemployed gamblers lounged in front of the casinos and moaned about hard times. Only the Sportsman's Club remained open.

Judge Hill, wearing his black robe, took a seat on Murphy's bench. In the courtroom were Breckinridge and two aides. His presence, Breckinridge admitted, was unprecedented in Kentucky judicial history.

The handsome judge made no excuses to the prospective jurors. Speaking quietly but firmly, he told them:

"This Court feels the necessity of a thorough examination of this grand jury."

He began asking questions and hit pay dirt with his first one. A woman acknowledged she had a relative who worked "in a place where they make book." She was excused.

Several prospective jurors pleaded they were "too nervous" to serve. Still others recalled associations that disqualified them. Poor health was a problem for others.

In many respects, it was a typical Campbell County panel. Among those excused, a former police chief of Southgate, the wife of a former sheriff, the wife of a city of Newport employee, the wife of a Dayton city councilman, three men who said they had friends among Newport gamblers, a woman who said she had such a friend, and a woman who had served on a previous jury within the year. When the panel was exhausted, five names had not answered, twenty-two individuals had been excused, and only nine jurors tentatively seated.

The Judge drew fifteen additional names from the jury wheel and ordered subpoenas served. Breckinridge commented:

"When it becomes difficult to seat a jury because the jury is to investigate gambling, the situation speaks for itself."

Next day the process continued. One of the nine tentatively seated was excused when he suddenly recalled that his brother-in-law was a policeman. Five of the fifteen additional jurors were excused. Only one had a respectable problem — "my baby was due to arrive yesterday, your Honor."

The assembled jury consisted of five men and seven women and the Judge gave it instructions. He wanted, he said, a probe "of a possible conspiracy by all officials who were charged with the duty of enforcing the laws of Campbell County and Newport."

Speaking slowly without notes or prepared text, the strange judge in the unfamiliar black robe continued:

"A conspiracy, simply stated, is a concerted action or agreement among officials to permit lawlessness without taking an active step in stopping such a situation."

"If, in your investigation, you find that such agreement exists, you may return an indictment against any of the personalities concerned. That will include certainly your sheriff, your chief of police. It will not only include the leaders of this particular situation, but the members themselves down to the man on the beat."

The judge looked down upon the citizens he had assembled and continued:

"It has been my behavior in the past to instruct on those things which have been most prominent in a community in regard to law violation, and I don't think the court is required to be more stupid than anyone else..."

"I don't know what your personal feelings may be about the laws against vice and gambling, and so forth, but it is not for the court to question the wisdom of the legislature who passed these laws.

"You will have scars here for years as a result of the nefarious practice of openly operating gambling places. I ask this jury to consider whether or not children could be raised in an atmosphere of wholesale, wide open violations, and corruption without being tainted in some manner."

"I did not come here to preach you people a sermon. I didn't ask to be sent here. I was ordered to be here by the Chief Justice, but since I am here, I hope you will feel I am not a foreigner in your community come to tell you how to run your business."

"I am merely here to instruct you and work with you relative to a problem which is nationally significant. I've had certain labels applied to me — a tough judge, a mountain judge, and Wyatt Earp. I hope you will find that I am a kind person, but I do insist on doing what I am supposed to do under the law and I hope this community will accept me in that kind of light."

Breckinridge commented later:

"Judge Hill took this jury and converted it before our eyes. The men started shaving, wearing neckties. The women wore their Sunday best. They began to take on the appearance of a responsible section of middle class people."

Hill did more than stir the civic conscience of the jurors — he made them aware of their strength. To aid the jury, he promised to call upon all agencies of the state and federal governments concerned with law enforcement. He listed them, causing a Cincinnati reporter at the press table to snarl:

"He's naming everybody but Dick Tracy."

Wise watched from the rear of the courtroom as the Judge gave specific instructions to investigate the conduct of the Commonwealth's Attorney. The jurors, added Hill, were to report to him the moment such an investigation began. He would then appoint a commonwealth's attorney pro tem to replace Wise.

Under Kentucky law, the commonwealth's attorney must assist the grand jury in all matters except those in which he is involved. Thus when the jurors at last entered the grand jury room, Wise followed them in.

John Anggelis advised the ministers to say upon beginning testimony that evidence against Wise was to be presented. Presumably the jurors would then notify Judge Hill.

Seifried, his face still impassive, rapped on the door of the jury room and announced the Social Action Committee wanted to testify. Instead, Wise called in Newport's most famous madam, Vivian Schultz. At the time Hattie Jackson testified in Frankfort, Wise had commented that the testimony of such a person was unworthy of consideration. Yet as a first witness before the special grand jury he called the woman who had brought Hattie to Newport. Obviously, he expected her to discredit Hattie.

Apparently the women members of the grand jury didn't like the idea and after an argument, audible in the courtroom, Vivian was dismissed and the ministers called. Barkhau was first, followed by Baker. Both men said they wanted to talk about Wise. Each time Wise left the room only to return when the witness finished.

We were almost literally holding our breath. If anything was accomplished, Wise had to be replaced. The commonwealth's attorney was hanging on desperately, obviously aware of the stakes involved.

Cesare Bernardini, the third witness, put an end to the farce. He reminded the jurors that they were supposed to notify Judge Hill when an investigation of Wise began. He was ready, he said, to discuss the conduct of Wise. The jury came out to report, but Judge Hill had left for his Cincinnati hotel. Thereupon the jury recessed until next morning.

That night at Hill's request, I drank bourbon with him in his hotel room high above the Ohio. The judge talked about the bad old days in Harlan County when coal mine violence was common. After a few drinks, I asked him, as one hillbilly to another, why he was seemingly unafraid of the gangsters who'd strutted Newport's streets for decades. He replied:

"Before I left Harlan some of the boys came to me and told me they'd get the word out that if anyone gave me trouble up here, they'd have a plane ready and would fly up and clean out the town."

The judge chuckled. "One thing about the boys in Harlan — when they say they'll kill somebody, they kill him."

Next day the jurors assembled early and Wise led them into the grand jury room. When Hill arrived at the appointed hour, Wise had been with the jurors for fifteen minutes. I asked Hill if Wise's presence with the jurors was improper under the circumstances.

"If he was investigating a murder case," replied the judge, "then his presence would be all right."

He sent the bailiff to command the jurors' presence in the courtroom. Wise was asked what had taken place. He replied:

"I told the grand jury what the situation was."

Judge Hill took control of the situation, whatever it was, and asked the foreman:

"Are you considering any evidence against Bill Wise? Or have you considered any evidence against Mr. Wise?"

The foreman was William Horn, reportedly a friend of Wise. He was vague in his reply:

"Not personally," he stuttered, "everybody included."

"You considered evidence against all officials, including Mr. Wise?"

"That is, in general, what so far we have heard," said the unhappy Horn.

"I think the situation calls for a commonwealth's attorney pro tem," Hill said dryly. He ordered the jury to adjourn, pending the selection of such a person.

Wise rushed from the rear of the room and protested loudly. He had other matters to present to the special grand jury, he said.

"The jury is adjourned," said Judge Hill. He stood, an impressive figure in the black robe. Wise stared up at him, then turned on his heel and walked away.

In the next twenty-four hours, Hill and Breckinridge, with input from Henry Cook, considered various members of the Campbell County Bar. They selected Frank V. Benton III, thirty-five years old, married, and the father of four children. He was a graduate of the University of Kentucky School of Law and had been associated for ten years with a law firm founded in 1890 by his grandfather. Even Wise commented:

"He is a fair man and competent."

Thus it was that on Monday, August 21, one month from the day

Hattie Jackson made her charges, Benton took over from Wise. I was the first witness.

*****

Automobiles in downtown Newport often bore two bumper stickers. One, "Root The Reds Home," referred to the hot National League pennant race and the hope of the community that the Cincinnati Reds would bring the World Series to town. The second, "Local Self Government," referred to the political campaign being waged in Campbell County. More and more, however, "Switch to Honesty," the battle cry of the reformers, was appearing on suburban cars. The Ohio valley quivered in the grip of an unprecedented heat wave. Many Kentucky cities rationed water.

My appearance before the special grand jury left me encouraged. A division was apparent. The seven women jurors and three of the men were friendly and interested. Two of the men were sullen. The foreman tried to trip me up with a question about Vivian Schultz and retreated into silence when corrected as to facts. Notes were taken. And no one asked me if my purpose in being there was to sell newspapers.

Seventeen witnesses appeared that first day. Several of them were State Policemen who had made a "private visit" to Newport in June and toured brothels and casinos. By the next day the jury was ready with its first indictments. The first batch listed thirty-eight counts of leasing or renting property for gambling purposes and was directed at dummy corporations allegedly owning various casinos. A former mayor, Robert Siddell, was named in twelve counts. A second batch of seven indictments was returned. They charged violation of a state law requiring business establishments to register the names of owners. Heading the list of owners indicted was Red "the Enforcer" Masterson.

Calling the indictments "incidental," Benton said time was needed to physically prepare hundreds of indictments based on federal wagering tax records. The jury adjourned until August 31st.

But the pressure continued. In Washington, the Senate Permanent Subcommittee on Investigations chaired by Senator John McClellan opened hearings into illegal gambling. The spotlight immediately focused on Newport. The area was described by Internal Revenue Service officials as the principal center of the layoff betting business in the United States.

And on that same day special agents of the Intelligence Division of the IRS struck at Screw Andrews' numbers empire.

They raided the Sportsman's Club.

Screw Andrews was born in 1911 in Cincinnati, the youngest of ten children. Their parents had been born and married in Italy where their name was Andriola. Screw's first brush with the law came at age 13 when a gun with which he was playing discharged and killed a bystander. Ultimately, he had more than forty arrests to his credit.

The Cincinnati area in which he was raised had been corrupted in the twenties by George Remus, king of the bootleggers. Remus once estimated he paid out over twenty million dollars in graft to operate in Cincinnati and "Little Mexico" across the river. He literally taught officials of three states — Ohio, Kentucky, and Indiana — to expect payoffs as normal income.

Andrews grew into a large man, more than six feet tall with wide shoulders. He had blonde hair and wore glasses. Women found him attractive and he gained a reputation that won him his nickname, but he had contempt for the people he exploited and cold, cold eyes.

A big role in the expansion of the illegal liquor business after World War II was played by Andrews who reopened old routes through the mountains first used by the moonshiners of the Twenties. Sources in Tennessee and the Carolinas were tapped. Quite naturally he began to operate numbers in the joints that sold his liquor. It was necessary to use force to consolidate the business. Steve Payne, a black man, was his chief competitor. Payne operated out of the Sportsman's Club on Central Avenue in Newport. On May 14, 1947, the Club was raided by cops friendly to Screw. Payne's body was found in a ditch early in 1948. He'd been shot several times in the head and chest. Less than a month after the murder, title to the property passed to Irvine "Nig" Devine.

A mysterious figure, Devine was a close associate of "Trigger Mike" Coppola, boss of the East Harlem numbers racket. As such he was able to obtain Coppola's money and muscle to finance Andrews. The Sportsman's Club soon passed through the hands of a dummy to Andrews.

Another rival was A.L. Schmidt, known as "White Smitty." Newport City Solicitor, Morris Weintraub, on August 7, 1948 led a raiding party past the Sportsman's Club to hit Smitty's headquarters. Smitty was indicted, but Commonwealth's Attorney Wise was unable to obtain a conviction. Weintraub, of course, happened to be Andrews' attorney. "White Smitty" escaped jail and thereafter worked for Screw.

One major rival remained. Melvin Clark survived one murder attempt, killing the attacker. He told his girl friend that the dead man had been acting on Screw Andrews' orders. Clark pleaded self defense, beat the murder charge, but was convicted of carrying a pistol and, as one officer put it, "was probated out of Kentucky." He returned and opened a new joint in 1954. Six months later Screw Andrews gunned him down. Screw pleaded self defense and was acquitted.

Federal wagering tax records show that in February 1959, after a few bombs exploded in Newport and Cincinnati, Andrews consolidated all numbers activity under his direction. One of his services to Coppola came when he, Gil Beckley, and "Sleepout Louie" took a gambler's widow to New York to meet the gangster who was looking for a new wife. Coppola quickly married her. Later, on her death bed, she would write:

"Screw Andrews is Mike Coppola's main and most important man in Newport. Screw handles all the dirty work for Mike and Tony Salerno."

Morris Weintraub became counsel of the Newport Housing Commission and when federal urban renewal funds became available, he helped arrange the sale of three clubs owned by Screw to the city for $450,000. Screw announced plans to build a plush new club overlooking the Ohio at the northern end of York Street. Mayor Mussman, who had a real estate business on the side, arranged for Screw to buy the site from the city. Zoning restrictions were trimmed to make it possible to issue a building permit. The old Sportsman's Club was demolished and Screw moved into one of the other buildings and paid rent of $1,053 a month to the city. Pending completion of the new club, it remained the center of numbers racket activity.

*****

At 11:30 p.m. on August 22nd, a picked squad of Special Agents from five states surrounded the interim Sportsman's Club. It was crowded with more than two hundred black Shriners, part of a huge convention in Cincinnati. A banner welcoming them hung across Central Avenue. A black undercover agent had scouted the joint for a month and was stationed near the front door. When a lookout rushed in shouting "Raid," steel doors were closed. Sledge hammers crashed against the obstacle in vain, but the undercover agent opened it. The raiders poured in. Three men sprinted to the restroom area where gamblers were flushing numbers tickets down the toilets.

A second raiding party hit the nearby Corner Liquor Store, also owned by Andrews. Records were seized.

The Shriners were lined up, questioned, and released. Several numbers writers tried to sneak out with them but the undercover agent pulled them from the line. Teams of agents began interviewing the twenty-five employees who remained. Andrews was not among them. A systematic search began. The Special Agents, armed with blueprints, found eleven slot machines behind a secret panel. The slots were mounted on metal frames and fastened to wooden turntables. When the panel was lifted, the slots turned into playing position. Other secret panels were discovered. Behind some were bales of records. Others concealed safes. Locksmiths were brought in. It took several hours before they could be opened. In one safe fifty-five thousand dollars in cash and guns were found; another held twenty-one thousand and more guns.

A long narrow room, cleverly camouflaged, was discovered in the heart of the building. It contained a table and chairs — and twenty telephones. The phones rang for hours as customers called in to learn the winning numbers.

A machine was found that pushed numbered ping pong balls upward until three rolled free into a chute, giving the night's winning number. The agents examined the device and found a hidden compartment in which pre-selected balls were stored and released at will by the operator. The number, selected in advance, was the one receiving the least play from the suckers. It took the agents only a few minutes to become experts at blowing up any number they chose.

The search continued through the night. The agents checked their blueprints and became convinced there was leftover space somewhere. Again, they hunted through a closet. The shoe of one agent hit a piece of wire on the floor. It was about ten inches long and insulation had been cut from the copper at each end. Trying to figure out its purpose, the agent noticed two nail heads about eight inches apart, shoulder high, in the very back of the closet. He placed the ends of the wire against the nails. Something buzzed within the wall, the back of the closet swung open. Inside was a small room literally packed with minute details of the numbers racket. Those records would go to a special federal grand jury to be convened in Cincinnati.

The search was still going on when I arrived. A friendly agent let me in and apologized because I'd not been notified in advance. Security had been very strict, he said, and, besides, it was past your deadline.

Morris Weintraub came in and promptly demanded that the agents throw me out on the grounds I was trespassing. When the agents laughed at him, Weintraub ordered me out.

"Are you ordering me out in your capacity as Counsel for the Newport Housing Commission or as the attorney for Screw Andrews?" I asked politely.

Weintraub got very red in the face and proceeded to call me every dirty name I'd ever heard, and some I'd never heard before. He was even more foul-mouthed than Lester. I felt the blood drain from my face. My stomach started to cramp. I clenched my fists. Weintraub kept cursing. I took a deep breath, held it a minute, expelled it, and said nothing.

"I'm gonna get a court order barring you from the premises," shouted Weintraub and dashed for the door. Two agents stared at me. One of them said:

"You don't have to take that kind of shit. Why didn't you knock hell out of him?"

I replied: "If I had as much as touched him, he'd be back with a warrant and I'd be in jail with the rats. They've been trying to get me to do something foolish for three years. I'm not about to start now."

"Good point," acknowledged the agent, but there was still a question on his face.

In my heart I also wondered. Was I really playing it smart or was I afraid? Since that day in 1952 when I'd been assaulted by a crooked cop, I had refused to react to provocation. There were reasons, of course, with which I could justify my failure, but were they just excuses? I really needed to hit somebody hard.

After a bit, Weintraub returned without a court order. The agents refused to admit him until he acknowledged his purpose in being there was to represent Screw Andrews. Frank Benton, the new commonwealth's attorney pro tem, dropped in and gave me a quote. Noting the Club had been operating within two hundred yards of the police station, he said:

"This raid alone shows how gamblers have openly flaunted the law and how arrogant they have become."

After being assured that the agents now had enough evidence to put Screw and his cohorts into prison for years, I left the building, and walked to the site of Screw's new club on the chance Screw would be there. Walls were going up and a workman told me the structure of glass and steel would be completed by December. I was able to confirm the existence of concealed spaces which I'd suspected after an earlier visit when blueprints were left unguarded. It was going to be a splendid palace, but somehow I didn't believe Screw Andrews would be around to operate.

Since there was no one around worth hitting, I drove to Cincinnati, wrote my story, and sent it press rates collect by telegram to the *C-J*. It got lead play on the front page next day.

After a while I began to feel better, but I cautioned myself that until Ratterman was elected all apparent gains could be lost. It was not time yet to declare victory.

TWELVE
30 August '61

Morris Weintraub was suddenly a very busy man. In the absence of Lester, he was forced to go to Washington to represent two gamblers from the Belmont Snax Bar. The Permanent Subcommittee on Investigations subpoenaed them in the belief they operated "a typical Newport medium-sized handbook." Investigators for the committee reported the men handled $1,165,022 in wagers over a twenty-one month period.

The two men took the Fifth Amendment over and over, refusing to answer any questions. If, however, the witnesses didn't want to talk, Weintraub did. Finally, Senator McClellan commented somewhat sourly:

"These are the most silent witnesses and the most talkative attorney we've had in a long time."

During the hearing, an IRS official said that Newport was "strangely silent." A staff member credited the IRS only to have Senator Sam Ervin note that a newspaper in the area had been conducting "something in the nature of a crusade" and that a grand jury was conducting investigations.

Ervin hailed from Morganton. N.C., not far from Happy Valley and had been a friend of my father. Later, he would win national recognition as chairman of the Watergate Investigating Committee.

Meanwhile, Sheriff Roll's aching feet became a problem. He removed his shoes so photographers could get a picture. Given 136 subpoenas to serve, he'd found only two witnesses and had become exhausted.

The Sheriff obviously needed help, Judge Hill declared. He asked the governor to send in State Police. Combs obliged, proclaiming a state of limited emergency in Campbell County. The Reverend Mr. Pomeroy observed:

"It was unfair to ask Mr. Roll to find witnesses who were to be questioned about Mr. Roll's integrity."

I was on hand to record the historic moment when State Police returned officially to Campbell County after many decades. It occurred at 2:10 p.m. when Detective Algin Roberts parked in front of the courthouse. Fellow officers followed within hours. The temporary overthrow of existing legal machinery was now complete. First had come a special grand jury, then a special judge, followed by a commonwealth's attorney pro tem, and finally State Police to act for the sheriff.

No time was lost as witnesses were rounded up. On August 31, the special grand jury returned indictments totaling sixty-five counts against fifteen gamblers. Among those named were the two who had taken the Fifth in Washington.

For the "liberals," it was obvious the situation was getting out of hand. Attorney Davies and Hirschfeld held a press conference to attack Benton's grandfather, who, they said, had incorporated the firm that owned the Yorkshire Club in 1944. That didn't impress any of the assembled reporters so Davies changed the target.

"Messick went to see Red Masterson," said Davies. "Masterson treated him like a gentleman and Messick insulted him by asking how many men he'd killed."

Masterson had only killed two men, Davies continued, and had been acquitted for doing that. He looked at me and added:

"If you'd been up here then, they'd probably killed you too. You've ruined half of Newport."

"I had a little help," I replied modestly.

Masterson, incidentally, was one of those indicted that day.

The special grand jury's normal life of six working days was about to expire. Judge Hill issued an order extending the jury's tenure by nine days. The grand jury then went into recess while more indictments were prepared. The spotlight swung back to Frankfort where Breckinridge announced plans to hear another ghost from Newport's past — James Harris, former marshal of the suburban town of Wilder.

Jiggs Buckman asked for delay. His client, Sheriff Roll, worn out by his fruitless search for witnesses, was in the hospital. Commissioner Davis asked for proof. Buckman staged two dramatic walkouts before returning with a medical report allegedly confirming Roll's illness. The hearings were adjourned until September 26. If Hattie Jackson had blown the lid off Newport, Harris was reportedly prepared to blow up the pot. Thus Roll's "illness" blocked a public airing of Harris' story.

But if Harris was stopped in Frankfort, Hattie returned to Newport the following day.

Flanked by Breckinridge on one side and Sergeant Sherrard on the other, with a State Policeman bringing up the rear, Mrs. Jackson came up the stairs to the courtroom where she had been convicted of pandering. In front of her face she held an open newspaper while excited photographers snapped pictures. Sherrard told me she was "scared to death."

Intense heat had driven the jurors from the tiny room where usually they met and into the larger courtroom. All fans in the building had been brought there.

Word spread quickly and within minutes gamblers, policemen, and prostitutes crowded into the hall to gaze through the tiny windows of the courtroom door at the spectacle of Hattie Jackson squealing her heart out. And more than one cursed Judge Murphy for wanting her back.

Sherrard, standing guard outside the door, became worried as the crowd swelled. He reported his fears to Judge Hill who ordered the windows in the door covered. Sherrard called for reinforcements. When, some ninety minutes later, the witness finished her testimony and left the courtroom, guards formed a human wall around her. They pushed a path through the throng to the police car. Hattie stretched herself on the rear seat and covered her head with newspapers.

The desperation of the pro-vice faction increased. Orders went out to close all bingo games in Campbell County. Who gave the order could not be ascertained. Similar action had been taken in earlier years to quiet reform fervor, but this time the reformers weren't blamed. The Catholics of Newport had become sophisticated enough to know who was responsible and why it was done. Resentment was widely voiced.

On September 8, "Big Jim" Harris testified in Newport for almost an hour. He, like Hattie, had appeared before the federal grand jury probing the Ratterman case. What he said was, of course, secret but at a press conference later in Henry Cook's law office, Harris said he told the grand jury of payoffs to various officials he had made while running a bawdy house in Wilder. He named names, but, unfortunately, anyone quoting them ran the risk of a libel suit since his comments weren't privileged.

Admitting that he was a gambling operator while wearing a marshal's badge, Harris said his troubles with the law began when he tried to operate on a larger scale than the syndicate desired. The syndicate permits small operations, he said, but cracks down when anyone gets too big. He admitted that bedrooms in his Hi-D-Ho Club had been wired for sound, but he said this was necessary to prevent the hookers from cheating.

Wise followed Harris before the grand jury. Benton said to allow him to do so was "an unusual privilege" but one that Wise had requested. The commonwealth's attorney emerged from the grand jury room breathing fire and announcing plans to sue every newspaper that had carried Hattie's charges about him. With the money he would thus receive, he would retire to Florida.

No one paid much attention. It was Friday afternoon. I filed my story and caught a Piedmont plane to North Carolina where my presence had been urgently requested.

*****

The two-engine prop-jet took off, circled west where the land was bright and turned southeast where shadows grew. A steward — Piedmont didn't use women in those days — provided some crackers and a soft drink in lieu of dinner. I leaned back and tried to sort out the events of the past hectic weeks. Things had developed at a bewildering pace and I'd been too busy to put them into perspective. I was returning to my home state because the Blue Ridge Electric Membership Corporation, the co-op founded by my father, was celebrating its twenty-fifth anniversary. As part of the ceremonies, a portrait of my father would be unveiled. My mother thought it essential I be there, the more so because my brother had declined to attend.

Well, I needed a break. Unbidden, the memory of Danny Davies declaring that in the old days I might have been murdered in Newport came to mind. Well, apparently, from what my friend Howard reported, my murder had been seriously considered but rejected on the grounds it would cause too much heat. A bribe offer was made instead. When that failed, a war of nerves had been conducted in hope of creating an incident that could be used to discredit me. On three occasions I had received mysterious invitations from female callers who promised valuable information if I would meet them late at night at some joint. I'd gone to one rendevous but I'd taken Bernardini with me. Nothing happened. When I refused to react to other provocation in a suitable macho manner, the word had gone around that I was a "queer." This explanation perhaps satisfied the gamblers and their friends, but it didn't stop my reporting. Morris Weintraub's outburst the other day had been an example of the frustration felt by the "liberals."

In darkness now, the plane stopped at the Tri-City Airport in Tennessee, then flew over the Blue Ridge. I looked down at scattered lights and remembered hiking those mountains while surveying power lines. I had loved the Blue Ridge, its immense sweep and eternal silences, but I had also hated it as a prison from which I longed to escape. Well, I had escaped. Was I happier as a result?

We landed at Hickory where Mother and my sister met me. Mildred was head of the English Department at Lenoir High School and had decided to devote her life to caring for Mother. I regretted her decision for I felt she had great potential and was surrendering all opportunity to develop it, but it relieved me of responsibility. Mother looked happy and very excited at the ceremony upcoming.

We stopped for dinner at some "fish place" Mother had heard about. The tables were covered with red checkerboard oilcloth — that's about all I remember of it. With Mother talking as if trying to make up for years of silence, we rode on to Happy Valley. The old house with its wide porches and attic full of rats had been demolished. On its site Mildred had built a small white house which seemed eminently suitable for two people, but Mother was already planning a new home across the creek which would be large enough, she said, to house her grandchildren when they came visiting.

I tried to tell about my recent adventures but Mother wasn't very interested. She knew all about the Syndicate from watching soap operas and wanted instead to talk about people I'd almost forgotten. I let her ramble and she was happy. Next day, wearing our finest, we drove to a high school near Granite Falls where the annual meeting of the cooperative was to be held. The organization now served more than 18,000 members in eight counties. Annual revenues were in excess of two million dollars. Over 3,600 miles of power lines had been built.

We were ushered to a stage on which several other guests were seated. About 1,200 members were assembled in the auditorium, many of them attracted, I was sure, by the possibility of winning a door prize of a refrigerator or electric range. Mother volunteered to formally thank the cooperative when the portrait was unveiled. Thinking I had nothing to do but sit, I relaxed. There was a long speech extolling the virtues of my father and as it neared an end, Mildred leaned over and whispered:

"Mother says she can't do it. You'll have to."

At that moment, the black curtain over the easel was removed and the image of my father stared out as if in challenge. The audience applauded politely. Dad was pictured wearing a dark suit with a bowtie and holding some papers. And then I was on my feet before a microphone. In writing stories, I had learned that when I got my lead, the facts assembled themselves in proper fashion. Perhaps the same would be true when speaking. I stared at the sea of faces gazing blankly up at me and began talking.

I told of the days when my father would hitchhike to Lenoir, of how he stirred interest and then enthusiasm among county leaders. I discussed the opposition they confronted, the power company's attempts to spread disinformation and doubt. And, abruptly, I realized that I'd gained the attention of my audience. For the first time I understood the thrill of public speaking. Maybe they had come to win a refrigerator, but, by God, they were listening to me.

I repeated a story I'd heard my father tell of one old mountaineer who didn't believe. When surveyors drove stakes he told them that while the stakes made good kindling, they were too far apart. When the power lines were built he said the wires would be good to hang clothes upon if they weren't so high and when, at last, the lines were energized and he was shown a lighted lamp. he burst out:

"It's a damn lie!"

I told how I had accompanied my father to Carter County in Tennessee. At a meeting in Mountain City a representative of the local power company had complained:

"These mountaineers are too poor to pay for electricity and too ignorant to use it."

I wrote the quotation down and on the following night my father used it to great advantage at a mass meeting in Shady Valley.

Men and women, I observed, are often confused when they lack the facts. In recent months I'd been involved in a struggle in Kentucky to give people the truth and overcome evil forces that sought to exploit them. The battle, I continued, was still not won, but the example my father and his friends had provided years before gave me confidence that virtue would triumph.

I saw my ending clearly now:

"About the time my father died," I said, "I left this area. In returning, I see things as my father would see them if he could return. And I can tell you that he would be very pleased, very delighted with the progress that has been made. But he would not be surprised. He had faith in the courage and wisdom of informed people when given an opportunity. I share that faith."

There was a roar of applause. Men and women stood, a tribute I realized that was more for my father than for me. The current manager of the co-op bounded over to shake my hand. Mother dabbed at her eyes. My sister patted me on the shoulder.

With our duty done, we were allowed to depart. Mildred drove us high up the mountain and parked at an overlook where I could gaze out at the blue ocean of ridges and refresh my spirit. Then, too soon, we went to Harper's Chapel where Dad was buried. The sight of the grave didn't move me. My mother and sister were Advent Christians who believed that one's soul remained in the grave with the body until the trumpet sounded for Judgment Day. Consequently they felt it proper when visiting the grave to update the occupant on recent events. It was my chance to tell Dad that I'd followed the trail of corruption from Waynesville to Frank Andriola's joint in Newport. I thought about it, but decided not to bother.

When we returned to the house, a representative of the co-op had left three electric blankets and a note thanking us effusively. Apparently the cooperative's management had been having difficulties after a rate increase and needed to invoke my father's memory to restore faith.

After another night of listening to Mother retell old stories, I flew out of Hickory without regret. Faye met me at the airport and on Monday I flew back to Newport.

*****

Newport, Ky. Sept. 12 - The big wind is beginning to blow through Newport. A special Campbell County Grand Jury voted 93 felony counts in 19 indictments Tuesday and spent the rest of the day voting on indictment of officials. The jury is expected to complete its work Wednesday with a final report and additional indictments...

The felony charges were for setting up and operating gambling houses. They were brought against every top gambler at the Beverly Hills, the Yorkshire, the Flamingo, and the Snax Bar. Once more the interlocking ownerships of syndicate clubs were revealed.

If I appeared a bit poetic in my lead, it was because I remembered that September 12 was an anniversary. On that day in 1960, members of the Newport Ministerial Association had agreed to continue the fight for one more year. They pledged to quit Newport if, at the end of that year, no progress had been made.

None of the ministers was leaving, I wrote, but every plane flying west to Nevada was crowded with gamblers hoping to find work in Las Vegas. Some were even going south where a new casino was opening in the Bahamas. Did they consider the outcome of the upcoming election a foregone conclusion?

Tension was thicker than humidity in Newport as the special grand jury met for the last time. Mayor Mussman demanded the same privilege accorded Wise earlier and appeared before the grand jury. He came out smiling and told reporters:

"I feel like I clarified some things they didn't know about second class cities and conditions in Newport."

Print reporters and television cameras waited as the hot afternoon dragged on. Some of the reporters amused themselves by betting small sums on who would be indicted and who would escape. Finally a knock sounded on the door of the grand jury room to which the jurors had returned despite the heat. The uniformed bailiff opened the door, closed it, and went in search of Judge Hill. The wait was over.

Still wearing the unfamiliar black robe, the judge took his seat. The jurors filed in, their report was read.

Wise escaped indictment. The jury declared:

"He does not make full use of his abilities and powers in all instances involving gambling and other vice violations... Mr. Wise has appeared before us and he indicates that he is proud of his abilities as an attorney and as a prosecutor. It is not consistent with this expression of pride that he would adopt the apathetic attitude of many of our public officials towards gambling and prostitution as a way of life in this county.

"We do not believe that this is what the people want as we have so often heard it expressed. We ask the next grand jury to continue this investigation of public officials. We are convinced that many public officials have conspired, combined, confederated, and agreed together to pervert, corrupt, or obstruct justice by permitting these sordid conditions to exist. We have named 13 of these officials. We voted on others and, while a majority of our body favored indictments against other officials, the required nine votes were not received in these cases..."

Indicted on charges of conspiracy to pervert, corrupt, or obstruct justice were Mayor Mussman, City Manager Hesch, ex-police Chief Gugel, ex-detective Chief Fredericks, detectives Ciafardini, Upshire White, Edward Gugel — son of the former Chief — three other police officers, and three of four city commissioners. The fourth was a woman newly appointed to fill the vacancy caused by her husband's death.

Judge Hill told the jurors, "I'm proud of you," and said he would order the next grand jury to continue the probe. He dismissed them. I got to one of the women and learned that my earlier estimate had been correct. The seven women had been unanimous in wanting to indict everyone. Two men opposed indicting anyone. The remaining three men split on individual names with two of the three needed to vote an indictment.

Mayor Mussman, no longer smiling, called the indictments an example "of what can happen when witch hunting and politics take over in place of reason and rule by law."

Wise didn't look very happy either. When reporters clustered around him in search of a statement, he pointed his finger at me and shouted:

"I will not talk in front of that man."

It was the first time Wise had lost control of his feelings where I was concerned.

The Cincinnati reporters led Wise towards a women's restroom. I started to follow. Judge Hill, who had doffed his robe, stood with Breckinridge observing the scene. Hill called to me. I walked back to them.

"Let's get out of here, Hank; our job is done," Hill said.

The three of us walked out of the Campbell County Courthouse and headed for Breckinridge's car in the parking lot across from the Playtorium.

The big wind had blown through Newport.

Back in Louisville, Mark Ethridge wrote a memo to Jim Pope and Ben Reeves which was passed on to me.

The indictments returned yesterday at Newport, regardless of whether convictions are secured or not, climax one of the best pieces of work we've ever done on these papers. Hank has done a wonderfully fine job. Such a job that, in my mind, he is entitled to a Pulitzer Prize for it.

THIRTEEN
6 October '61

The World Series opened in Cincinnati and some of the joints in Newport tried to capitalize on it.

I was in the area for other reasons. Lately things had been even more bizarre than usual.

A week earlier, the Newport City Commission apparently reacted to Syndicate pressure and appointed Upshire White Police Chief. Ciafardini was passed over, an indication, perhaps, of the low esteem in which Charles Lester was now regarded. White had called a press conference to request that in the future his first name be spelled "Upshere." He was serious.

Even for Newport this had seemed unusual — city officials under indictment appointing as police chief a detective also under indictment.

Meanwhile, defense attorneys filed one hundred motions asking for the dismissal of all indictments returned by the late special grand jury. The lawyers got together with Wise and selected a special judge, Louis Reuscher, to hear the motions. His qualifications consisted of service as circuit court clerk — in 1900.

Breckinridge only a few hours earlier had secured a temporary injunction from the Court of Appeals barring Reuscher. And just minutes before, the Newport Ministerial Association swore out a warrant charging Wise with nonfeasance.

A state of confusion reigned in the courthouse when I arrived. Thirty-five witnesses had shown up in answer to subpoenas for the hearing on defense motions. No one knew who was in charge. Special Counsel Hirschfeld advised the witnesses not to leave and blamed the problems on Breckinridge. My old comrade, Cesare Bernardini, who was tired of being called as a witness every time Danny Davies had a client, produced his subpoena.

"Breckinridge's name isn't on this," he told Hirschfeld, "so don't give us any of that crap."

Reuscher, who seemed disappointed at his failure to be judge for a day, asked Judge Murphy to dismiss the witnesses. Murphy said he had no legal standing in the case, but he thought the witnesses could legally go home. And there the matter would stand until November when the Court of Appeals ordered Judge Hill to handle it.

While all this was going on, Commissioner Davis made his recommendations in the ouster hearings of Gugel and Fredericks. He found them guilty, and commented:

"It is utterly incomprehensible that open gambling establishments could flourish within the city of Newport to the extent described in the record without the knowledge of the two respondents here involved..."

Upon being informed that some of the nightspots might reopen to capitalize on the World Series crowds, I decided to stay over. That night I made the grand tour.

On Monmouth Street, the Frolics Club advertised its stripper named Neptina who was supposed to do an "aqua-tease." When I entered the place a large glass tank of water stood ready but there was no sign of Neptina. Nor was there a single customer. Only the orchestra and a bartender were present. When I asked about the show, the bartender replied:

"Unless somebody shows up, there won't be one."

When no one showed up, I went down the street to the Tropicana. The neon nudes were dark but the marquee bore the sign:

Welcome Series Visitors

There wasn't a single sucker in the joint.

Over on York Street, the Flamingo and Yorkshire were also empty. A dozen diners were lost in the vastness of the Beverly Hills theater-restaurant.

I decided Newport was learning what the national publicity caused by the Ratterman case had cost them.

Immediately after the Reds lost the series, winning only one game, the Beverly Hills announced it was discontinuing its "policy of Floor Shows, Dinner & Dancing for an indefinite period." The casino had been closed since July; now the whole place was shutting down. There was more than met the eye in the announcement. It was timed to a propaganda campaign claiming that without gambling, Newport would become a ghost town. The Beverly's action meant that several hundred more people would be unemployed on election day.

Along York Street where once casino parking lots overflowed, there were now blocks where day or night not a car could be seen. FBI Special Agent Staab told me one day:

"It reminds me of a western movie after the gold supply has been exhausted. At any moment you expect to see a dust storm blow up and tumbleweeds come rolling down the street past the deserted saloons and gambling dens."

On October 10, the governor signed an order ousting Gugel and Fredericks. He invoked full penalties. This meant that neither man could hold public office for four years. It didn't bother Gugel who headed for Arizona but it prevented Wise from giving Fredericks a promised job as commonwealth's detective.

The ouster hearings against Stuart and Roll resumed on October 16. Final evidence introduced were federal wagering tax records showing that handbooks in Campbell County paid taxes on almost six million dollars in wagers each year.

What the actual handbook "handle" was no one knew. Treasury agents told me the amount reported varied according to the size and openness of the operation. Screw Andrews' records had disclosed that the Sportsman's Club had paid taxes on only one-seventh of the wagers accepted. Another bookie less well known had admitted reporting only one-fifteenth of his take. The average, believed the agents, would be in the neighborhood of one-tenth. That would make the yearly handbook total a cool sixty million. When the value of casino gambling at the rug joints plus bustout gambling and prostitution was added the total would be in excess of one hundred million.

With that kind of cash available it was easy to understand how Newport had bought immunity from local and state prosecution for so many years.

Just for fun I waded through the mass of records and found the file of The Spotted Calf, the cafe which advertised itself on matchbook covers at the Newport Gun Club. For June, 1960, the period during which I'd visited the club while being "protected," the operators reported accepting $5,532.

Commissioner Davis permitted attorney Leary to offer his defense for County Police Chief Stuart. It took two minutes. Stuart presented a March, 1958 order signed by County Judge Jolly which stipulated that the county patrol could "assist the police departments of the incorporated areas whenever called upon by the chief of police."

This order, said Leary, meant that Stuart could not enforce anti-gambling laws in any city unless requested to do so by the police chief of that city. Breckinridge responded that such an order was invalid inasmuch as it prohibited Stuart from doing his statutory duty.

Buckman asked that the hearings move to Newport so he could present a number of witnesses in defense of Roll. Davis agreed. When the proceedings continued, Buckman assembled a large group of politicians, officials, and Cincinnati reporters. All were willing to swear that Roll was a fine fellow. Under cross examination, however, they were also willing to swear that wide open gambling existed which apparently everyone but Roll knew about. After six such witnesses, Buckman dismissed the rest.

Ultimately, Combs ousted both men and later, after the heat had died, pardoned them. After all, they were good ole boys and had a lot of friends among the voters in Campbell County.

*****

Meanwhile, something really unusual happened.

On October 13, Stripper April Flowers was arrested in Cincinnati in a hotel room with Charles Polizzi, Jr.

The father of the thirty-year-old Polizzi was an early member of the Cleveland Syndicate and had once been part owner of record of the Beverly Hills, the Yorkshire, and the Lookout House. Yet here was young Charles, armed with a pistol for which he had a permit, escorting April to Lexington where she wanted to tell all.

Cincinnati police were happy enough to allow the couple to continue their journey. FBI Special Agent Frank Staab interviewed them at a Lexington motel. Polizzi explained that a contract had been let for April and he was protecting her from hit men. He could do so, he added, "because my old man has a lot of clout."

Staab and Assistant U.S. Attorney Mitchell Meade recorded April's version of the events before and after Ratterman's arrest. The federal grand jury was not in session, however, and April, after passing a lie detector test, was sent on her way without testifying.

Why the grand jury was not meeting was a question the "liberals" of Newport thought they could answer. Word passed around the stricken city that Frank Sinatra had personally intervened with Bobby Kennedy to delay the investigation. Sinatra was well known in Newport, having dropped thirty thousand dollars at the Beverly's crap tables several years earlier.

Source of this information was an alleged friend of Judge Paul Stapleton who was a high official in Justice. On a visit to Stapleton's office, the Judge called the official for my benefit, just to prove he could.

"If Ratterman was framed, why hasn't the federal grand jury done something about it?"

That was the question the "liberals" used in their election propaganda, confident all the while that the grand jury would not meet until after the election. This argument seemed to make sense and the reformers were suddenly alarmed.

I was at work in the City Room one October day doing routine stuff, and glad for a respite from Newport's turmoil, when I received a call from a frustrated Mitchell Meade. The young assistant U.S. Attorney confirmed the grand jury would not meet until after the election and he was convinced that Ratterman would lose if it did not.

"Can you do anything?" he asked.

What he wanted me to do was get Bobby Kennedy on the phone and persuade him to call the grand jury back into session. I tried. This time I could not reach the Attorney General and had to settle for a conversation with his press secretary, Ed Guthman. Ed almost fused the line when I told him the tale about Sinatra, but said a decision to delay had been to avoid the appearance of meddling in local politics. I argued that the federal grand jury could indict everybody in Newport after the election and nothing would change. Unless Ratterman was elected, all the progress made in four years of struggle would be lost.

Guthman was sympathetic but not very optimistic. I called Meade back and told him I had failed. Meade had another idea. If I could get April's story into the paper, it might create enough heat to change minds in Washington. She was in St. Louis at the moment. He'd been in daily contact with her and knew her telephone number.

"Give me her number and I'll give her a call," I promised.

At that moment, City Editor Herchenroeder handed me another press release to rewrite. I pushed it aside and called St. Louis. April answered. I looked around the room. Ora Spaid was not doing anything. I told him to listen in.

April recognized my name and when I told her that Meade had given me her number, she was willing to talk. I made notes furiously. So did Ora. The story came easily as if it had been told before.

She had, she said, appeared several times at the Tropicana and knew everyone rather well. She knew, for instance, that Gay Fine, a waitress, was the girl friend of Detective Ciafardini and Ciafardini came to the Club almost every night. He had been there late in the evening of May 8, but Gay was busy and he had left.

A couple of hours later, she continued, she had just begun her final act when Carinci appeared. He told her to cut the act short and go to his apartment to entertain "a dear friend." When she changed out of her mirrored costume and started to dress, Tito tossed her a robe and told her to hurry. He accompanied her up the elevator. She noticed that the casino was closing down early.

"They were running out the customers and the shills," she said.

Carinci left her at the door of his apartment and muttered something about getting a beer. In the living room she found another dancer, Rita Desmond, and a man later identified as Thomas Paisley.

(Paisley was the mutual friend of Carinci and Ratterman who had arranged the meeting of the two men at Carinci's request after Carinci asked help in getting out of the gambling racket.)

April said that the couple told her to go into the bedroom. She went in and found a man on the bed. He was fully clothed and seemed to be unconscious. She'd never seen him before. For that matter, she'd never seen Paisley before either.

"Hey, wake up," April said. When the man on the bed didn't respond, she went back to the living room to mix a drink from Carinci's private bar. Paisley and Rita had vanished so she took her drink back to the bedroom.

The man on the bed was still asleep. She shook his shoulder "and he mumbled something." Sitting down on the edge of the bed, she began to talk in an attempt to waken him.

At no time, April emphasized, did she take off her robe. About five minutes had passed, she estimated, when she heard voices in the outer room and a group of men rushed in. She recognized Ciafardini.

April went into the living room, leaving Ratterman fully clothed on the bed. She heard a noise from the bedroom "as if someone was fighting." A minute later, Ciafardini joined her.

"Pat, what's going on?" she asked.

The detective "gave me a hard look and winked as if I knew what it was all about."

"We're going to jail," he said.

The man from the bedroom, later identified as Ratterman, came out wrapped in a bedspread and held upright by two officers. April, wearing only her robe, went along. So did Carinci. In the police car, Carinci cried.

(Carinci apparently was an emotional individual. Another dancer told me that he often called her to his apartment to play her flute as he tried to relax.)

I asked April if Ratterman had given her the famous ballpoint pen and told her to use the phone number on it to call him up. She replied she'd not seen the pen until just before the police court trial when Lester told her what to say about it.

Upon being released by the police from jail about 3:25 a.m, April and Carinci returned to the Tropicana where April found her red convertible parked out front. Her clothes had been packed and stored in the car. She protested. Marty Buccieri, co-boss of the nightclub, finally ordered her bags carried back to her room. Carinci explained the original plan called for her to leave town after a picture had been made of her and Ratterman. Since no picture was made, she would be needed to testify at Ratterman's trial.

After receiving a phone call from Police Court Judge Rolf, Carinci said he had to go to Rolf's home. Another meeting followed with "Sleepout Louie" Levinson at the Flamingo Club. April was not present but Carinci told her about it.

She was told what to say at the police court trial and was promised a trip to Puerto Rico if she cooperated but got nothing.

"The racket boys are after me now," April said. "They want me to give them an affidavit retracting my statement to the FBI. I'm afraid for my life."

I asked the voice in St. Louis if she knew why the federal grand jury had postponed hearing her.

"No," she replied. "I wish they'd hurry up. I won't be safe until I testify."

I asked a few more questions, thanked her, and hung up. From the front of the room, my city editor bellowed:

"Hank, you got that story ready?"

"Coming up," I said.

Ora was busy telling Bob Clark, his nearest neighbor, all about April's revelations. I picked up the press release and knocked out a short article. Then I wrote April's story and took it in to Ben Reeves.

The assistant managing editor read the story twice and put on a worried expression.

"This is pretty hot," he said.

I waited.

"Would she sign an affidavit?"

"I guess I could ask her."

"Why don't you do that?" said Reeves.

I went back to my desk and got April on the phone. She sounded reluctant but when I mentioned that Meade wanted a story published, she agreed. I told her I'd be down next day.

Reeves approved the trip. On the following morning, I flew to St. Louis and took a cab to the shabby hotel in the theatrical district where the stripper was staying. A big man with young muscles refused to let me upstairs without April's permission. I used the house phone. The woman refused to see me. She'd told me the truth, she said, but she didn't want to swear to anything. I asked why.

"That prostitution charge they brought against me in Newport is still hanging over me," she said. "What's more, if I signed an affidavit and the federal grand jury didn't do anything, they might get me for perjury. A girl can't be too careful."

I argued in vain. The big bruiser at the desk became restive. Obviously, he didn't want his guests disturbed. Hell, maybe Chuck Polizzi, Jr. had assigned him to guard her.

Frustrated, I went back to the airport. Upon arriving in Louisville, I went home and re-wrote my story. Then I called Ed Zingman, the attorney who handled libel matters for the *C-J*. I read the story to him, and told him that Religion Writer Ora Spaid had listened to the conversation and could confirm my quotes. Moreover, I said, I'd been to St. Louis and identified April as the person I talked to.

"Go ahead and run it," said Zingman.

After all, he was a law partner of Lieutenant Governor Wilson Wyatt who had made April a Kentucky Colonel and then decommissioned her.

Next day I reported again to Reeves and told him Zingman had approved the story. Still, he hesitated. In spite of my frustration, I realized suddenly the problems of an editor who must risk his career on the ability and integrity of a reporter.

"Would the FBI confirm it?" asked Reeves.

The *C-J* wasn't on speaking terms with the Federal Bureau of Investigation and had not been since the days when the Bureau aided the late Scott Hamilton on his witch hunt. Yet I had a special relationship with Frank Staab.

"I'll try," I promised.

I called the FBI office and asked for Staab. A secretary asked who was calling. I told her, and wished too late that I had arranged a code name with Staab.

The veteran special agent picked up the phone and in a loud voice said:

"Hello, Hank Messick."

I thought I understood. In a louder than usual voice, I told him I had some information I wanted to share. He said that was kind of me and I read the story I had written about April. When I finished. Staab said loudly:

"Thanks very much, Hank. That's good information, but there's nothing there we don't already know. It's all true but we already have it."

I wondered if the FBI recorded incoming conversations.

Back to Reeves I went and told him the FBI confirmed the story in every detail. Reeves sighed.

"Okay, we'll run it. But change the lead. We've already said that Ratterman was framed."

The newspapers' editorial writers had said so, but I had not. Nevertheless, I changed the lead to make it read that April Flowers claimed she was framed as well. My editor accepted that version, took the copy, and with a sigh of relief, I called Mitchell Meade in Lexington and Jack Cook in Newport to tell them to read *The Courier-Journal* next day.

Reeves played the story below the break on the front page with a two column head. The Associated Press picked it up and the Cincinnati newspapers spread it all over their front pages. I received ecstatic calls from Cook and Breckinridge. Late on the day the story ran, I got a call from Meade.

"Guess what?" he asked.

"What?" I replied.

"The federal grand jury will reconvene at 9:30 a.m. on Friday, October 27. Day after tomorrow. Congratulations."

"I guess I've got another story." I said, reaching for my pencil. "Give me the skinny."

*****

Lexington was an easy drive from Louisville in Bluegrass country. Personally, the grass didn't seem much different there than elsewhere, but it was part of the tradition. Rolling pastures surrounded by plank fences painted white dotted the area. Inside the fences, thoroughbreds pranced. Each farm had its oval race track and its quota of rugged looking men and women armed with stop watches.

Not surprisingly, such people liked to bet but, being busy, they usually phoned in their wagers. On an earlier visit I had at the request of Bill Hummel, chief of IRS Intelligence for Kentucky, visited a handbook in downtown Lexington. The joint did a big business, but the IRS had been unable to crack it. With a little luck, I got inside and discovered the telephone operators were in the attic. A staircase unfolded from the ceiling at the press of a button. Following my visit, the IRS raided the joint.

On this day the first witness heard by the federal grand jury was April. She was whisked in and out by a back route to avoid the mob of reporters and TV cameramen. We could see her through a door in the courtroom. She wore a two piece gray suit and was smiling.

Another witness was stripper Bonnie Green who had found a husband since her appearance in Newport in May. Escorted by two federal marshals, she was allowed to leave through the main door and walk down a long corridor to the elevator. As all male eyes watched the retreating figure, she rotated her hips in an exaggerated but professional grind. Reporters grinned at each other.

A third witness was Newport Special Counsel Hirschfeld, law partner of Danny Davies and the man who had prosecuted Ratterman in police court. Hirschfeld didn't look happy when he emerged. Asked for comment, he said:

"This isn't Campbell County where everyone stands around babbling."

And no one stood around lying either. At least they didn't since August when the federal grand jury indicted the Bridewells on perjury charges.

George Ratterman was the final witness. He looked lean and alert as he came out of the courtroom. The jury, he said, had wanted to review the testimony he had given months before. He was on his way to San Francisco where on Sunday he was to do analysis for a professional football game telecast.

A period of inactivity followed the departure of the witnesses. It became an hour. Were the grand jurors debating who to indict?

About 4:00 p.m. a young reporter from the Lexington bureau of the *C-J* came dashing up. He was out of breath, but upon seeing me he relaxed. The Associated Press out of Washington was saying that a number of indictments in the Ratterman case had been returned.

I told him Washington had jumped the gun and that, in any case, I was there to take care of it. Gladly, he left it to me.

Meade came out and took me aside. The delay, he explained, was because the grand jurors were writing a formal report. Such reports were discouraged in federal court on the grounds they tended to prejudice the cases of those indicted, but Judge H. Church Ford considered the Newport situation worthy of comment and had given the jurors permission to say what they pleased. Not knowing that a report was being written, the Washington officials had announced indictments at a prearranged time.

It was one more indication these grand jurors had minds of their own.

About a half an hour later, the doors to the courtroom were opened and the press allowed inside. Judge Ford took a seat and the twenty-three grand jurors arranged themselves before him. Foreman Laurie

Blakey presented the report. The Judge ordered it read. It began bluntly enough:

"The foul odors of vice, corruption, and bribery cover Campbell County officialdom like a pall."

Other highlights:

"Testimony indicates that both elected and appointed officials are receiving monthly payoffs to influence them in the non-enforcement of the laws..."

"We have reached the inescapable conclusion that there has been no effort whatsoever on the part of the local police of Newport, or the County Patrol, or the sheriff of Campbell County to enforce criminal laws of the Commonwealth of Kentucky relating to gambling and vice."

"We have also reached the conclusion that there has been no effort on the part of the commonwealth's attorney, county attorney, or city attorney to do anything whatsoever to carry out their sworn duties to enforce the law..."

"The primary force which can rectify this disgraceful situation lies in the people of Campbell County, Kentucky and in their ability to elect officials who will enforce the laws..."

There was much more — references to layoff betting, to the numbers racket, to lawyers who should be disbarred. And, finally, there were indictments.

Charged with conspiring to violate, and with violating, the civil rights of Ratterman were Lester, Buccieri, Carinci, and police officers Ciafardini, White, and Quitter.

It was almost deadline for the street edition. I went over to the Lexington bureau, wrote my story, and sent it in by teletype. The newspaper gave it an eight column banner.

FOURTEEN

November '61

On the day before the voters cast their ballots, the regular Campbell County grand jury was impaneled by Judge Murphy. Ten women and two men were selected.

Noting that "a valid order" to continue the investigation of officials was on the books — thanks to Judge Hill — Murphy said he would divide the work of the grand jury into two parts. Routine affairs would be taken up first and Wise would officiate. When that was completed, a commonwealth's attorney pro tem would be appointed to handle the investigation. Named foreman was the operator of a small firm which manufactured seat covers in Newport. The man wore a seat-cover advertisement on the back of his jacket, making him easy to identify.

The grand jury should wait until after the election to begin its work, the judge added.

I was the only reporter present at the impaneling of the grand jury in contrast to earlier occasions. It was, I thought, an indication that everyone realized the final judgment rested with the voters. What that judgment would be was the question on everyone's mind. Proponents of the status quo were loud in their predictions of a liberal triumph, but the leaders of the Switch to Honesty Party were quietly confident. In Louisville my editors, excepting Pope, had assured me Ratterman had no chance. Newport had always been a hell hole and would remain one.

I filed my story and spent the balance of the afternoon wandering around the almost deserted town. Nothing seemed to be operating.

Screw Andrews' $300,000 palace at the foot of York Street had been completed, but it was padlocked. Screw had neglected to pay the contractor and liens against the structure had been filed. Presumably, if Ratterman lost, the numbers racketeer would pay his debts and open for business.

As darkness gathered, I walked by Vivian's place. The little lighted doorbell was not burning.

Jack Cook spotted me and called me to his car. Ratterman had disappeared, he said. Since the episode in May, the candidate had been kept on a leash. He was supposed to go nowhere alone and to be in touch at all times with some member of a watchdog committee. About an hour ago, he had vanished.

"The bastards may have killed him," said Jack, worry in his voice. "It's about the only way they could still win."

I got into the car and discussed all the possibilities. Suddenly I had an inspiration.

"I understand the opposition is holding a rally in the basement of the Playtorium," I said. "Do you suppose he went there?"

"It would be bearding the lion in his den," said Jack, "but it's just the thing George would do. Let's go look."

The parking lot in front of the Playtorium contained a half a hundred cars. We parked and Jack led the way. The basement had been the casino before gambling was moved next door to the Snax Bar. We found it full of people. Free beer had been provided and everyone was drinking as if the issue to be voted upon next day was wet or dry. Mayor Mussman attempted to preside, but the "liberals" seemed equally divided between Republican Howe and Democrat Peluso. Tempers were rising among the unemployed gamblers, pimps, and prostitutes.

Conspicuous among them by the seat-cover advertisement on his back was the foreman of the new grand jury.

I proved to be a unifying influence, someone all could dislike. They formed a long congo line and weaved their way around me. On command, the line halted and everyone held his nose. The message was pretty plain.

Mussman, his face flushed and his collar open, confirmed that

"Saint George" had been in a few minutes before and had tried to make a speech. The mayor thought the attempt both stupid and typical of a do-gooder.

"We don't go to his rallies," said Mussman.

"Red Masterson does," I replied.

I stared at the swarming mob and realized that I was no longer afraid. It was an exhilarating sensation. In all my past trips to Newport I had carried a hard ball of fear in the pit of my stomach. Now it was gone.

The drunks broke up, forgot about me, and began shouting insults at each other. Several arguments started and in the murky light I saw steel flash.

"Let's get out of here," said Jack Cook.

I was reluctant to go. My new found courage made me enjoy the mob scene. Old Newport was dying before my eyes. Cook tugged at my arm.

Once outside, Jack found a telephone and confirmed that Ratterman was back in touch with his guardians. I went to my hotel where on a television news program was Tony Warndorf, a candidate for Newport city commission. He had been foreman of the trial jury that had acquitted Sheriff Roll in 1960. Now he was denouncing do-gooders and the restrictions they imposed. He stated with a straight if flushed face:

"Laws! To hell with them. There's not one that wasn't made to be broken."

That seemed to sum it up nicely.

Election day dawned clear and cold. Still feeling brave, I went over early and spent the morning wandering from precinct to precinct. The Switch to Honesty Party had been organized so Ratterman could have observers at the polls to challenge unqualified voters and make sure the election was honest. They were kept busy. At one precinct a large number of women who had formerly worked in brothels razed by the urban renewal program, were successfully challenged. Danny Davies blustered in vain. Of one hundred and forty registered, only sixty were qualified.

So it went all around town. Automobiles bearing large American flags and green "Local Self Government" stickers were everywhere in evidence. Presumably they were carrying voters to the polls. Some were carried to several precincts only to be denied the right to vote more than once. Ratterman's headquarters were in a rented office two blocks from the courthouse. About noon, someone hurled a brick through the plate glass window. Campaign workers decorated the hole with red, white, and blue ribbons.

When I visited campaign headquarters, the staff bowed low as I entered. When I asked why, one of the women, a pretty one, gave me a kiss.

"For the April Flowers story," she said.

All the Ratterman people were happy and confident. Everything was going according to plan. The turnout in the county outside Newport was unusually heavy.

At lunch in the Playtorium. I overheard two gamblers talking about a friend who wasn't eligible to vote and was afraid he would be challenged if he tried.

"I told him," said one man, "to go down to the poll and wait. Sooner or later, the challenger will go out for coffee. Then you can sneak in and vote before she gets back."

In mid-afternoon I broke off to write the second half of the story that would appear next day. It was so worded that it would stand regardless of who won. At its end I noted that whatever the outcome of the election, "it was a foregone conclusion by gambler and reformer alike that Newport as a 'sin city' is dead." After filing the story, I called the *C-J* to tell them what was coming and what I expected to happen.

"Ratterman is going to win," I added.

Ben Reeves thought me very funny.

Optimism continued to grow at Ratterman headquarters as darkness fell. At the courthouse, where the official vote would be tabulated, the mood was surly. Reporters from Cincinnati gathered there to await results. I went back to the office with the broken window. Arrangements had been made for Ratterman's poll watchers to phone in unofficial results as quickly as they were counted.

By 9:00 p.m. those results were in. Ratterman carried Campbell County with 12,610 votes. Peluso was far behind with 7,070. Howe got

6,663. The biggest surprise was not the reform candidate's showing in Newport where he trailed Peluso by only 500 votes, but his victory in Southgate, home of the Beverly Hills.

Howe had expected to hurt Ratterman in wealthy Fort Thomas but George won his home town by a four to one majority. The more than 26,000 votes cast in the election was an off-year record. There was one bit of bad news. Four reformers running for city commission were narrowly defeated. Yet even that made clear the basic fact that Newport had stagnated while the county around it increased in population. The balance of power had shifted to the suburbs.

There was a telephone booth just outside. I arranged my notes and put in a collect call to the *C-J*. Old reliable Dick Hunter was on rewrite and I dictated the top half of my story. He took it efficiently and offered his congratulations.

"At least the editorial boys backed one winner," he said.

"What do you mean?"

"The Republicans swept both the city and county down here," he explained.

"Wonderful!"

And it was wonderful. The corrupt democratic machine that had ruled Jefferson county for generations was beaten. I hoped my earlier stories about the county police force, the jail, and city police scandals had been a factor. For me, the night had brought double victory.

I called Faye to give her the good news.

"Does this mean you can come home and stay awhile?" asked the mother of my three children.

"Yes," I replied. "I suppose it does."

"Then it is good news," said my wife. "I'm delighted for all of us."

"See you tomorrow," I said. "Right now, I'm going to a victory party."

"We'll have our own when you get home."

As I hung up, I saw a group of men approaching down the street. They proved to be Cincinnati reporters. When the trend towards Ratterman became apparent, the official count at the courthouse had been suspended. Perhaps those counting had simply wanted to delay the inevitable, or maybe the idea was to give Lester — now back in town — time to think of something. In any case the reporters asked my help in obtaining the results. I was glad to share the good news.

Shortly thereafter I was taken to a spacious home in Fort Thomas where champagne was flowing. Gathered there were many familiar faces — Protestant ministers, Catholic priests, wealthy business types, and men and women from "the Bottoms." I looked for Chris Seifried but did not find him. Dudley Pomeroy came over to shake hands.

"Did you think the day we first met that so many things would have to happen before you won?" I asked.

"God moves in mysterious ways," he said with a grin. "What are you going to do for an encore?"

"I'd like to check out the Cleveland Syndicate. Find out if there really is such a thing and, if so, how it developed. I don't know if the paper would let me, however."

Others present were also looking ahead. In two years the terms of Murphy and Wise would expire. If they could be replaced by men such as Benton, the gains made today could be consolidated. There was every confidence this would happen. It did.

After awhile the excitement ebbed and I persuaded someone to take me to my hotel. Next day, as if to provide a footnote, a moving van backed up to Vivian Schultz's front door and loaded up a lot of beds. Women members of the Committee of Five Hundred trailed the van to storage.

Back in Louisville I was greeted with some respect by my city editor. He told me that Mark Ethridge wanted to see me when I arrived. Downstairs in the richly appointed office, Ethridge shook my hand and promised I would receive a substantial pay raise and other goodies. Bingham, he added, shared his appreciation for the work I had done.

I was pleased — and tired enough to accept good fortune at face value.

In December, as if to add bourbon to the branch water, a federal grand jury indicted ex-Sheriff Roll on four counts of failing to file income tax returns.

And a few days later, another federal grand jury indicted Screw

RAZZLE DAZZLE

Andrews, two of his nephews including one named Frank Andriola, and four black men on thirty-five counts of wagering tax evasion.

It was only then that James Pope dropped the shoe he had been holding for a year and announced his retirement. Bingham appointed Norman Isaacs to be executive editor of both newspapers.

"There goes your Pulitzer," said Faye when I brought the news home.

"There goes the *C-J*," I replied. "From now on, it'll be all razzle-dazzle - all show and no substance."

(My prediction came all too true. The Bingham family proved incapable of managing the newspapers and after several years of frustration, sold them to the Gannett chain.)

We sat in silence for several minutes. I looked at Faye's troubled face. The fate of a great newspaper meant less to her than the question of how I could make a living and send our children to college. It would be difficult if not impossible to keep working at the paper, but I would give it a try.

We stared at each other. I forced a laugh.

"One thing is sure. They can't bring back the Old Newport."

"Not immediately, anyway," said Faye.

AFTERWORD

An exodus of good reporters began immediately after Isaacs took charge. I hung on grimly until Mark Ethridge, as one of his last acts of kindness before leaving the newspapers, arranged for me to receive Ford Foundation grants to study organized crime in the United States over a two-year period.

Several books resulted from my investigations. The first one, *The Silent Syndicate*, traced the evolution and development of the Cleveland Syndicate which since 1940 had controlled Newport. Another, *Syndicate Wife*, concerned Michael "Trigger Mike" Coppola, the man who had financed Screw Andrews aka Andriola.

Andrews and his colleagues were found guilty of reporting for tax purposes only one-seventh of his wagering tax income. All went to prison after appeals failed.

The trial of those charged with conspiring to violate Ratterman's civil rights ended in a hung jury. In a second trial a year later, Lester and Buccieri were found guilty. Ultimately the Sixth Circuit Court of Appeals upheld the convictions and commented, "The evidence was sufficient to convict all the defendants on all of the charges."

Carinci did not escape. New indictments were brought charging him and his associates at the Glenn Hotel with not reporting a profit of $1,302,685 earned on razzle-dazzle from 1958 through 1960. The joint where Ratterman was arrested burned mysteriously in 1962. Carinci was sent to prison at Terre Haute, Indiana. His prison stay was interrupted by a new trial on additional charges. This time he pleaded guilty.

Ratterman, in cooperation with Federal agencies, closed down Newport gambling completely. The climax came in 1962 when sheriff's deputies raided all bookie joints having a federal wagering tax stamp, and IRS agents simultaneously hit every place not having one. Citizens rallied to his support. Both Wise and Murphy, in office since 1940, were defeated in re-election bids by reformers pledged to support the sheriff.

With gambling and vice eliminated, the entire northern Kentucky area boomed. New industry moved in and the urban renewal program replaced the old buildings in the "Bottoms." Even a university was built just east of the Beverly Hills Country Club. Yet a strange phenomenon was noted - no one in authority wanted to credit the upsurge in economic activity to the elimination of gambling. For decades, Kentucky had pretended "Little Mexico" didn't exist so how could one admit it was gone. Only a few old timers talked about "the good ole days."

Victory is never permanent. As I wrote in *Syndicate in the Sun*, "It is an unhappy fact that reform movements often begin to disintegrate in the moment of victory." As this is written, legal gambling is spreading across the United States and voices are urging that gambling boats be legalized on the Indiana side of the Ohio River. The anything-for-a-buck mentality that made Old Newport a hell hole has gained respectability. Gambling, legal or otherwise, has inevitably brought corruption. History will almost certainly repeat itself as a new generation ignores the lessons of the past.

As the Kefauver Committee said in 1951: "It is the nature of the business of gambling, and not its legality or illegality, that makes it so attractive and lucrative for gangsters and hoodlums."

APPENDIX

This appendix is a collection of letters written to James S. Pope, Sr., the Executive Editor of the *Louisville Courier-Journal* in 1961. The letters commend Hank Messick's work in exposing the syndicate's workings in Newport and Campbell County, Kentucky.

MOEBUS, COOK, KIRCHHOFF AND NEISCH
ATTORNEYS AT LAW

STANLEY C. MOEBUS
HENRY J. COOK
MARTIN ROY KIRCHHOFF
D WRAYBURN NEISCH

DONALD LOSEY
HARRISON M. STACY

September 22, 1961

8 EAST FOURTH STREET
NEWPORT, KENTUCKY

11 SOUTH FT. THOMAS AVENUE
FT. THOMAS, KENTUCKY

PRIVATE BRANCH EXCHANGE
AX 1-2487

Honorable James S. Pope, Sr.
Executive Editor
Louisville Courier Journal
Louisville, Kentucky

       Re: Hank Messick

Dear Mr. Pope:

I have come to know Hank Messick personally since my return to Newport, Kentucky, on May 1, 1961. However, I have known him by reputation much longer and by the articles he has written in the past three years while covering our County of Campbell. His stories of the wide open commercialized gambling, vice and official corruption running rampant here have opened the eyes of all Kentuckians and they have had tremendous impact upon our state and federal officials. It is my opinion that Hank's articles were instrumental in bringing about the help we are now getting from both these sources.

My experience with news writers has been widespread. My law career commenced in 1936; I was a candidate for U. S. Congress at the same time Wendell L. Willkie was running for President; my candidacy for Circuit Judge was sponsored by the Campbell County Civic Association in 1950 and I served by presidential appointment as United States Attorney for the Eastern District of Kentucky from 1955 to 1960. In all that period of time, I have come to know many experienced and competent reporters, but none compare with your Hank Messick. His educational background, innate ability and pure bulldog tenacity serves him well in his desire to "dig" out the news and his articles reflect all the traits necessary to classify him as an excellent reporter.

I commend Hank for the job he has done for all the citizens of Campbell County, expecially while working under the circumstances here. He has taken verbal abuse and derision from those persons interested in retaining the sordid conditions we believe now are on the way out. Some of these persons who have treated Hank in this manner are elected and appointed city and county officials, who's duty it is to enforce the very laws we seek enforced.

         Very truly yours,

         Henry J. Cook
         MOEBUS, COOK, KIRCHHOFF & NEISCH

HJC/gc

OFFICE PHONE 5-2024 RESIDENCE PHONE 7-1951

LAW OFFICES
JOHN C. ANGGELIS
300-303 BANK OF COMMERCE BLDG
LEXINGTON, KENTUCKY

September 29, 1961

Mr. James S. Pope, Sr.
Executive Editor
Courier-Journal
Louisville, Kentucky

       Re: Mr. Hank Messick

Dear Mr. Pope:

Mr. Hank Messick, Courier-Journal reporter, made a tremendous impression on me when his articles on the Newport vice were read. It sounded almost fantastic to read that a newspaper reporter had the courage and the conviction to invade the shocking Newport vice in its backrooms, alleys and houses of prostitution, in order to give a factual report to the Commonwealth of Kentucky.

I write this letter not only as a concerned citizen but as the attorney for the Newport Ministerial Association. It may be stated simply that Mr. Messick's constant invasion of syndicated crime in the Newport area was the singular factor which gave encouragement and leadership to the ministers and laymen who were looking for a battle plan against open and notorious syndicated crime. His leadership and valor can also be contrasted with his unimpeachable character by refusing to be intimidated or bribed.

Mr. Messick's extraordinary efforts of three years with the ministers and laymen prepared the way for over two hundred indictments which were returned by the recent special Grand Jury. These indictments are proof of the great job done by Mr. Messick on the Newport assignment.

It is a distinct pleasure for me as a citizen and as the attorney for the Ministerial Association to write

Mr. James S. Pope, Sr.
September 29, 1961
Page --2--

this letter of commendation not only to praise Mr. Messick's success, but with the hope that he will continue the fight with his outstanding factual reporting.

                                        Sincerely yours,

                                        JOHN C. KNUCKLES

JCK
bjh

NEWPORT MINISTERIAL ASSOCIATION
Box 600
NEWPORT, KENTUCKY

September 22, 1961

Mr. James S. Pope, Managing Editor
Louisville Courier-Journal
Louisville, Kentucky

Dear Sir:

The Newport Ministerial Association desires to commend your Reporter, Harry Messeck, for his untiring efforts and his innumerable accomplishments in behalf of law and order in Newport and Campbell County during the past three years. His work has been most vital to every accomplishment made by our Association and its Social Action Committee.

Mr. Messeck has confronted every gambler and gambling establishment, personally, without regard to his own safety. He has investigated gambling activities and fearlessly reported his findings under threats from the underworld. He has reminded the law enforcement agencies of the city and the county of the evidences of lawlessness he has found, personally and by the printed page in spite of the ridicule these agencies of government heaped upon him. He has publicly testified, in courts, before grand juries and hearings, to what he knows of vice in the area, without fear. He has done his work in the face of indifference on the part of reporters and editors of both local newspapers and has taken ridicule from them. Through his efforts, Mr. Messeck has practically forced the local papers to face the issues in Campbell County and publicize them.

It is our hope that this commendation will be of assistance in gaining national acclaim for Mr. Messeck. He deserves it if any one does.

Sincerely yours,

Rev. Donald J. Witzl,
Secretary

DJW:cs

OFFICE
EDWARD G. HILL
CIRCUIT COURT JUDGE
26TH. JUDICIAL DISTRICT
HARLAN, KENTUCKY

September 16, 1961

Mr. James S. Pope, Sr
Executive Editor, Courier Journal
Louisville, Kentucky

Dear Sir:

I wish to commend Mr. Hank Messick for his diligent work as your reporter during the recent grand jury probe of vice and gambling conditions in Newport and Campbell County, Kentucky. I do not pose to have the knowledge of the technical qualities of newspaper reporting; however, I might advise you that it has been my practice since I have been Circuit Judge to hold "open house" in my court so far as the news media are concerned, and by virtue of this policy, I have been in a position to observe many reporters.

I found Mr. Messick to be fearless and agressive and his astute ability as a reporter brought to light well-hidden, salient facts relative to the gambling and vice conditions in Newport and Campbell County, Kentucky.

I might say it is my thought that Mr. Messick went far beyond his call of duty as a reporter while working under perhaps physical threats and a negative atmosphere.

Respectfully yours,

Edward G. Hill

EGH/s

COMMONWEALTH OF KENTUCKY
OFFICE OF THE ATTORNEY GENERAL
FRANKFORT

JOHN B BRECKINRIDGE
ATTORNEY GENERAL

October 3, 1961

Mr. James S. Polk, Sr.
Executive Editor of the Courier Journal
Sixth and Broadway
Louisville, Kentucky

Dear Mr. Polk:

    I am taking the liberty of writing in connection with the major public service which, in my opinion, Mr. Hank Messick has rendered in informing the public of the conditions obtaining in Newport, Campbell County, Kentucky. Mr. Messick's diligence, patience and relentless pursuit and, through you, publication of the facts has perhaps contributed more than any other single factor to the action of the recent special Campbell County Grand Jury.

    It is my understanding that Mr. Messick has suffered personal indignities and abuse, as well as being subjected to vilification and vandalism, to say nothing of threats of physical violence at the hands of those whom the record clearly establishes are capable of executing such acts. He has, nonetheless, continued to expose himself in the pursuit of news and to publish his findings in the face of the possible consequences.

    The concert of federal, state, local authorities and an aroused citizenry which has finally been brought to bear upon the nation-wide criminal elements operating out of Newport could not, in my opinion, have been effected without the groundwork having been laid by the press. Mr. Messick's articles have constituted a major contribution within the Commonwealth to this end result. His continuing activities will greatly facilitate an

Mr. James S. Polk, Sr.
Page Two
October 3, 1961

ultimate conclusion reestablishing law and order in the community; needless to say, his work has perhaps but begun.

    I trust you will not consider my remarks presumptious, but I am cognizant of the importance of recognizing such outstanding services when they have been rendered - and Mr. Messick has been performing in this particular area over the thankless years.

    With every best wish, I remain

              Sincerely yours,

JBB:ghc

Thomas Emery's Sons, Inc.

Established 1840   Carew Tower   Incorporated 1925

Cincinnati, Ohio
ZONE 1

December 26th, 1961

Mr. James S. Pope, Sr.
Executive Editor
Louisville Courier-Journal
Louisville, Kentucky

Dear Mr. Pope:

The purpose of this letter is to commend you and the Courier-Journal for the excellent coverage afforded the citizens of Campbell County during the past year with regard to our efforts to improve our local government and to rid our community of the flagrant vices which have prevailed there for a number of years.

Your reporter, Mr. Hank Messick, has done a magnificent job in this respect. All the citizens of Campbell County owe him a debt of gratitude. His coverage has been extremely thorough.

Last month I was elected sheriff of Campbell County. In the early stages of the campaign for that post the opposition to reform in our community had attempted to cloud the basic issue by creating a scandal between a dancer named April Flowers and me. Mr. Messick served to remove this cloud in the minds of the voters by his published interview with Miss Flowers prior to the election last fall. For this interview in particular, and for his many other examples of timely and accurate reporting, we owe him much.

I should like to thank you personally, and I speak in accord with the feelings of a great majority of the citizens of Campbell County, for assigning such an excellent reporter as Hank Messick to our community.

                                        Sincerely,

                                        George W. Ratterman

GWR/ns

SOCIAL ACTION COMMITTEE
NEWPORT MINISTERIAL ASSOCIATION
NEWPORT, KENTUCKY

September 29, 1961

Mr. James S. Pope, Sr.
Executive Secretary
Courier Journal
Louisville, Kentucky

Mr. Pope:

The Social Action Committee of the Newport Ministerial Association wants to express its appreciation for the support the Courier Journal has given the efforts to rid Newport of vice and corruption.

We especially want to commend your feature writer Hank Messick for his untiring efforts to ferret out the news, and for the fine manner in which the articles were written. Hank's efforts and his articles were instrumental in gaining the support of all the major church denominations in Kentucky, and we feel they also had an effect on Governor Combs and Attorney General Breckinridge's decision to bring about the "ouster proceedings". This hearing has led to an investigation by the Campbell County grand jury, the returning of over 100 indictments including the Mayor, City Manager, three Commissioners, and a number of police officials of Newport.

These indictments have caused an almost complete cessation of gambling, prostitution and illegal sale of alcoholic beverages in Newport and Campbell County. If there is any one factor which can be pointed out as having the greatest impact in bringing about all this, we feel it is Hank Messick.

On the third anniversary of your support, we just want to say thanks to you and to Hank.

Sincerely,

Christian F. Seifried

Christian F. Seifried, Chairman
184 Kentucky Drive

DEPARTMENT OF PUBLIC SAFETY
DIVISION OF KENTUCKY STATE POLICE
NEW STATE OFFICE BUILDING
FRANKFORT, KENTUCKY

November 10, 1961

Honorable James S. Pope, Sr.
Executive Editor
Courier-Journal
Louisville, Kentucky

Dear Mr. Pope:

   During the last few months while in Newport to testify before the Campbell County Grand Jury relative to vice conditions, I had an occasion to meet your reporter, Hank Messick. It occurred to me at that time that this man probably had made the greatest single contribution to the many investigated events of late which have ultimately led to the actual shut down of Newport's varied and sordid vice operations.

   Hank began reporting on conditions in Northern Kentucky in 1958, and I know that he has been before the Grand Jury each year since that time, giving accounts of conditions which he has personally witnessed. I also know that he has been subjected to much abuse and numerous threats. In spite of this, Hank has pugnaciously pursued his objective of reporting fearlessly the truth. Even though a reporter traditionally has the responsibility to dig out the truth, I think that the service which he has rendered in this instance has called for an abundance of courage and a dedication to the task that few men have.

   Not only would I like to commend you and your newspaper for the great service which you have done for our Commonwealth by virtue of making Hank's stories possible, but I also would like to commend Hank to you and to those who consider nominations for a Pulitzer Prize. It is my firm conviction that Hank Messick is most deserving of such a nomination, and that both Kentuckians and Americans owe him a deep debt of gratitude for having begun the removal of a blight which is symptomatic of a decay of our moral fiber.

           Sincerely yours,

            Colonel David A. Espie
            Director

DAE:chj

THE H. J. HOSEA AND SONS COMPANY

BRIGHTON ST. AND C. & O. R. R.
NEWPORT, KENTUCKY U.S.A.
PHONE AXTEL 1-2739

September 26, 1961

Mr. James S. Pope, Jr.,
Executive Editor
The Courier-Journal
Louisville, Kentucky

Dear Sir:

We have had the pleasure of working with your reporter, Hank Messick, on the Campbell County situation for a number of months. During that time I have had occasion to read all of his stories and reports in your newspaper and have dealt with him personally on many occassions.

All of us feel that Mr. Messick has performed an outstanding journalistic task as has your newspaper. During all of that time he has exhibited great integrity, a determination to get the facts no matter whom they may have helped or harmed, and a sincere dedication to his task. He has been subjected to considerable personal abuse, great resentment from some sources, and, in some cases, a bitter antagonism that would have discouraged and impaired the functions of a lesser man. However, through all of the foregoing he has exhibited great personal courage and ability and has maintained an objectivity and complete fairness to all concerned.

We have the highest regard for your reporter, Mr. Messick and appreciate your sending him into our community. If any award is available for fine journalistic endeavor he is certainly entitled thereto and we will be the first to so attest.

Again we thank you and Mr. Messick for giving us much needed assistance in our effort to make our community a better place in which to live and rear our children.

The undersigned is president of the Committee of 500 of Campbell County, Kentucky.

Very truly yours,

Henry J. Hosea

HJH/VF

INDEX

Ackerman, Bishop Richard H. 110
Accardo, Tony 74
Alcoholic Beverage Control 67, 70, 113
Andrews, "Screw"(Frank Andriola,) 7, 23, 52-54, 61, 74, 106, 122, 139, 146, 147, 159, 172, 178, 190, 194-196
Anggelis, John 135, 145, 155, 195, 200, 201
Asheville Citizen 6
Associated Press 14, 185, 187
Atlanta 16
Aunt Mattie 14

Bahamas 173
Bailey, George 23, 76
Baker, Reverend Donald 55-58, 60, 64, 70, 117, 156
Barkhau, Reverend (Dr.) Harold 47, 60, 66, 70, 77, 156
Beckley, Gilbert 149, 160
Belmont Snak Bar 52, 54, 71, 95, 96, 102, 103, 165, 173
Bennett, Reverend George 59, 64, 68, 70, 77, 146
Benton, Frank V. III 157, 163, 194
Berman, Joe 149
Bernadini, Cesare 60, 81-84, 90-92, 156, 169, 177
Bertelsman, Otis 104
Beverly Hills Country Club 45, 50, 52, 59, 61, 85, 95, 113, 134, 136, 141-142, 146, 149, 153, 173, 177-178, 180, 193, 197
Bingham, Barry, Sr. 20, 25, 33, 34, 38, 61, 72, 75, 194, 195
Bingham, Sally 21
Bingham, Worth 21
Black Mountain 10
Blackey, Laurie 187
Blue Ridge 10
Blue Ridge Electric 9, 169
Bottoms, the 44, 194, 197
Breckinridge, John 73, 136, 145-148, 151-176, 179, 185, 204-205
Bridewell, Ralph 89, 91-92
Bridewell brothers 57, 147-148, 187
Buccieri, Mary 121, 130-131, 183, 188, 196
Buckley, Jerry 91
Buckman, J. D. "Jiggs" 145, 148, 167, 179
Burke, Edmund 36
Bynum Hall 8

Canton 6
Campbell County Grand Jury 53, 84, 107-108, 151-172
Carinci, Tito 50, 117, 119, 121, 125, 126-128, 131, 141, 142, 149
Carrollton 64, 86

Castro, Fidel 72-73, 97
Central Avenue 61
Chapel Hill 1, 8, 10, 35
Chandler, A. B. "Happy" 18, 25, 66, 69, 72-73, 133, 141
Churchill Downs 26, 39, 115
Ciafardini, Pat 95, 116-118, 126, 128 142, 147, 174, 176, 181-182, 188
Cincinnati Enquirer 60
Cincinnati Post & Times-Star 146
Cincinnati Reds 158, 178
Clark Bridge, 24, 30
Cleveland Browns 110
Cleveland, Dr. Frank 119, 120
Cleveland Syndicate 48, 52, 61, 73, 94, 137, 145, 149, 170, 176, 180, 194, 196
Clark, Bob 183
Clooney, Rosemary 20
Coffin, Dean Oscar "Skipper" 1, 3, 5, 8, 14
Colorado A&M 5
Columbia Street 51
Combs, Governor Bert T. 72-73, 108, 113, 135, 141, 146, 153, 179
Commitee of 500 111-112, 114, 116, 194
Cook, Henry 61, 116, 125, 133, 142, 147, 152, 168, 199
Cook, Jack 60, 64, 120, 123, 127-132, 185, 190-191
Coppola, "Trigger" Mike 139, 160, 196
Cottonmill Song 11
County Police Merit Board 35
Courier Journal (C-J) 16-17, 21-23, 30, 33-34, 37, 41, 52, 54, 56, 62-63, 66, 69, 72, 74-75, 84, 92, 97-98, 106-109, 120, 124, 126, 129, 141, 163, 184, 187, 192-193, 195
Court of Appeals 152, 176, 196
Croft, John 146, 149
Cumberland Falls State Park 142

Dade County Florida 29

Dalitz, Moe 149
Daniels, Jonathan 17
Davies, Danny 82, 90, 101, 125, 166, 177, 187, 191
Davis, John L. 145, 149, 167, 177, 179
Desert Inn 137
Desmond, Rita 125, 182
Detroy, Lawrence "the Barber" 111
Devine, Irvine "Nig" 159
Dixie Highway 39
Drahmann, Virginia 151
Dream Bar 68
Duke University 17, 100
Durante, Jimmy 113
Durham Herald 14, 31, 75

Earvin, Sam 165
Eismann, Bernard 145
Engelhart, Gordon 35
Espie, David A. 208
Esquire Magazine 47
Ethridge, Mark 17, 21, 25, 34, 38, 72, 75, 80, 111, 175, 194, 196
Evangelical United Brethren Church 58

Federal Bureau of Investigation (FBI) 7, 31, 99, 121, 122, 149, 185
Federal Bureau of Narcotics 12
Fine, Gay 181
First Baptist Church 7, 53, 77
First Presbyterian Church 59, 77
Flamingo Club 49, 52, 67, 77, 91, 103, 146, 173, 177, 183
Flowers, April 117, 120, 122, 125, 126, 134, 140, 141, 180-186, 192
Ford, Judge H. Church 187
Ford Foundation 196
Fort Thomas 193-194
Frolics Club 177,
Fourth Street Grill 83
Frankfort Bureau 87
Fredericks, Leroy 52, 87, 102, 109, 136, 145, 147, 149, 174, 177-178

Freedom Hall 98
Frenchie 72
Fulton, John 36

Giancola, Carl A. 101
Gibson, Mae 2, 5, 12
Gino 57
Gilmore, H. T. 29
Glenn Hotel 116-117, 119, 121, 130, 196
Glenn Rendezvous 44-45, 49, 67, 84, 88
Graham, Otto 110
Granite Falls, N.C. 170
Great Smoky Mountains 6, 10
Greater Cincinnati Airport 66
Green, Bonnie 186
Greensboro 9, 11
Gugel, Edward 174
Gugel, George 51, 76, 95, 109, 136, 143, 145, 147-149, 174, 177-178
Guthman, Ed 181

Haddad, Frank 37
Hall, Elmer 126-128, 132-133,
Hamilton, Scott 185
Hammett, Dashiel 87
Hanson, Karen 24
Happy Valley 1, 3, 9, 11, 13, 16, 48, 53, 78, 85, 98, 143, 169
Happy Valley High 14
Harbor Bar 82, 90
Harlan County 100, 156
Harper's Chapel Cemetary 14, 172
Harris, James "Big Jim" 167
Harwood, Dick 143-144
Hay, Charles 145
Hay, Nancy 129
Haywood County 4, 6, 8
Hazelwood 4
Helliwell, Arthur 114
Herchenroeder, John 20, 32, 34, 38, 40, 98, 181
Hermann, Bob 35

Hesch, City Manager 47, 51, 66, 76, 95, 143, 174
Heutis, Carl 74
Hi-D-Ho Club 168
Hicks, Mary 14
Hickory, N.C. 169
Highchew, Sylvester 89-90
Higgins, Lawrence 111
Hill, Judge Edward G. 100-101, 152-174, 177, 189, 203
Hinglebrok, Ann 110
Hirschfeld, Thomas 125-126, 129, 131, 166, 179, 187
Hobson, Henry 37
Hodges, Juanita Jean, 117, 120
Hoffa, Jimmy 96--97, 140,
Honorable Order of Kentucky Colonels 24
Hoover, J. Edgar 13
Horn, William 157
Hosea, Henry J. 209
Howe, republican candidate 190, 192
Hummel, Bill 186
Hunter, Dick 104, 120, 123, 193
Hurricane Hazel 17

Intelligence Division IRS 159, 161
IRS 139, 159, 197
Isaacs, Norman 21, 145, 195, 196

Jackson, Hattie 146, 147, 148
Jeffersonville 24
Jefferson County 40-42
Jefferson County Police Dept. 26
Jefferson County Jail Commissary & Charitable Fund, Inc. 42
Jessel, George 24
John Birch Society 18
Johns, Cardos 30, 35
Johnson, Grover 87
Johnson, Claude 115, 118
Johnson, Lyndon 97
Jolly, County Judge Andrew 78,

101, 109, 179
Josten, Margaret 125

Kefauver Committee 6, 13, 44, 48, 197
Kelly, Pat 75
Kenan Stadium 8
Kennedy, Senator John F. 96
Kennedy, Attorney General Robert 96, 100, 122, 124, 139, 180
Kentucky Derby 24
Kentucky Hotel 73
Kettering Laboratories 119-120,
Kleinman, Morris 149

La Grange 41
Lake Junaluska 12
Las Vegas 20, 45, 137, 173
Layman, Walter 27-28, 30
Lela 56
Lenoir 10, 171
Lenior High School 169
Leahy, Coach Frank 110
Leary, Joseph 145, 179
Lester, Charles E. 52, 54, 67, 96, 100, 114, 125-126, 129, 130, 133, 140, 165, 188, 194, 196
Levinson, Ed 68
Levinson, Louis "Sleepout Louie" 49, 52, 68, 149, 160, 183
Lewis, Jesse K. 93, 102, 108, 135, 145
Lexington 186
Licking River 90
Lindsay, Nick 35
Lindsay, Vachel 35
Lookout House 180
Louisville Times 21, 30, 43, 75, 106, 143,
Lukens, James 96

Market Street 39
Marrs, Myron "Bub" 26-27, 30, 32-34, 35-38
Marrs-Messick case 34

Masterson, Albert "Red" 52, 94, 112-113, 125, 128, 141, 147, 149, 158, 166, 191
Mayberry, Mayor 66, 76
Maysville 16-19
Maysville Messenger 17
McDonald 74
Meade, Mitchell 146, 180-181, 184-185, 187
Meehan, John 63, 133
Merchant's Club 52, 94
Messick, Hank Jr. 17
Messick, Jon 17
Messick, Marda 5, 79
Messick, Mildred 10, 11, 169
Messick, Faye 4-5, 10, 23, 25, 32, 34, 43, 63, 79, 136, 172, 193, 195
Messick, Finley 14
Messick, Paul 11, 13, 14
Miami Herald 6
Monmouth Street 44, 177
Morganton 10
Morris, Hugh 145
Mountain City, Tn 171
Muehlenkamp, George 101
Murphy, Judge Ray 59, 70, 81, 86, 95, 100-105, 109, 142, 147, 150-174, 176, 189, 194, 197
Mussman, Ralph 47, 78, 79, 109, 125, 131, 149, 160, 173, 174, 190, 191
"My Old Kentucky Home" 19

Neptina 177
Netherland Plaza Hotel 58
Newport City Commission 176
Newport Gun Club 89, 179
Newport Housing Commission 160, 162
Newport Ministerial Association 48, 53, 55, 93, 119, 173, 176
Newport Nightgown 114
New York Herald-Tribune 124, 131-132
New York Times 23, 35
Nixon, Richard 17, 97, 140

N & O (Raleigh) 144
North Wilkesboro 9
Northern Kentucky University 45
Notre Dame 110, 115, 134

Ohio River 197
Old Fort Mountain 10
Ormes, Andrew 74

Paisley, Thomas J. 127, 129, 141-142, 182
Payne, Steve 159
Patterson 9
Peloquin, Bob 138
Peluso, Johnny "TV" 190, 192-193
Pendennis Club 115
Playtorium 52, 54, 59, 61, 71, 126, 131, 175, 190, 192
Polizzi, Charles Jr. 180, 184
Pomeroy, Reverend Dudley 53-54, 59, 77, 93, 109, 135, 166, 194
Pope, James 20, 28, 38, 40, 42-43, 47, 54, 62-63, 72, 80, 106, 109, 175, 189, 195, 198
Portwood, Alfred 67, 69, 70
Powell, Tom 67-68, 77
Purple Gang 91

Quitter, Joseph 116, 188

Raleigh 16
Raleigh Times 17
Rankin, Jim 30, 75
Ratterman, Ann 125, 132,
Ratterman, George William 109-110, 112, 115-116, 117-120, 124-129, 131, 132-134, 139, 140-141, 149, 164, 178, 180-182, 185, 187-189, 190-192, 196-197, 206
Ratterman, Father P.H. 118, 119
Ray, Officer 1-14
REA 79
Reed, Justice Stanley 16, 19-20

Reeves, Ben 115, 127, 175, 183-185, 192
Religious News Service 78
Remus, George 159
Reuscher, Louis 176
Roberts, Algin 166
Roberts, Oral 98-99, 107
Roll, Norbert 96, 102, 104, 109, 136, 148, 165, 178-179, 191, 194
Rolf, Judge Joseph 125, 132, 183
Rollins, Bill 124, 126, 128, 132,
Rollins, Steid 17, 33
Russ, Editor 2, 5, 7, 8, 9, 13, 14
Russell, Phillips 8, 9
Russell, Solon 41-42

Salerno, Tony 160
Sanders, Harlan 26
San Fransico 187
Saturday Evening Post 81
Schmidt, A. L. "White Smitty" 160
Schmidt, Peter 52-53, 59, 61, 95
Schultz, Vivian 55, 57, 83, 92, 147, 156, 190, 194
Seifried, Chris 46, 54-55, 59, 61, 71, 76, 79, 113, 117, 145, 156, 207
Senate Permanent Subcommittee on Investigations 159, 165
Shady Valley 171
Shaw, Logan 26
Sheraton-Gibson 87
Sherrard, B. L. 147, 167
Shively 26
Shoemaker, Don 4, 6
Shriners 161
Shuford, Ab 3
Siddell, Robert 158
Sigma Delta Chi 38
Sinatra, Frank 180-181
Skaggs, Dolph 29
Smith, Al 96
Snow, Willie 32
Social Action Committee 47-48, 60, 66,

67, 70, 90, 94, 101, 105, 114, 145, 153
Southgate 193
Spade, Peter 87
Spade, Sam 87
Spaid, Ora 23, 30, 38, 78, 181, 184
Spearman, Walter 8
Sportsmans Club 61, 146
Spotted Calf Cafe 89, 90, 105, 179
St. John's United Church of Christ 60
St. Louis, MO 181, 184
Staab, Frank 121, 122, 140, 178, 185
Stapleton, Judge Paul 95-96, 151
Stardust Club 67
Steeplechase 74
Steinman, Jack 105
Stuart, Harry 136, 145, 178-179
Sutton, Carol 40
Switch to Honesty Party 189, 191

Terrace Hilton 81, 138
Terre Haute, IN 196
Thiem, Jack 147
Three Four Five (345) Club 83, 92
Time 124, 128
Tri-City Airport 169
Tropicana 115, 131, 146, 177, 181
Tucker, Sam 149
Twist, Kid 88

Underwood, David "Dog" 6-7, 12, 13, 15
United Effort Day 77, 107
University of Kentucky School of Law 157
University of Iowa 5, 9
University of North Carolina 5
U.S. Supreme Court 16-17, 31, 33
Uzzell, T. A. 6

Van Arsdale, Judge B. C. 30, 39
Vance, Kyle 88, 103

Wallace, Lew Foreword

Warren, Earl (Chief Justice) 16, 18-19
Warndorf, Tony 191
Warrior Creek 9, 14, 143
Washington DC 181, 187
Watergate Investigating Committee 165
Watterson, Henry 21
Waynesville, NC 2, 6-9, 11-12, 14, 172
Waynesville Mountaineer 1-12
Weintraub, Morris 160, 163, 165, 169
WHAS TV 21
White, Upshire (Upshere) 95, 116, 147, 174, 176, 188
Wilder, KY 167-168
Winston Salem 9
Wise, William 59, 63, 71, 87, 105, 107, 130, 141, 142, 147, 152-174, 176-179, 189, 194, 197
Withrow, Thomas 129-131
Withrow, Mrs. Thomas 130, 133
Witzl, Donald 103, 202
World Series 68, 158, 176-177
Wyatt, Wilson W. 69, 72-73, 108, 141

Xavier University 118, 127, 131

Yorkshire Club 48-50, 52, 131, 146, 173, 177, 180
York Street 50, 58, 67, 160, 177-178

Zingman, Ed 29, 34, 184

www.ingramcontent.com/pod-product-compliance
Lightning Source LLC
Chambersburg PA
CBHW030321100526
44592CB00010B/514